Palgrave Studies in Literary Anthropology

Series Editors

Deborah Reed-Danahay
Department of Anthropology
The State University of New York at Buffalo
Buffalo, New York, USA

Helena Wulff
Department of Social Anthropology
Stockholm University
Stockholm, Sweden

This book series aims to publish explorations of new ethnographic objects and emerging genres of writing at the intersection of literary and anthropological studies. Books in this series will be grounded in ethnographic perspectives and the broader cross-cultural lens that anthropology brings to the study of reading and writing. The series will explore the ethnography of fiction, ethnographic fiction, narrative ethnography, creative nonfiction, memoir, autoethnography, and the connections between travel literature and ethnographic writing.

More information about this series at
http://www.springer.com/series/15120

Ulf Hannerz

Writing Future Worlds

An Anthropologist Explores Global Scenarios

Ulf Hannerz
Department of Social Anthropology
Stockholm University
Stockholm, Sweden

Palgrave Studies in Literary Anthropology
ISBN 978-3-319-31261-3 (hardcover)   ISBN 978-3-319-31262-0 (eBook)
ISBN 978-3-319-70627-6 (softcover)
DOI 10.1007/978-3-319-31262-0

Library of Congress Control Number: 2016953616

Cover image © WideWorld / Alamy Stock Photo

Printed on acid-free paper

This Palgrave Macmillan imprint is published by Springer Nature
The registered company is Springer International Publishing AG Switzerland

Series Editors' Preface

Palgrave Studies in Literary Anthropology publishes explorations of new ethnographic objects and emerging genres of writing at the intersection of literary and anthropological studies. Books in this series are grounded in ethnographic perspectives and the broader cross-cultural lens that anthropology brings to the study of reading and writing. By introducing work that applies an anthropological approach to literature, whether drawing on ethnography or other materials in relation to anthropological and literary theory, this series moves the conversation forward not only in literary anthropology, but in general anthropology, literary studies, cultural studies, sociology, ethnographic writing and creative writing. The "literary turn" in anthropology and critical research on world literatures share a comparable sensibility regarding global perspectives.

Fiction and autobiography have connections to ethnography that underscore the idea of the author as ethnographer and the ethnographer as author. Literary works are frequently included in anthropological research and writing, as well as in studies that do not focus specifically on literature. Anthropologists take an interest in fiction and memoir set in their field locations, and produced by "native" writers, in order to further their insights into the cultures and contexts they research. Experimental genres in anthropology have benefitted from the style and structure of fiction and autoethnography, as well as by other expressive forms ranging from film and performance art to technology, especially the internet and social media. There are renowned fiction writers who trained as anthropologists, but moved on to a literary career. Their anthropologically inspired work is a common sounding board in literary anthropology. In the endeavor to foster writing skills in different genres, there are now courses on ethnographic writing, anthropological writing genres, experimental writing, and even creative writing taught by anthropologists. And increasingly, literary and reading communities are attracting anthropological attention, including an engagement with issues of how to reach a wider audience.

Palgrave Studies in Literary Anthropology publishes scholarship on the ethnography of fiction and other writing genres, the connections between travel literature and ethnographic writing, and internet writing. It also publishes creative work such as ethnographic fiction, narrative ethnography, creative non-fiction, memoir, and autoethnography. Books in the series include monographs and edited collections, as well as shorter works that appear as Palgrave Pivots. This series aims to reach a broad audience among scholars, students and a general readership.

Deborah Reed-Danahay and Helena Wulff
Co-Editors, Palgrave Studies in Literary Anthropology

Advisory Board

Ruth Behar, University of Michigan
Don Brenneis, University of California, Santa Cruz
Regina Bendix, University of Göttingen
Mary Gallagher, University College Dublin
Kirin Narayan, Australian National University
Nigel Rapport, University of St Andrews
Ato Quayson, University of Toronto
Julia Watson, Ohio State University

Acknowledgments

This project of scrutinizing global future scenarios began in a more organized form in the early 2000s as a part of a wider interdisciplinary research program, "Kosmopolit: Culture and politics in global society," supported by the Tercentenary Fund of the Bank of Sweden. It has continued after that period, however, as a part-time engagement, much of the time on a back burner. It has been reflected in a number of visiting lectures, at the National University of Singapore, the Chinese University of Hong Kong, University of California-Berkeley, University of Illinois-Champaign/Urbana, University of Minnesota, University of Edinburgh, University of Oxford, University College London, the Institute for Social Anthropology of the Österreichische Akademie der Wissenschaften in Vienna, University of Vienna, Internationales Forschungszentrum Kulturwissenschaften in Vienna, University of Innsbruck, University of Basel, Université Libre de Bruxelles, the Max Planck Institute for Social Anthropology at Halle/Saale, the Friedrich-Alexander-Universität Erlangen-Nürnberg, Central European University in Budapest, Universitá degli studi di Milano-Bicocca, Universitá degli studi di Siena, University of Oslo, Linköping University, National Defence College at Stockholm, and Stockholm University; and in conference papers at meetings of the International Institute of Sociology and the Swedish Anthropological Association. I am grateful to my hosts on these occasions, and to all those listeners who offered constructive and generous comments in discussions. A number of more brief publications have resulted from such presentations (see Hannerz 2003, 2007, 2008, 2009, 2015a and b).

I thank Deborah Reed-Danahay and Helena Wulff for the invitation to publish this book in their series. Helena Wulff has followed the project from its beginning. And it has been a pleasure to work with Mireille Yanow, friendly and effective editor at Palgrave Macmillan, who has guided the manuscript on its way to publication.

CONTENTS

LIST OF FIGURES

Prologue: Atlantis and 1984

Over three hundred years ago, a compatriot of mine, Olof Rudbeck the Elder, published a book which for a while became reasonably well-known, in his home country as well as abroad. The *Atlantica*, published in Swedish and Latin editions, purported to demonstrate, with a wealth of learning both genuine and spurious, that world history was in large part Swedish history.[1]

By the standards of his time and place, Rudbeck was an impressive polymath. He was a professor of medicine, an expert botanist and an astronomer, lectured on a variety of other subjects as well, and had been a youthful and activist Rector of his institution, the University of Uppsala. Although he made some enemies along the way, he also had friends at the royal court. 1648, the year when Rudbeck had arrived at Uppsala as a student, in his late teens, was the year of the Westphalian Peace, which ended thirty years of war in Europe, and laid the foundations of a durable continental nation-state order. It also confirmed Sweden, successful in the war, as a significant power—something a bit like an empire, surrounding much of the Baltic Sea and briefly extending overseas, into West Africa (the Gold Coast) and North America (Delaware), as well.[2] A country like that could use a certain amount of historical glory, and Rudbeck's intellectual preoccupations somehow came to develop in a direction where he could provide it.

He was not alone at the time, of course, in trying to determine the location of the vanished kingdom of Atlantis, as once described by Plato. According to his findings, however, the site of Atlantis had actually been just north of Uppsala, at a known ancient cult place; and as his materials

just grew and grew, it became clear that Sweden had been settled early by
Noah's son Japhet and his descendants, that by way of later southward
cultural influences heathen Nordic deities had been transformed into
members of the antique Greek pantheon, and that the Greek and Latin
alphabets had developed out of the ancient runes, as available for inspection on the rune stones spread in the Swedish terrain. By way of the rivers
and the seas, Swedes had reached the Indus River in the east, and America
long before anybody else. Moreover, Buddha was a Swede.

Assembling all the evidence for this view of the past naturally took
some time, and Rudbeck was also continuously distracted by administrative quarrels at his university, so it was not until 1679 that the first edition
of *Atlantica* could be published. It was received respectfully by scholars
here and there in Europe, but by that time the career of his country on
the more contemporary map was already turning rather topsy-turvy. Then
between the early eighteenth and early nineteenth centuries all its more
distant territories were lost. The "Sweden as No. 1" brand lost most of its
credibility, the interest in a northerly version of the Atlantis story dwin-
dled, and Sweden could move on toward becoming the small, reasonably
clean and well-lit place that it has been since.

Another author, and a book from the mid-twentieth century: George
Orwell's *1984* provides intriguing ethnography from a fully culturally
engineered totalitarian society, ruled by Big Brother, controlled through
Newspeak, Doublethink, the Thought Police, and Two Minutes Hate
sessions in the offices. The global setting is one of three superstates:
Oceania, Eurasia and East Asia. It is over the first of these that Big
Brother rules; we see it through the eyes of Winston Smith, the anti-
hero protagonist. Smith is a Londoner, and London is the chief city of
Airstrip One, the third most populous of the Oceanian provinces. Smith
could remember when Airstrip One had been called England, or Britain,
but everything had been different then, even the names of countries, and
their shapes on the map.

Oceania, Eurasia and East Asia are more or less continuously at war
with each other, in alternating combinations: peace between two, war
against the third. Winston Smith remembers that Oceania, now at war
with Eurasia, was allied with it only four years earlier. Yet any knowledge
of these shifts in history, these changes of partners, is officially suppressed.
Now the truth, eternal until further notice, is that Oceania has never ever
been allied with Eurasia. But wait: midway through the book, the war with
Eurasia is over. So no, there was no such war.

Rudbeck and Orwell may be an unlikely couple, but with the *Atlantica* and *1984* they offer us varieties of a global imagination; and they exemplify quite instructively three themes which will be more or less continuously present in the following pages.

They both played with maps. Orwell drew new boundaries, between three superstates none of which existed at the time of his writing: nor does anyone of them exist now. Rudbeck situated places, people and knowledge where one might not have expected them to occur—Japhet and Buddha somehow connected to Sweden; Atlantis there, too; Swedes, on the other hand, on the Indus; and runes and classic alphabets culturally in touch.

The second theme involves time. Olof Rudbeck the Elder assembled a past, George Orwell invented a future. Here, in principle, we will be concerned with ways of looking ahead. But then the contrast between these two is more complex than it may seem. As anthropologists have known since the time of their ancestral figure Bronislaw Malinowski, myth becomes charter: starting from a few steps back into a past (which may in itself well be internally somewhat timeless) can be the way to speak authoritatively about what is, and what is to come. According to the slogan of the Party in Orwell's Oceanian state, "who controls the past controls the future: who controls the present controls the past." Along such lines, Rudbeck's *Atlantica* seems rather like an origin myth suitable for the present and desired future of an expansive mid-seventeenth century Swedish power.

Thirdly, the question is where we find these writings on a scale between fact and fiction. Neither of the two works seems entirely unambiguously placed on that scale. It is perhaps not entirely obvious what may have been seventeenth-century tongue-in-cheek in the composition of the *Atlantica*, but the work was hardly intended at the time to be understood as fiction. Yet for the twenty-first century reader, it can hardly be anything else. George Orwell's *1984* is fiction, although it has sometimes been read as potential non-fiction, a fantasy which threatens to become real.

These are the matters, then, which this book is about: how people and their practices and ideas arrange themselves, or get arranged, over territories and maps; the past, the present, but especially the future; how fact and fiction meet and mingle. Moreover, Rudbeck was an academic, while Orwell was a writer-journalist (reporting for one thing from the Spanish civil war, at the beginning of a period when the European map was temporarily redrawn). Both these lines of work, and the qualities of the border zone between them, are prominent in what follows. If Rudbeck exercised his scholarly creativity quite long ago, however, and Orwell wrote several decades before the real 1984, we will engage here with other writers from the near past, and in the changing present.

This is a book by an anthropologist. More specifically, according to an old distinction in anthropology between field workers and "armchair anthropologists," it is a work from the armchair, by someone who has perhaps reached the stage when he may no longer see and hear perfectly enough, and run fast enough, to be an ideal field worker. Field research has tended to be the stuff from which heroes and heroines are made in anthropology, while "armchair anthropologist" at least occasionally carries derogatory overtones.[3] Yet past and present, anthropology is dotted with people whose main scholarly contributions have been from the armchair, or the desk. The best thing, however, may be to divide one's time between both. Among colleagues, the anthropologist who has never had a field experience, or who has never really reported from one, has about the same credibility as a theoretical swimmer. So it matters, too, that the armchair project I engage with here came soon after a field study of the work of newsmedia foreign correspondents (thus people who to a degree have followed in Orwell's footsteps), and was in large part inspired by it.[4]

As field workers, anthropologists have been rather naturally oriented toward the local, the small-scale, the "micro": a myriad of little pictures. They also tend to be specialists on particular parts of the world. It may show here, too, that there are regions which I know more about than others. But I will not be so preoccupied here with empirical fact-checking. At times, I get a bit impatient with all the subtle detail offered by conscientious colleagues, and wonder whether one cannot actually say more about The Big Picture.

In this book, I engage with various attempts to do precisely that. The inclination of an anthropologist confronting such attempts may be to find faults: pointing to exceptions to any generalization, arguing that things are really more complex, finding beautiful theories destroyed by ugly little facts (frequently even by quite attractive little facts), discerning that breadth may go with shallowness, suggesting that intensive field work is the only way to get things right. In what follows, I may occasionally put on the anthropologist's cap with similar results. Nonetheless, I am also attracted to a metaphor of "zooming," moving between scales, and still hope, as an anthropologist, to learn more about how to do this in a credible as well as accessible way. Thus (as the title *Writing Future Worlds* also suggests) I am curious about styles in a certain genre of writing. In that sense one may see what follows as in part a kind of literary critique, a suitable armchair activity.

Anthropologists, it was pointed out quite long ago, have also been disproportionately engaged in "studying down," doing their field studies among people with less power, prestige and material resources than themselves—partly perhaps because they sympathized more with them and wanted to speak for them, partly certainly because these people were more accessible to the anthropological way of doing field research. So the argument has reasonably been made that there should be more of "studying up," finding out more about people who have more power, and about how they use it.[5] But then the notion has also emerged of "studying sideways": inquiring into the ways of life, work and thought of groups of people who are on more or less parallel tracks to that of the anthropologists, other knowledge producers.[6] My study of the foreign correspondents was of this variety. In a way I return to it now—again I am concerned with some journalists, but I am also interested in the work of certain scholars in other parts of Academia. Obviously Rudbeck was a forerunner here; the current exemplars are mostly linked to the disciplines of history and political science, even as their reputations reach out more widely. (Considering the impressive influence of their work, it is true that this also becomes to an extent a case of "studying up.")

I do not see this book as one written specifically for other anthropologists, but will be just as pleased if other readers will be interested in the way one anthropologist explores the terrain of issues at hand. On the whole, anthropology may have been rather open to outside contacts, although in different directions in different times, and more generally inward-turning in some periods than in others.[7] At present, I believe there is a deficit in interdisciplinary communication across some borders, and in the flow of ideas between much of Academia and the surrounding society. Studying sideways here, my goal is not to offer some sort of a compendium of a certain body of writings, covering all their arguments and conclusions evenly. Neither would I claim to be qualified to offer a critical review of works of history, or political science, or international relations, of the kind that would come from inside the respective disciplines, growing out of their particular traditions and debates. And I certainly do not intend to offer a comprehensive alternative to the perspectives offered in these writings. My intentions are rather different. Above all, I am interested in how the basically small-scale commentatorial enterprise of a handful of writers grows into a significant component of global public consciousness.

I would not claim to offer "*the* anthropological view" of this either. I am sure there can be many sideways perspectives toward the topic of this book, from anthropology or from geography, or political philosophy, or elsewhere. But the particular one emerging in what follows reflects my own selection of interests, and resonates with my experiences. This is how I read what those writers have written. Occasionally I have been told that I have been early in engaging with some of the coming growth areas of the discipline—if that is so, I think this has usually involved taking some of the key ideas from the heartlands of anthropology to its frontiers (or sometimes to its contested borderlands). In this project, I am again attempting to explore borderlands. Some anthropologist colleagues have been in these particular zones before me, but I think too few. In a way, insofar as I will recurrently connect my scenario readings with the work of other anthropologists (contemporaries or ancestors), I will draw them into the borderlands as well.

Again, too, anthropology has its key concepts, and enduring preoccupations. Above all, I think of anthropology as a study of human diversity—trying to describe the latter accurately, and to understand it as a whole and in its parts, not focusing too narrowly or prematurely on what is closest at hand, at home, or dominant. Intimately linked to a conception of diversity has been the central notion of "culture." Over the years the term has been defined, redefined, and debated. Thus anthropologists have turned into experts not only on the real, empirical entities called cultures, but also on the concept itself, its strengths and weaknesses.[8] Some critics within the discipline would now simply reject it as useless and even dangerous. I still find it useful for certain purposes—but I am aware that one of the disadvantages is that it is sometimes used, in some other academic fields and in varieties of public discourse, in ways which are not intellectually viable, or are politically dubious. What to do or not to do with ideas about culture will thus be one issue in what follows.

The subtitle of the book includes a notion of global scenarios. "Scenarios" fits here because it refers to something rather inclusive, with people as actors in one way or other, and not least because it points toward the future. The term "global" may deserve some more comment. On the one hand, the scenarios on which I focus are comprehensive; even if the coverage really turns out to be rather uneven, they take the idea of the world as an interconnected whole seriously. On the other hand, they do not simply assume that one can easily generalize about that whole. Occasionally, to emphasize this, I will use the term "geocultural." Unlike the kindred term "geopolitical," this term has not been in very common use in either a popular or an academic vocabulary, although it shows up now and then, here and there, rather haphazardly.[9] As I use it, I draw on the earthly sense of "geo" to make "geocultural" refer to the distribution of people with differing cultural repertoires over the global map. And I will in large part focus on the way people *think* geoculturally, about the world and its parts, and the main features of those parts. Some geocultural thinking is indeed very entrenched, taken for granted, and hardly very imaginative. But then we may sense that in some mapmaking there may be certain geocultural entrepreneurship involved, as in Orwell's and Rudbeck's activities. We should keep our eyes open for examples of the geocultural imagination.

Among the absolutely most entrenched geocultural ideas, however, are those of nations and nationalities. So against that background, what about me? The fact that this commentator-critic is Swedish may not, I think, matter so much (although apart from Rudbeck there will be references, in passing, to another couple of Uppsala professors, from different centuries, as well as a quick revisit to the city of my birth)—that he is non-American, probably more. In large part, the writings considered in the book are American. I have been a fairly continuous America-watcher for a long time. Yet coming from elsewhere, and spending my time mostly elsewhere, may entail seeing the United States from a certain distance, and probably more likely in a global context than many Americans do, much of the time. The scenarios are indeed of the world, and I will argue, for the world as well.

So what follows? Here is a preview:

Chapter 1, "The 'One Big Thing' Quintet & Co," allows a first inspection of some of these scenarios, and a meeting with the people who created them.

Chapter 2, "When pundits go global," sketches the wider context in which the scenarios are at work: the interconnected field of Academia, media and politics where their authors function as public intellectuals; the interdependence between scenarios and newsmedia; and the outreach across borders which establish the scenarios as global sociocultural phenomena in themselves.

Chapter 3, "Playing with maps," compares the various ways the scenarios draw borders in the world, defining the regional, continental or civilizational divides expected to matter in the future.

Chapter 4, "Side shows: Eurabia, MexAmerica," discusses two special cases: alarmist accounts of the way two major world regions are said to be transformed by penetration from outside forces.

Chapter 5, "Reporting from the future," considers the conditions of looking ahead toward what the world may become. Can scenarios predict, or warn of undesirable developments, or imagine what will happen in other ways? Where do scenarios stand between our understandings of fiction and non-fiction, and how are ways of scenario writing affected?

Chapter 6, "Contemporary habitats of meaning," engages with conceptions of "culture." What kind of understandings of culture are set forth in the scenarios, what kinds of critical responses have these met with? Starting out from a view of human beings as a learning species, how can we grasp contemporary world culture as an organization of diversity?

Chapter 7, "Culture: between XL and S," is about the ways some sets of meanings and their expressions are extremely widespread in the world, and at the other extreme some may be carried only by very small groups, or individuals. On the scale in between, however, recent history shows a variety of other shifting distributions of beliefs, agendas and commitments between groups and networks within the geocultural landscape.

Chapter 8, "Soft power," focuses on one widely popular conception of how countries can exercise influence on people in other countries: through the attractions of their culture. Some countries may choose between hard and soft power; for others, the latter may at least offer some hope.

Finally, Chapter 9, "Scenarios from everywhere," widens the horizon toward views of the global present and future from more commentators—Americans with roots somewhere else in the world, and a range of writers based in other continents.

NOTES

1. David King's *Finding Atlantis* (2005) offers an accessible account of Rudbeck's work and its reception—suggesting that Rudbeck "combined the reasoning of Sherlock Holmes with the daring of Indiana Jones."
2. As it happens, one of the writers whose work is the topic of this book, Paul Kennedy, includes a brief summary of Sweden's part in this period of history in *The Rise and Fall of the Great Powers* (1987: 63–66).
3. Susan Sontag's essay "The Anthropologist as Hero"—on Claude Lévi-Strauss, with a focus on his *Tristes Tropiques*—dwells on the peculiarity of classical field work as a human encounter; it is in her book *Against Interpretation* (1966).

4. My study of the work of foreign correspondents is most fully reported in the book *Foreign News* (2004a). Apart from that, my earlier field studies have been in the United States, West Africa, and the Caribbean.

5. "Studying up" was first advocated in a classic book chapter by Laura Nader (1972).

6. I first used the notion of "studying sideways" in a rather wide-ranging paper (Hannerz 1998) on various transnational populations; see also Rao (2006) on field work among Indian journalists, and Ortner (2010) in a study of film makers in Hollywood.

7. Caroline Brettell's *Anthropological Conversations* (2015) offers a rich and up-to-date view of anthropology's interdisciplinary connections.

8. I have developed my own view of the culture concept and its uses in a couple of essays (Hannerz 1996: 30–43, 1999); for other views see for example Brumann (1999) and Kuper (1999). We come back to it especially in Chap. 6.

9. Immanuel Wallerstein's (1991: 11) use of "geoculture" to refer to "the cultural framework within which the world-system operates" may be among the more prominent; but it does not seem very clear, and seems too narrowly tied to a mostly present-day global order.

CHAPTER 1

The "One Big Thing" Quintet & Co

Sometime in the late 1990s, when I was doing my study of the work of newsmedia foreign correspondents, I spent a morning with Bill Keller at the Manhattan headquarters of the *New York Times*. Keller was then the foreign editor of the paper, had made his name as a correspondent in Moscow during the *perestroika* and in Johannesburg during the South African transition from apartheid, and later served for several years as the paper's executive editor before returning to writing, as a columnist.[1] At the time, we talked about the strategic placing of foreign correspondents in what seemed likely to become important news sites. Keller mentioned that he had recently for the first time posted a correspondent in Istanbul. Turkey was an increasingly interesting meeting point between East and West, he said, although "you don't have to believe this stuff about a clash of civilizations."

That conversation, and that particular remark, offered me one window toward the way our contemporary understandings of the world are shaped, and toward the geocultural imagination. Keller's rather skeptical mention of "this stuff" referred to an argument which had already caught my attention some years earlier—to begin with, that day in 1993 when in one of the American newsweeklies I came across a story on a new, or new-old, view of the world that was attracting notice. Samuel Huntington, well-known Harvard University professor of political science, had just published an article in the journal *Foreign Affairs*, under the title "The Clash of Civilizations?" That sounded interesting, so had I made my way to the original article. With major conflict over political ideology now

11

gone, I found Huntington arguing, the most important cleavages, and the coming battles, would be between the large-scale cultural blocs of the world. There were seven or eight civilizations in the world now: Western, Latin American, Slavic Orthodox, Islamic, Hindu, Confucian, Japanese and African. About the civilizational status of Africa he was not really quite sure. But in any case, while states remained the major actors in the international order, the important thing about civilizations in Huntington's view was that they are very durable, and that they tend again and again to determine who goes with whom in wider configurations of conflict. In Huntington's worst case, it would be the West against the Muslims and the Confucians. And in a four-word formulation that would get particular attention, "Islam has bloody borders."

The Huntington thesis has indeed provoked considerable debate since then, and gone through its ups and downs. But it was possible at the time, in the 1990s, to see it as one belonging with a number of other pronouncements about present and future states of the world. Even before Huntington, the historian Paul M. Kennedy, reaching further into the past and not so very far into the future, had portrayed the overreach and subsequent decline of Spanish, French and British empires—could the United States be next in line? Then there had been Francis Fukuyama's remarkable suggestion that the world might have reached "the end of history." One journalist, Robert D. Kaplan, already well-known for his reporting on troubled regions, warned in a magazine article for the *Atlantic Monthly* that the world now faced a "coming anarchy." And then, in a book on the transformative power of liberated and electronically empowered markets, it was another foreign affairs writer, the *New York Times* columnist Thomas Friedman, who noted that, together with the work of Kennedy, Huntington, Kaplan and Fukuyama, his own book could actually be seen to belong in a genre. Friedman identified the genre as "The One Big Thing."

What had happened was that toward the end of the Cold War, and even more after it, people habituated for more than a generation to the metaphor of the Iron Curtain and the reality of the Wall could imagine their world anew—indeed asked, with relief or anxiety, what might happen next. And this small but lively intellectual industry had risen to the challenge, creating scenarios for a born-again world, suggesting what would be the coming big thing.

We entered an age of futures. As the world turned, there would be more of these scenarios. By the time the 1990s came to an end, the onrush of interpretive schemes may have slowed down a bit, but then there was

9–11, and another wave of global commentary. If the first wave had retrieved an old notion of civilizations to fit into a clash scenario, now "empire" was also back as a keyword in a number of writings, frequently as a suggestive way of referring to the uniquely powerful position of the United States in the world order or disorder. (Wars in Afghanistan, and particularly controversially in Iraq, contributed to this.) And especially since 2008, with economic upheavals spreading rather unevenly over the world, shifts in the global centers of gravity have become more conspicuous than they were before—mostly from West to East, to a degree from North to South. This again generates more scenarios. As the comment by Bill Keller suggests, too, the scenario formulations could move out from the original texts into wider fields of debate.

These are indeed global scenarios, or world scenarios, because they attempt to offer a Big Picture of global conditions and affairs. There were times, not so long ago, when futurist scenarios may have referred to the world in a vague, general sense, or to modernity or what would come after it, but often they were implicitly inclined to be ethnocentrically Western. Consider a famous book from a couple of decades earlier: Alvin Toffler's *Future Shock* (1970). The index here offers two page references to Asia, and three to Africa, in some 500 pages. Look up one of these, and you find that it only suggests a need to help "incipient futurist centers in Asia, Africa and Latin America," while another argues that "a professor who has moved seven times in ten years, who travels constantly in the United States, South America, Europe and Africa, who has changed jobs repeatedly, pursues the same daily regimen wherever he is." And so it goes: there is no actual discussion of differing characteristics among parts of the world, mostly a globetrotting mention to provide some rhetorical flourish.

The scenarios of the more recent period are not necessarily free of regional bias, but at least they seem more often to involve a fairly explicit sense of the world as a single place, interconnected but internally diverse. To some extent, at least in that first "One Big Thing" phase, that may have been because they were engaged in mapping the way things would be after the Cold War, as that had indeed been a confrontation which manifestly drew in much of the world in one way or another. But then the shift is also a response to the way that globalization became a central understanding, a key concept, in the last decade or so of the twentieth century. Even if the term has mostly been used so as to involve some regions much more than others, there is now less of the utter disregard of other parts of the world that the West could get away with in earlier eras.

Since the end of the Cold War, we have now seen about a quarter-century of global scenarios. It would be hazardous to try to predict the future of the genre. (One thing one can learn from it is precisely that predictions are difficult.) This book is rather more of a critical report on the products of that period, on a changing landscape of texts. From the original set of authors, there have been more books: children and grandchildren perhaps of "One Big Thing." But more writers have also joined them. In this chapter, we will first have a look at that initial "One Big Thing" quintet of Thomas Friedman's—composed of himself, Huntington, Fukuyama, Kaplan and Kennedy—and their most prominent texts. But we will also proceed to identify some of those other writers who have contributed significantly to the scenario genre.

SAMUEL HUNTINGTON: MODERNIZATION, CLASHING CIVILIZATIONS, AND A DOMESTIC CULTURE WAR

Of those five pioneers, only Samuel Huntington is no longer alive. He died on Christmas Eve, 2008, and earned many respectful newspaper obituaries in the days and weeks that followed. His *Foreign Affairs* article had grown into a book, *The Clash of Civilizations and the Remaking of World Order* (1996), and it was for this work that he was now most widely remembered.

But this had come fairly late in a long career. Particularly among his political science colleagues he was already very well known. His first book, almost forty years earlier, had argued for a professionalized military, and he had then turned more generally to problems of modernization. The early post-World War II generation of American modernization theorists in the social sciences had tended to see all the features of modernization as occurring in one happy bundle.[2] Huntington had objected that they could be in conflict, and that without political order, the rest of it might not follow. Later he had emphasized the religious underpinnings of a continued spread of democracy in the Christian West—here one might already have spotted the early steps toward his view of civilizational differences.

And then several years later, his last major book, *Who Are We?* (2004), had also become a focus of controversy. It had been clear already in his "clash of civilizations" writings that the argument involved a sort of large-scale identity politics, and that Huntington was a partisan in the domestic American culture wars of the period; since it was important for the West to stick together, he argued, there could be no room for multiculturalism. That theme was elaborated in the later book, critical particularly of the impact of Mexican immigration on the fabric of life in the United States, but also of an American elite which he found insufficiently patriotic. In Chap. 4, we will come back to this as well.

FRANCIS FUKUYAMA: NO MORE HISTORY?

In contrast, Francis Fukuyama was hardly so well known as he launched his contribution to the "One Big Thing" set of scenarios. His essay "The End of History?" (1989) appeared in the journal *The National Interest*, but it, too, was soon expanded into a book. Fukuyama was a third genera-tion Japanese-American. His grandfather had immigrated to the U.S. West Coast in the early twentieth century, he was born in the Midwest when his father was a sociology student at the University of Chicago, and then he grew up in large part on Manhattan. He went to Cornell University for his undergraduate studies (partly under the conservative philosopher Allan Bloom, with whom he remained in contact), then began to study litera-ture at Yale, and went to Paris to acquaint himself more with the thinking of Jacques Derrida and Roland Barthes. Apparently disappointed, he dis-covered the late Hegelian Alexandre Kojève instead. Then he earned his doctorate at Harvard, studying under Huntington.

But by the time he became famous, Fukuyama's work had taken a dif-ferent turn. After a period at RAND Corporation, the think tank, he had moved on to the U.S. State Department. In his "end of history" essay, he raised the question whether the ideological evolution of humankind was about to reach its end point, as liberal democracy became univer-salized, in combination with the market economy. This was world his-tory—never mind "what strange thoughts occur to people in Albania or Burkina Faso," or what challenges to the triumphant ideology might be promoted by "every crackpot messiah around the world." Fascism, which had been one of the twentieth-century alternatives, was long gone, in Europe as well as Asia. True, when Fukuyama's essay was published, the Berlin Wall still stood, and Gorbachev vas still in increasingly shaky power in the Kremlin. Yet in the Soviet Union as well as in the People's Republic of China, Marxism-Leninism had in fact been abandoned. And while the leadership of these great powers was showing signs of coming to terms, however ambiguously and reluctantly, with the decline of their past way of thinking, one could see

the ineluctable spread of consumerist Western culture in such diverse contexts as the peasants' markets and color television sets now omnipresent
throughout China, the cooperative restaurants and clothing stores opened
in the past year in Moscow, the Beethoven piped into Japanese department
stores, and the rock music enjoyed alike in Prague, Rangoon, and Tehran.
(Fukuyama 1989: 3)

It would be a mistake, however, to assume that this essay is entirely celebrationist in tone. Particularly the end is of a strikingly different kind. "The
end of history will be a very sad time," Fukuyama concludes. Economic
calculation and technical problem-solving will replace daring, courage,
imagination and idealism. In the post-historical world there will be neither art nor philosophy, "just the perpetual caretaking of the museum of
human history." Yet perhaps the prospect of centuries of boredom, and
nostalgia, could somehow serve to get history going once again?

The National Interest provided space for some critical comments on the
essay, including one by Samuel Huntington. And then the essay grew into
a book—that, we can already conclude, is typical of the scenario genre.
The title now, in 1992, was The End of History and the Last Man. The
argument had become more complex, although the basic message was
the same. Since then, with his reputation solidly established, Fukuyama
has continued to write and edit more books: Trust (1995a), for example,
a comparative analysis of the importance of extensive social capital for
economic development; The Great Disruption (1999), on the changing
American social order; America at the Crossroads (2006), a critique of
neoconservative foreign policy; and Blindsided (2007), a collaborative
volume on the problems of anticipation. By the time of The Origins of
Political Order (2011) and Political Order and Political Decay (2014),
the end of history did not really seem to be in sight; the challenge was
rather "getting to Denmark," a perhaps semi-mythical country where
the state apparatus worked well, where the government was accountable,
and where the rule of law was trustworthy. But from many parts of the
world, the road there was obviously long and narrow. He also took the
initiative of starting a new journal devoted to politics, policy and culture,
The American Interest, in 2005. And Fukuyama has made a couple of
career moves between leading academic institutions—getting with time
to the Hoover Institution of Stanford University, and thus back to the
West Coast where his grandfather had landed, but under quite different
conditions.

PAUL KENNEDY: LOOKING BACK A LOT, LOOKING FORWARD A LITTLE

Born and educated in Britain, the historian Paul Kennedy was well into his scholarly career before he moved across the Atlantic to become a professor at Yale University, where his specialty developed as "international security studies." A very productive scholar, he had already published a number of books before those of more direct interest to us here. The first one of the latter, *The Rise and Fall of the Great Powers*, was published in 1987 (thus perhaps a little before the Cold War was quite over), and the subtitle identifies the period it covers as from 1500 to 2000, so the claim to futurist coverage was rather modest. But then in the debate which that book provoked, it became increasingly clear to him that to really engage with the future, one would have to deal with certain issues which had not claimed so much attention in the past. Moreover, the style of history which centered on states and empires as major actors was no longer to be taken for granted. The next book, then, had a more clearly forward-looking view: *Preparing for the Twenty-first Century* (1993). The emphasis was on issues of demography, technology, ecology and energy. Yet Kennedy noted that culture, religious beliefs and social attitudes could in the end determine how peoples and countries responded to challenges. Leadership would be important. And again he was after all cautious about looking far ahead. As demographic projections tend to involve a generation or so, he noted, he would talk about the next thirty years, approximately the period until 2025.

Not so much later, with a group of co-workers, Kennedy focused on a set of countries—Indonesia, India, Pakistan, Turkey, Egypt, Algeria, South Africa, Brazil, Mexico—which they felt had perhaps not drawn sufficient interest in the days of bipolar great-power politics, but whose near future would have an impact on the world as a whole. These would be the "pivotal states" (Chase et al. 1999). One could note several of them were among those which would soon be known together as BRICS—Brazil, Russia, India, China, South Africa—and others among them were among those for which the acronym MINT has more lately been suggested: Mexico, Indonesia, Nigeria, Turkey. In the former grouping, when Kennedy & Co wrote, Russia and China were already so much great powers that they hardly needed to be included. (And one could indeed also discern that with various kinds of internal unrest in the times that followed, the continued path of many of these countries remains uncertain.)

Then after this, Kennedy (2006a) took on writing an overview interpretation of the United Nations, with its ramifying organizational order and agendas, which recognized its weaknesses, and yet took a favorable view of this "parliament of man" and its part in a workable future. Meanwhile, he also kept on writing for a wide range of papers, journals and magazines, ranging from the *New York Review of Books* to the *Atlantic Monthly* and the *Los Angeles Times*. As a migrant from the United Kingdom, Paul Kennedy has also taken time out to coach boys' soccer.

THOMAS FRIEDMAN: FREQUENT FLIER WITH AN ATTITUDE

Huntington, Fukuyama and Kennedy have been at home in Academia (although they have not always been there), working perhaps largely in the library, at the desk and in the armchair. Friedman and Kaplan are from the world of journalism. Thomas Friedman first reached prominence as a foreign correspondent reporting from the Middle East—Beirut to begin with, then Jerusalem—and earned his first two Pulitzer Prizes on that basis.[3] But then he returned home to the United States, to cover first the State Department, and after that the White House. Since becoming world affairs columnist at the *New York Times* in the mid-1990s, however, he has certainly again spent much time on the road and in the air—he refers to himself as a "tourist with an attitude." Apart from his frequent commentary in the daily paper, he has continued to write book after book. The one in which he made the reference to a "One Big Thing" genre was *The Lexus and the Olive Tree* (1999). Of later work, *The World is Flat* (2005) and *Hot, Flat, and Crowded* (2008) are those most relevant to our interests here. A yet later book, the co-authored *That Used To Be Us* (with Michael Mandelbaum 2011) is more centered on domestic American matters, as it reflects a critical period in his country's life.[4]

The Lexus and the Olive Tree is not about a real car crashing into a real tree—the Japanese luxury car model which he inspects as it comes off the assembly line in Toyota City stands for "all the burgeoning global markets, financial institutions and computer technologies with which we pursue higher living standards today," and the ancient tree he remembers from his old reporting beat in the Middle East, not least from the borderlands between Palestinians and Israelis. This is what Friedman says about olive trees:

> They represent everything that roots us, anchors us, identifies us and locates us in this world—whether it be belonging to a family, a community, a tribe,

a nation, a religion or, most of all, a place called home. Olive trees are what give us the warmth of family, the joy of individuality, the intimacy of personal rituals, the depth of private relationships, as well as the confidence and security to reach out and encounter others. (1999: 27)

But then there are complications as well:

We fight so intensely at times over our olive trees because, at their best, they provide the feelings of self-esteem and belonging that are as essential for human survival as food in the belly. At worst, though, when taken to excess, an obsession with our olive trees lead us to forge identities, bonds and communities based on the exclusion of others, and at their very worst, when these obsessions really run amok...they lead to the extermination of others.

In this book, however, there is more about the Lexus and what it stands for, and not really so much about the olive tree. And further into the book, the dominant, dramatic metaphor becomes that of "the Electronic Herd": stock, bond, currency and multinational investors, often anonymous, connected by screens and networks, capable of stampeding through the open spaces of the global market, still understanding its rules—those which, whether you like them or not, constitute the Golden Straitjacket. Among his favorite informants, it turns out, are hedge fund managers. (After 2008, possibly, one would be less likely to be impressed by their insights.)

Even so, Friedman allows that the Electronic Herd does not shape action on the current and emergent world stage alone. Although he does not give them equal time, he identifies three major forces: markets, nation-states, and what he terms "super-empowered individuals." And notably, in a book published two years before what would become "9–11," he points to a fairly obscure Saudi millionaire, Osama bin Laden, as an example of the latter.

The next in Friedman's series of bestselling books was *The World is Flat* (2005), with the subtitle "A Brief History of the Twenty-first Century." At first seemingly pre-Columbian, the title is actually inspired by a comment by a leader in the booming Indian information technology industry, in an interview in Bangalore: "Tom, the playing field is being leveled."[5] The flattening of the world, then, makes life simpler for that Electronic Herd. It can run, and run, and run—but with the global power of computers, software, e-mail, networks, teleconferencing and all that, distances do not really matter any longer. What matters are the new circumstances of competition in the world marketplace.

And then a few years later came *Hot, Flat, and Crowded* (2008). The leveled playing field is still there, and thus the market; but it has been joined by climate change, and a mushrooming world population. Three Big Things are more than One Big Thing, so there is a move toward some greater recognition of complexity. One can keep up with what is on Thomas Friedman's mind continuously, of course, through his column on the *New York Times* Op-Ed page. Frequently he reports on his encounters with national leaders, and other Very Important Persons. Friedman, one could say, is much involved in "studying up." But then again, considering his own status, it becomes more like "studying sideways"—perhaps tourist with an altitude, too.[6] (The recurrent format where he uses a column as a personal letter to some prime minister, president, king or other, in a fairly informal tone, may imply something like that.)

ROBERT KAPLAN: HERE COMES ANARCHY

"The Coming Anarchy," by Robert Kaplan, began as a magazine article, in the February, 1994, issue of the *The Atlantic Monthly*. By then Kaplan was already well-known for his book *Balkan Ghosts*, published in the previous year. And in 1993, another book of his had also appeared: when I was in Jerusalem, as part of my study of foreign news reporting, one of the most knowledgeable Middle East correspondents based there mentioned, quite admiringly, Kaplan's *The Arabists* (1993b). Here was a subtle longitudinal inquiry into the complexities of twentieth-century American diplomacy in the Middle East, with emissaries struggling not to "go native" in local political thought worlds—and not to become too ensnared by established opinion, or passing fashions, from the Foggy Bottom headquarters of the State Department either. But in fact there had by then already been a couple of other books, based on this reporter's travels in Central Asia and Northeast Africa. Kaplan had started out as a newspaper stringer, but before that he had also served in the Israel Defense Forces for a year. He describes himself as of working-class background; his brother would become a CIA veteran.

The books, and the magazine articles, would keep coming. In the new century, there were *Imperial Grunts* (2005) and *Hog Pilots, Blue Water Grunts* (2007), as Kaplan turned to reporting on the U.S. military, in its stationings around the world; and *Warrior Politics* (2001a), with the subtitle "Why Leadership Demands a Pagan Ethos." *Monsoon* (2010) describes the Indian Ocean region as one of particular future strategic importance, *Asia's Cauldron* (2014) takes Kaplan onward to the present and future troubles of the region of the South China Sea. Like both Huntington and Friedman, he also found time to devote one book to domestic American matters—*An Empire Wilderness*, in 1998.

In the mid-1990s, however, spreading upheaval and disorganization was Kaplan's One Big Thing. By the time *The Coming Anarchy* appeared in book form, in 2000, it was a smallish collection of essays, with the rather long title essay up front. The other chapters had mostly also appeared first in *The Atlantic Monthly*. The preface noted that the times following an epochal military and political victory will be "lonely times for realists." (2000: xi) So the overall message of this book, as Kaplan puts it in the subtitle, is to shatter the dreams of the post-Cold War years. In the title essay, again, he goes to work on this by way of a journey through West Africa, mostly along the Atlantic coast, traveling by bush taxis, carrying only a rucksack. Here he finds it all: "disease, overpopulation, unprovoked crime, scarcity of resources, refugee migrations, the increasing erosion of nation-states and international borders, and the empowerment of private armies, security firms, and international drug cartels" (2000: 7). But these problems do not belong only there. They are representative of world-wide demographic, environmental and societal stress, of a kind that would "soon confront our civilization."

And then he shifts to buttressing his argument, in large part by citing a wider range of scholarly expertise on the spread of the global ills he has identified. Here he also finds what becomes a favorite metaphor: the affluent parts of the world are riding in a stretch limo, but outside it, as they pass by, is the rest of mankind.[7] The imagery goes well, of course, as a contrast with Kaplan's own mode of travel, in those decrepit bush taxis. According to that anthropological vocabulary again, if Friedman "studies up," Kaplan makes rather more a point of "studying down." He can place Fukuyama's people, imagining that they are approaching the end of history, in the stretch limousine; and although he is critical of Huntington for painting his picture of clashing civilizations with too broad a brush, he can see race, ethnicity and religion combining with other sources of conflict—outside the stretch limo is "a rundown, crowded planet of skinhead Cossacks and *juju* warriors, influenced by the worst refuse of Western pop culture and ancient tribal hatreds, and battling over scraps of overused earth." (2000: 29–30)

This, then, is what Kaplan's "lonely realists" would see. Indeed, the 1990s were not good times in much of Africa. Some years into the twenty-first century, it still has its problems, although for one thing it has had elections (or what has at least passed for elections) in a number of countries, so there are at present fewer soldiers in power. Some countries show noteworthy economic growth. The pandemic reach of that entire cluster of interrelated threats has not really materialized. Even as we can still recognize them and be concerned over them, it seems anarchy has at least not yet arrived. Perhaps there were indeed too many optimists crowding into the stretch limo, but the "realists" may to a degree have been overly pessimistic, after all.

Other chapters in *The Coming Anarchy* contribute to the picture of Robert Kaplan as an observer of the world—past, present, future. In his own home country he sees a corporate elite, and a mass mostly interested in being entertained; and he wonders about the prospects for democracy. He finds his old copy of Gibbon's *History of the Decline and Fall of the Roman Empire*, and considers the possible parallels with America. Henry Kissinger's early study of Metternich and post-Napoleonic European politics allows him to review favorably Kissinger's own politics, in the Cold War and in the hot war of Vietnam. Order is more important than justice, and between adversaries there may have to be a balance of fear. In every society throughout history, Kaplan argues, there are a crucial percentage of frustrated young males driven to impulsive physical action, and the professionalization of the military leaves them out. Without an acceptable, civilizing outlet for their inclinations, the rest of society may need to be protected by more prisons, electronic surveillance, and gated communities. And then he turns to a Joseph Conrad novel to provide what he feels is a real understanding of the complexities of the Third World. He is convinced that academic social science cannot do it nearly as well.

By the time Kaplan reaches the South China Sea in *Asia's Cauldron*, the bush taxi is not often in sight, although he takes time out for a quick motorboat trip to an island slum in the backwaters of Malaysia. Otherwise his company now seems more like that customarily kept by Thomas Friedman. In another of his books, however, he has taken time to linger and browse in the stacks of a scholarly library. As we will see in Chap. 3, in *The Revenge of Geography* (2012), he pays his respects to some of the early classics of geopolitics.

...AND SOME OTHERS

To repeat, apart from the original "One Big Thing" quintet, and mostly after their early writings in the scenario genre, a number of other writers have been similarly concerned with the global future. The borders of the genre are somewhat blurred, and the reasons for inclusion and exclusion must be a little arbitrary. They will evolve and become more explicit as we go on, but at this point some of the additional contributors to the genre can be introduced more briefly.

Three are political scientists. Benjamin Barber's central contribution to the genre is *Jihad vs. McWorld* (1995)—a bestseller, and one may be a little surprised that it was not on Thomas Friedman's list a few years later (but perhaps it was because it had Two Big Things, at the time one too many; and it really argued for a Third). A Harvard Ph.D., Barber has had varied later academic affiliations, as well as connections to other kinds of organizations. In his book title, "McWorld" stands for a totalizing, dominant market; that much is fairly clear, even as Barber ties rather a lot of things together in that bundle as well. "Jihad," more surprisingly and more debatably, is made to stand for just about any more or less defensive assertion of difference: nationalism, nativism, xenophobia, parochialism, even "culture." (The contrast may remind us of Friedman's *The Lexus and the Olive Tree*, but perhaps we find Barber's more striking.) This is hardly political science in a conventional sense, but more of a cultural critique of contemporary and emergent consumer society. Much as Barber recognizes the power of both his Jihad and his McWorld, however, he is himself above all an advocate of a strong civil society, a democracy so far most safely based in the sovereign nation-state. The concern with the overwhelming power of commerce returns in one of Barber's later books, *Consumed* (2007), with the subtitle "How Markets Corrupt Children, Infantilize Adults, and Swallow Citizens Whole"; the book is dedicated to the author's teenage daughter, Cornelia, an expert shopper. Before that, there has also been *Fear's Empire* (2003), clearly a post-9–11 book, a critique of a foreign policy built on military "shock and awe" principles and friendly dictators rather than multilateralism and democracy.

That perspective is hardly entirely different from that of the second political scientist, Joseph Nye, who has had his academic base at Harvard University, like Samuel Huntington. For us, the key concept in Nye's large body of writings is "soft power"—as contrasted, of course, with hard power. The latter is political power in a narrower sense, not least military power, as well as economic power; all command power. Soft power rests on the ability to set the political agenda in a way that shapes the preferences of others. It co-opts rather than coerces people; "if I can get you to *want* to do what I want, then I do not have to force you to do what you do *not* want to do" (Nye 2002: 9). In large part, soft power involves culture. Nye cites values of democracy, personal freedom, openness and upward mobility as characteristic of American soft power, projected in a multiplicity of ways, but not least through popular culture. In that area, the German publicist Josef Joffe, editor of *Die Zeit*, whom Nye quotes approvingly (and to whom we will return), concludes that what America has at present is a soft power that "rules over an empire on which the sun never sets." Chap. 8 will be devoted to that notion.

The third political scientist is Thomas P.M. Barnett, yet another Harvard Ph.D. Barnett (2004: 5) describes himself as a child of the 1960s who, captivated by 1970s superpower summitry, set his sights on a career on international security studies. He specialized in Soviet studies—only to be "abandoned by history" (for the time being, perhaps). Then in the post-Cold War years he divided his time between government service and Washington think tanks. The Naval War College was a major early affiliation; by way of that he also became involved in research consultancy with a brokerage firm on Wall Street. Barnett first came to wider public attention in 2002 when *Esquire* identified him as a "best and brightest" thinker, and then the same magazine published his article "The Pentagon's New Map" the following year. Another year, and the article had grown into a book, with the same title. If *The Pentagon's New Map* (2004) has hardly had quite the same impact as Huntington's, Nye's and Barber's writings, it offers notable variations on major themes, as well as insights into organizational contexts of the making of, and the debating over, scenarios. In later work, Barnett (2005, 2009) has focused less on mapping the world, and more on policy implications. Working out of an Indiana base, he has been more of a freelancing writer, blogger and speaker, with consultancy affiliations.

Among the non-quintet people who figure in the scenario genre are also some more historians. Samuel Huntington actually did not invent the notion of "the clash of civilizations" himself—he borrowed it from the historian Bernard Lewis, originally British but based in the United States (at Princeton University) for most of his active academic life. Lewis was a classic kind of Orientalist, who had early been given access to the Ottoman archives in Istanbul, and who went on to write prolifically on the Middle East for decades to come. He coined the term "clash of civilizations" in an article titled "The Roots of Muslim Rage," again in *The Atlantic Monthly* (1990). That article drew wide attention, and it as well as other writings of his have been cited frequently in the overall debate about global scenarios. Lewis himself, however, has mostly remained a commentator on Islam, the Middle East, and the Arab World rather than a globalist, so he is somewhat marginal to the concerns of this book (although he will make a personal appearance at one point). We may remember that when Edward Said, prominent Palestinian intellectual in New York exile, published his book *Orientalism* (1978), Bernard Lewis was a main target for his critique.

We might note, too, that Lewis was an early migrant from Britain to academic life in the United States, and that others have followed him later. Paul Kennedy, of the "One Big Thing" quintet, was one of them, and there have been more, not least historians. But insofar as they have been inclined to keep some connection to their country of origin, one may think of them as mid-Atlantic.[8]

Timothy Garton Ash is perhaps rather unusual in establishing his reputation early in his career, and on the basis of his participant observation in Central European society in its period of 1980s transition rather than a stay in the archives—really more the career pattern of an anthropologist rather than an historian. Mostly he is in Oxford, but he also has a California connection, at Stanford. In the 1980s, much of the time, he was behind the Iron Curtain, doing "history of the present" (and journalism), spending time not least in somewhat subterranean hideouts and hangouts. Then the fall of 1989 came, and his friends in the old opposition became national leaders. It was Ash who made the famous comment that in Poland, the transition period away from Communism had been ten years; in Hungary ten months; in Czechoslovakia ten days. Among his writings drawing on that period are *The Uses of Adversity* (1989) and *We The People* (1990). In 2006 he was awarded the George Orwell Prize for his political writing.

The book most directly relevant to our interest in global scenarios, however, is *Free World* (2004), about what unites North America and Europe, with Britain in an intermediary position—Ash stands out here as a firm Atlanticist. This was a book very much of its precise times, in a field of heated debate. The war in Iraq had been a very divisive venture among what had long been more or less close allies, and this was quite often portrayed as a conflict between America and Europe. Another mid-Atlantic historian (sort of—he had moved, for a while at least, from Washington to Brussels, when his wife was an American diplomat at the European Union headquarters), Robert Kagan, had just argued, on the first page of his book *Paradise and Power* (2003), that "on major strategic and international questions today, Americans are from Mars and Europeans are from Venus: they agree on little and understand one another less and less." Yet another commentator in the period, Robert Cooper, sometimes described as a British "diplomat-intellectual," was not so mid-Atlantic, but rather more clearly anchored on the European side. He, too, however, should be included in our cast here. In his book *The Breaking of Nations*, also of 2003 (and again an Orwell Prize winner), with the subtitle "Order and Chaos in the Twenty-first Century," his argument was that Europeans and Americans were in different stages of human political evolution: by the beginning of the new century there co-existed pre-modern, modern, and postmodern states. That scheme actually was not so different from the classifications offered by some other scenarists, yet Cooper's way of bringing time and evolution into a contemporary map raises some special questions.

Our final mid-Atlantic historian, Niall Ferguson, spent some idyllic childhood years in postcolonial Kenya but grew up mostly in Glasgow before his academic life started out at Oxford. It was the 1980s then, and Ferguson quickly moved into stridently conservative student circles. He developed a specialization in economic history, but has also branched out from it quite freely, and shown notable skills of synthesis. His first book to draw significant attention was a reinterpretation of World War I and its aftermath, *The Pity of War* (1998), where Ferguson suggested that for Britain to get involved in that conflict had perhaps not been a good idea. If it had not done so, the result may have been a post-Great War continental Europe under strong German influence, but it could have been a Germany where Nazism would not have arisen. That was an argument bound to provoke a debate, and it did. (The controversy gained new life in 2014, with the centenary of the outbreak of the war in question.) Then Ferguson evidently saw a more promising future on the other side of the Atlantic, and established himself first at New York University, later at Harvard, but with occasional returns to Britain. The two books *Empire* (2003) and *Colossus* (2004a) mark his move to the American scene. In an era of empire-bashing, the former offered a contrarian view of the benefits the old British variety had brought to the world. The latter, most relevant to our concerns here, asked why the United States would not live up to its imperial potential. In addition to his books, Ferguson has continued to make himself visible through other media forms.

Apart from these contributors to the global scenario genre, another number of names may be listed together, and one may quickly sense what they have in common: Amy Chua, Josef Joffe (already mentioned in passing), Parag Khanna, Bernard-Henri Lévy, Amin Maalouf, Kishore Mahbubani, Dominique Moïsi, Simon Tay, Fareed Zakaria...[9] The reason for turning them into a single set, and it may not be very strong, is that in one way or other, they have roots outside North America—all those enumerated before in this chapter are natives either of the United States or Britain, and in the latter case they are almost all academic migrants to America. In contrast, Lévy and Moïsi are French, Amin Maalouf also from France but before that from Lebanon, Joffe is German, Mahbubani and Tay are from Singapore. Khanna and Zakaria are now Asian-Americans, but both came from India in relatively young years. Amy Chua is American-born, but by parents who had recently arrived from the Philippines and who were of Chinese ethnic background. Someone with the name Oliver Todd may not sound as if he belongs on this list, but he does: he is another Frenchman. In Chap. 9, the question will be raised whether these commentators on the global present and future, with their particular linkages, can bring other sensibilities and points of view into what has in large part been a genre anchored in the United States.

INVASION ALARMS

Finally, if most of the scenarists identified so far tend to be more or less global in their scope, a couple of smaller sideshows are linked both to them and to each other; one is European, the other American. Samuel Huntington, it could be said, had something to do with both. His "clash of civilizations" theme tended to focus on a clash between Muslims and the West, and then there was that later book, *Who Are We?*—to repeat, critical of multiculturalism, suspicious of the consequences of Mexican immigration to the USA.

In both instances, alarms are raised about homelands, home continents, being invaded. In the European case, the key term is "Eurabia." Its origins may not be entirely clear, but one British-based writer publishing mostly under the name Bat Ye'or has promoted it particularly energetically, for one thing in her book *Eurabia* (2005). The well-known Italian journalist Oriana Fallaci (2006) also took a liking to the term and played a part in spreading it through her anti-Islamic texts in the years before her death. But other writers have contributed to the European invasion scenario as well. Bruce Bawer published his *While Europe Slept* in 2006, Christopher Caldwell his *Reflections on the Revolution in Europe* in 2009. More specifically concerned with Britain, and the growth of a "terror state within," Melanie Phillips' *Londonistan* also appeared in 2006.

On the whole, a certain type of American concern with Europe Eurabizing may go well with that early twenty-first century view of a deepening split between America and Europe. A Canadian-born columnist(-humorist) writing mostly for North American publications, Mark Steyn, goes some way toward this imagery in his book *America Alone*—again a 2006 publication—although he sees Islam eating its way into American life as well. But generally, American alarmism at home is more often directed toward an invasion from south of the border. If most newcomers to the United States, now and in the past, have been intent on joining the American mainstream, the Hispanics, it is argued, remain separate.

It is notable that on both sides of the Atlantic, the writers in question warn not only of the hordes from abroad, but also of their treacherous domestic allies. So more complicated culture wars are actually fought here. We focus on them in Chap. 4.

NOTES

1. Later yet, Bill Keller has engaged with the problems of American criminal justice, by way of a new non-profit organization (see Funt 2015).
2. Midcentury modernization thinkers, that is, were mostly optimists. Toward the end of the century, a generation or so later, commentators on "modernity" tended to be more often critical.
3. Friedman's first Pulitzer Prize in 1983 was for coverage of the civil war in Lebanon. The second, in 1988, was for his reporting on Israel. The third, in 2002, was for his writings on the world-wide terrorist threat; this, of course, was after 9—11.
4. Friedman's co-author Mandelbaum, a prominent Johns Hopkins University political scientist with a number of books on international politics, has also served in the U.S. State Department.
5. Friedman's interlocutor was Nandan Nilekani, of Infosys; if Nilekani needed any more claim to fame, which is doubtful, being Friedman's source for this insight made him even more of a public figure.

6. A book-length critique of Friedman's work from the left carries the title *The Imperial Messenger* (Fernández 2011). See also two chapters in the book *Why America's Top Pundits Are Wrong*—to which we come back in the next chapter—by anthropologists Angelique Haugerud (2005) and Ellen Hertz and Laura Nader (2005), and one critique from the viewpoint of a China specialist (Wasserstrom 2014).

7. Kaplan apparently has the stretch limo image from Thomas Homer-Dixon, Canadian environmentalist/security studies scholar.

8. To avoid misunderstanding: not mid-US seaboard here, but rather in the BBC sense of mid-Atlantic accent (neither distinctly British nor clearly American). Simon Schama and the late Tony Judt are other prominent British historians who have migrated to the United States.

9. One might have thought that someone with a name like Fukuyama also belongs on this list; but apart from the name, there seems to be hardly anything Japanese about Francis Fukuyama, a third-generation American.

CHAPTER 2

When Pundits Go Global

In October, 2005, *Prospect*, the British journal of opinion, and the American journal *Foreign Policy* jointly published a list identifying one hundred leading "global public intellectuals"—an example of the kind of world-wide rankings recently proliferating in many fields. It was striking that when that list was opened up to a mail vote by the readership on who would be the Number One, the choice for top global intellectual turned out to be Noam Chomsky, American theoretical linguist transformed into political critic—no doubt radically opposed to much of what his country stood for at the time. And when the two journals again organized such a vote, in 2008, it was very unexpectedly won by Fethullah Gülen, a Turkish Muslim thinker-organizer in American exile who was probably at the time entirely unknown to most of the readers. (He has appeared more frequently in the news later, due to the problematic relationship between his Hizmet movement and the Turkish government.) Obviously there had been a campaign to bring out a vote for Gülen. And since then, having shown its vulnerability to such manipulation, the list, recurrent in somewhat varying forms, has probably lost much of its attractiveness.

That first list, however, could be taken to show the interest in questions of the global future in a public sphere supposedly transcending borders. The list included four of the members of that "One Big Thing" Quintet—Thomas Friedman, Francis Fukuyama, Samuel Huntington, Paul Kennedy (only Robert Kaplan was missing). Of the other people significantly participating in the global scenario genre, as enumerated in the previous chapter,

Niall Ferguson, Timothy Garton Ash, Bernard Lewis, Robert Kagan, Robert Cooper, Kishore Mahbubani and Fareed Zakaria were likewise on the list. That is, almost one-eighth of the list was taken up by individuals engaging in a more or less similar kind of pursuit.[1] Apart from them, it included a remarkable range of people, from Pope Benedict XVI and the writer Salman Rushdie to the Slovenian philosopher Slavoj Zizek and the "dissident feminist" Camille Paglia. The one anthropologist on the list, Clifford Geertz, will appear occasionally in the pages which follow.

So this is what this chapter is about: the way the global scenarios reach out to a wider public, and in what sense they are not only *about* the world but also *for* the world. It is about the social life of scenarios, their production and circulation, their passage through the world terrain. So let us first give some thought to who those people are who were identified in the previous chapter.

With the exception of the rather brief presence of Amy Chua (see Chap. 9), and of a few writers contributing to the body of alarmist writings about Eurabia, all are men—and one may wonder why this is so. Probably it reflects the lingering male prevalence in some varieties of journalism, and in certain academic fields. Would more women scenarists might have offered us something different? One could suspect that gender issues might have been more in evidence—in different ways, they would seem especially important to the internal workings of some civilizations, and to prognoses of global crowding.

As far as age is concerned, Bernard Lewis, the Orientalist, born in 1916, is certainly the oldest among the writers appearing here. Samuel Huntington was born in 1927, his Harvard colleague Joseph Nye is a decade younger, and Benjamin Barber a couple of years younger yet. Then there are a number of people born in the 1940s and 1950s, loosely characterizable as "baby boomers": Robert Kaplan, Francis Fukuyama, Thomas Friedman, Timothy Garton Ash, Robert Cooper, Robert Kagan. Niall Ferguson and Fareed Zakaria are 1960s people, and Parag Khanna was born in 1977.[2]

For most of these authors, in other words, many of the dramatic moments and periods of the Cold War were somewhat before their time of mature awareness (the uprising in Hungary, the building of the Berlin Wall, the Cuban crisis, the height of the wars in Southeast Asia.) They could travel, one may suspect, with a lighter personal baggage of historical memories than Huntington could do—already established as a theorist in the 1950s and 1960s, and remaining preoccupied with bloc politics—or for that matter Bernard Lewis, having lived through a long period when his Middle East was still under European colonialism.

The scenarists are not always easy to place on a right-left political scale, and occasionally someone may noticeably change position, and company.[3] But certainly they are in different loci, some more neoliberal, others conservative or neoconservative, perhaps someone identifiable as center or vaguely center-left. Of those active in the United States, a majority are based in that Northeastern Seaboard corridor, between Massachusetts and the District of Columbia, where much of American political, academic and media strength is concentrated.

It is probably fair to say that the circle of scenarists exhibit a degree of mutual awareness, and a certain network density. Thomas Friedman, of course, showed such awareness at an early point when he identified the "One Big Thing" genre, but we hardly have to rely on his intuition, or on my classification of the genre and identification of its membership. These commentators have continued to quite often refer to each other, comment on each other, review each other, debate with one another, and occasionally interview one another. They also write blurbs for (or are at least quoted on) the back covers of each other's books: Samuel Huntington for Robert Kaplan; Francis Fukuyama for Thomas Friedman, Samuel Huntington and Robert Kagan; Robert Kaplan for Francis Fukuyama; Robert Kagan for Robert Cooper; Robert Cooper for Robert Kagan; Joseph Nye for Timothy Garton Ash and Thomas Barnett; Timothy Garton Ash and Paul Kennedy for Niall Ferguson.[4]

This does not mean that their comments on each other's products are always friendly—after all, what they offer are often competing "One Big Things." We have already seen Robert Kaplan seating Fukuyama's followers in that "stretch limousine" on their way to the end of history, and finding Huntington's portrayal of clashing civilizations overly simple. When Robert Kagan (2000) describes Kaplan's work, the tone is not really kindly:

> Robert D. Kaplan has made a career out of exposing the dark side of the post-Cold War world. A travel writer by profession, though one with considerably loftier ambitions, Kaplan has spent the last decade and more visiting the world's hellholes, cataloguing their miseries, and holding them up for discomforting perusal before what he regards as a pampered, self-satisfied Western elite naively clinging to the notion of progress.

And in a new afterword for the paperback edition of *Jihad versus McWorld*—a book which begins with the sentence "History is not over"—Benjamin Barber complains that commentators lumped his book "together with Pandemonium prophets like Robert D. Kaplan…and Samuel P

Huntington…, dismissing us all as Pandoric pessimists." So there is no simple consensus here, but rather an arena for arguments.[5]

Then again, however, they are also more or less identifiable as "public intellectuals," as in that *Prospect/Foreign Policy* ranking list. The term should not mean just that they are thinking celebrities—public intellectuals define the issues of the day, make values explicit, probably argue for agendas, all relevant to a wider citizenry, even to humankind.[6] But they do share a certain public prominence—so how do they get there? Answering that question involves taking some interest in how the landscape of knowledge production and distribution is now constituted.

THE HABITAT OF PUBLIC INTELLECTUALS

Changes in that landscape may well turn out to be One Big Thing as the twenty-first century moves on. The media and the universities were two areas of very powerful development in the twentieth century. William Randolph Hearst created a newspaper empire, and then built his monumental California home Hearst Castle on a hillside overlooking the Pacific Ocean. A little further up the coastline, after having built railroads across America, Leland Stanford founded Stanford University, to become one of the world's finest—but it then became the hothouse of Silicon Valley, which by the time the next century came along had created a technology that could possibly shake the foundations of both academic and print media businesses.

What universities and the newsmedia will eventually do in the Internet age, then, may remain to be seen—the question will reappear briefly in Chap. 5. So far, however, for most people occupationally engaged in them, they are quite separate. One's work is in either one or the other. Some academic writers may be all the rage on campus, in seminar rooms and in learned journals, for a period, but without reaching very far off-campus. (They may then become parts of the accumulated living wisdom, or they may soon be assigned to the dustbins of intellectual history.) In contrast, for the public intellectuals we are concerned with here, boundaries are more blurred. Scholarly work and media visibility are interrelated, and in addition, think tanks of various leanings as well as consultancy work are emerging as features of the same landscape.

Then, too, gates may open to fields of politics and government. The kind of authors we have identified could possibly exercise some influence of their own. They may be public intellectuals, but another label would likewise be relevant—they tend also to be "organic intellectuals," in the sense once proposed by Antonio Gramsci: people who refine and explicate the perspectives of a certain political class of which they are in some way themselves members.[7]

Several of them—Huntington, Kagan, Nye, Fukuyama—have served in Washington in one administration or other.[8] The acknowledgements of Robert Cooper's book *The Breaking of Nations* inform us that its second part was "originally intended to be a short note for the Prime Minister to read at Christmas" (Cooper 2003: vi); this was at a time when Cooper was one of Tony Blair's closest foreign policy advisors at No. 10, Downing Street. And in Benjamin Barber's book *The Truth of Power* (2001), we have an account of the interactions of the Clinton administration with American intellectual life, drawing on Barber's own experience. Watching the C-SPAN broadcast of a White House prayer breakfast one morning, Barber is no doubt very pleased to find President Clinton praising the insights of *Jihad vs. McWorld*, and holding up a copy of the book for everybody to see. (The picture of the scene is in the book, as well as Clinton's appreciative inscription in a book of his own speeches which Barber received from him.) Barber had a number of personal encounters with the president, and was for some time in and out of various White House office rooms. He is also quite forthright about his attempts to get the position as Chair of the National Endowment for the Humanities. He does the networking, but evidently his political profile has been too high and too far to the left. And so the job goes to a Mississippi musicologist, less controversial, a specialist on Delta blues.

Furthermore, those who have not been so directly involved in government may at least have become accustomed to being read and listened to there. Rumor has it that President Clinton read Robert Kaplan's earlier book *Balkan Ghosts* (1993a), and that it played a fateful role in the American reluctance to intervene in the early 1990s conflicts in the dissolving Yugoslavia; that his "coming anarchy" article from *The Atlantic Monthly* circulated quickly by fax among ministries and embassies across the world; and also that his *Imperial Grunts* was what George W. Bush spent a Christmas holiday reading. In June, 2006, too, Kaplan reports, he was among a handful of guests at Camp David, the presidential rural retreat, to brief President Bush, Vice President Cheney, Defense Secretary Rumsfeld, and Secretary of State Condoleezza Rice about what to do with the Iraq War, in a stage of disaster—"I recommended adopting a counterinsurgency strategy."[9]

As for Thomas Friedman, when the *Washington Post*, competing newspaper, portrayed him in late 2001 (under a rubric beginning "Thomas Friedman Comes Out Swinging..."), it quoted an anonymous White House official: "We ignore him at our peril...He's a very thoughtful guy with more than a dash of Tabasco. Sometimes what he writes is important and sometimes it's drivel. But his audience is really important." (Kurtz 2001) And then a decade or so later, on a Friday afternoon in August 2014, Friedman could have an hour with President Obama to himself, covering world affairs, and display the interview afterwards on the *New York Times* website.[10]

With regard to contacts and passages between Academia, the media, think tanks and consultant businesses, let us just note a few instances. Robert Kaplan may be primarily a journalist, but his curriculum vitae also includes a period as visiting professor at the United States Naval Academy, Annapolis, and a few years on Pentagon's Defense Policy Board. After that he has been a fellow at the Center for a New American Security in Washington, and more recently Chief Geopolitical Analyst at Stratfor, a global intelligence firm based in Austin, Texas.[11] Timothy Garton Ash is a Professor at Oxford University, England, and a Fellow at the Hoover Institution, Stanford University, and has also written a weekly column for the *Guardian*, the British daily (a column which is "widely syndicated in Europe, Asia and the Americas," his website says). Francis Fukuyama is now also at Stanford, but lets his views become known through his blog linked to *The American Interest*.

Moreover, there is Niall Ferguson. Reviewing one of Ferguson's books in the *New York Review of Books*, Paul Kennedy (2006b) notes that his compatriot is "what the British press dubs a 'telly don,'" having hosted successful television series linked to his books. Much before that, while Ferguson was still at Oxford but gaining fame with his controversial book on World War I, a *New Yorker* correspondent could report on his interviewee's forthright comment on what he had learned from his research on the early history of the Rothschild financial family:

> Studying the Rothschilds made me realize, why be a passive, unworldly academic author who expects to be able to sit all day in an ivory tower writing great works that no one will read? After all, history is a business, too. (Boynton 1999: 50)

So about a decade later, the front cover of the December, 2008 issue of *Vanity Fair* (in the middle of the financial crisis) could announce an article by Ferguson: "Is This the End of Banks?" And earlier in that year, it seems, he advised John McCain's unsuccessful presidential campaign.[12]

BOOK LAUNCHES

Having a sense of these positionings of the global scenarists at the intersections between Academia, the media and politics is important as one views the passages of their writings into public life. Generally, the academic response to the "One Big Thing" cluster of writings has not actually been overly enthusiastic. Scholarly journals mostly do not review or otherwise comment on the works of the journalist contributors to the genre—this disregard might seem a bit myopic, considering their impact on public understandings which more or less correspond to particular academic disciplines. Among the texts by academics, Huntington's "clash of civilizations" scenario has probably received more attention than most of the others, and the professoriate gave it mixed reviews. In the *American Journal of Sociology*, the historical sociologist Edward Tiryakian (1997) was mostly favorable, concluding that the study "draws on a large literature and utilizes important empirical documentation," and that it is "a major launching pad for reconceptualizing the world order and its major units of analysis." Pierre Hassner (1996/97), French international relations specialist, found inconsistencies with Huntington's previous work, thought there could be another synthesis with these, and thus ended with a request: "play it again, Sam!" [13]And Robert Marks (2000), writing in the *Journal of World History*, described it as "bad history in at least five ways." In Marks' view, Huntington ignored alternatives to the civilizationist approach to world history; his selection of sources was poor; he used historical anecdotes from numerous times and places as evidence for grand generalizations; the fit between civilizations and states as actors is not very precise; and the book was "politics masquerading as scholarship." So the reviewer concluded that "a little knowledge (in Huntington's case, of history) certainly can be dangerous."

To the best of my knowledge, no major anthropological journal reviewed Huntington's book at the time of its publication, but later on, in a book with the title *Why America's Top Pundits are Wrong*, a group of mostly American anthropologists somewhat polemically discussed the writings by Samuel Huntington, Thomas Friedman, and Robert Kaplan, as well as some number of pundits whose errors were committed in other fields (Besteman and Gusterson 2005). One of the editors, Hugh Gusterson, devoted a chapter to the "clash of civilizations" thesis, with the title "The Seven Deadly Sins of Samuel Huntington"—the errors thus enumerated had to do with basic definitions; stereotyping cultures; ignoring change; denying multiculturalism; maligning Islam; phony scientific methods; and the West as the Best. [14]

Marks' and Gusterson's criticisms certainly overlapped in some ways, so five and seven may not in this case add up to twelve, It seems clear enough, however, that disciplines can have bloody borders, too.

The academic reception, however, has hardly been what has mattered most to the fate of books in the global scenario genre. Even when the authors are academics, they have published these books mostly with trade presses, not university presses.[15] They are books for the corridors of power and the market place rather more than for the ivory tower, and the first two of these three can possibly be combined. When authors are political animals, with agendas, reaching out through the market place need not be just a question of maximizing sales. The underlying assumption can indeed be that accessing a wider public now makes a political difference, and that this kind of writings is a worthwhile way of shaping opinion. This could in itself be a matter of some debate: have international relations, some of them at least, become too important to be left to statesmen? Are the scenario topics now really the concerns of a wider public, not something confined to a narrow circle of specialists, with points of view inclined toward *Realpolitik*?[16] Possibly there has been a more general democratization of international politics, as some may claim, or it may have come to involve a more varied set of actors and interest groups. Or the wider audience may exist with regard to some issues more than others. One of the authors, Robert Cooper (2003: 102), makes the general point that even if "in the end, what matters is domestic politics," it has become increasingly difficult to separate what is domestic from what is international, as the two are so often entangled with one another—in the economy, in diaspora issues, in human rights commitments, or whatever. In any case, if a wider audience is to be reached and influenced, ideas must be packaged right. In a hybrid genre, the scenarios can also offer politainment.

As far as their launching is concerned, we have already noticed that in a typical trajectory, a scenario first appears in a brief version in some more or less authoritative American journal of opinion—*Foreign Affairs, Foreign Policy, The National Interest, The Atlantic Monthly.* (And again, Thomas Barnett's short sketch of "the Pentagon's New Map" was in *Esquire.*) Then soon enough the article grows into a book, elaborating on the first conceptualization.

At this stage, the scenario formulations have moved out into the world. Perhaps I first became curious about this wider impact toward the end of the 1990s—as I traveled I could find piles of the Huntington book in bookstores not only in New York but also in Frankfurt, or Florence, or Tokyo, in the original or in translation. Soon enough, not only Huntington but a number of the works of scenario authors took the step into airport literature, the titles we find in the bookstalls at Chicago-O'Hare, London-Heathrow, Singapore-Chengi or Stockholm-Arlanda, sharing table space with volumes on business leadership or successful global corporations. Obviously these bookstalls are premium sites for displaying titles of particular interest to the world's frequent flyers. (Questions could be asked about this—who selects the books for these outlets? And even if the books are picked up there, are they actually read—from cover to cover? Depending on the length of the flight?)

Frequently, however, as an article becomes a book, it may be just as important that the original has also already offered the message encapsulated in some even briefer formulation. And what above all enters the popular imagination are those seductive soundbites and catch phrases, fast food for thought: "the end of history," "clash of civilizations," "Americans are from Mars, Europeans are from Venus," "the world is flat," "soft power." Preferably, it seems, they should be unexpected, paradoxical, counterintuitive. History normally does not end, we do believe the world is round, both Europeans and Americans are earthlings rather than from other planets, real power is not so soft. Even the clash of civilizations may sound paradoxical, to the extent that we expect civilizations to be civilized.

It is tempting to believe that the scenarios in this commodity form draw considerably on ways with words acquired on the arenas of media and politics. Yet perhaps organizational logics and dramatic competences of different kinds can converge here. We can choose to listen here to a commentator who has much in common with the scenarists, although not quite a contributor to the genre. Michael Ignatieff is another historian, with a Harvard doctorate, and the son of a Russian *émigré* who became a Canadian diplomat. He has taught at his alma mater, has written prolifically—both fiction and non-fiction—and gained some fame as a broadcaster during a sojourn in Britain.[17] One of his books earned him an Orwell Prize, another was shortlisted for a Booker Prize. More lately he has served a period as leader of the Liberal Party in Canada, a period which did not end well as his party lost a national election badly. And so he went back to Harvard.

Following the philosopher Isaiah Berlin (with whom he studied at Oxford), Ignatieff (2007) has argued that it is the academics who have a demand on them to be interesting, and the politicians who must "work with the small number of ideas that happen to be true and the even smaller number that happen to be applicable to real life." In academic life, false ideas are just false, Ignatieff suggests, but if they are useless one may still enjoy playing with them—an intellectual's responsibility for these ideas is to try and work out their consequences. Politicians, in contrast, "cannot afford to cocoon themselves in the inner world of their imaginings." A sense of reality is a street virtue when acting on one's ideas can waste resources and ruin lives.

Ignatieff may exaggerate the inner-worldly playfulness of scholars a bit, and overestimate the sharp sense of reality of at least some political practitioners. Street wisdom does not always include a sense of what is around the corner. (I am reminded of one classic statement by the veteran politician Donald Rumsfeld which, at least out of context, I actually find quite insightful: "There are things we know that we know. There are known unknowns; that is to say there are things that we now know we don't know. But there are also unknown unknowns. There are things we do not know we don't know."[18]) It may still be possible that the campus experiences of several scenarists have been an asset in their more public endeavors as well, and time spent at off-campus think tanks seems likely to be of similar value.

NEWSMEDIA AS GATEKEEPERS

Books in the scenario genre may indeed do well in the market place. As one reviewer put it, reflecting on a new batch of titles: "These are times that try men's souls yet put wolfish smiles of profitable anticipation upon the lips of non-fiction publishers." (Beattie 2011)

Yet the game can be a little treacherous. Those capsule formulations may not always be understood precisely in the way their authors had in mind. Repeatedly the authors complain that they have been misunderstood. Looking back at the reception of his "end of history" argument, Fukuyama (1995b), lists Margaret Thatcher, Mikhail Gorbachev, the first President Bush, and Hosni Mubarak among the persons who, noting in their speeches that history still goes on, had rejected what they, or perhaps their speech writers, had thought was his thesis. And a friend had sent him a cutting from a newspaper in Dhaka, Bangladesh, where a columnist had noted that a Bangladeshi had been bumped from a British Airways flight; thus there was still racism in the world, so history had not ended. Joseph Nye (2003), trying to explain his concept once more, starts out from an exchange between George Carey, ex-archbishop of Canterbury, and Colin Powell, U.S. Secretary of State, at the World Economic Forum, Davos, about the uses of soft power.

But then not all the users of the new key concepts and catch phrases may have them straight from the original texts. The scenario producers may have their powerful readers, and also lay audiences of quite ordinary readers, Yet we should remind ourselves of that encounter of mine with Bill Keller, the *New York Times* editor, with which I began Chap. 1. There are also those people like him who take a special interest in such products, consuming them, commenting on them, passing them on. And perhaps doing somewhat parallel work themselves.

As I engaged in my study of the work of foreign correspondents, I could note that in shaping the view of the world and its parts, the correspondents and their editors, on the one hand, and the scenario writers, on the other, faced some of the same challenges, and could become entangled with one another as they sought solutions. Early in that study, I had a chance to talk to Tom Kent, then the international editor of the Associated Press, the news agency, in his mid-Manhattan office. It was in the mid-1990s, and he brought up one recent set of events. "In the past," he said, "if there had been a war between the Hutu and the Tutsi, our first question would have been, who is ours and who is theirs?" There was indeed some likelihood, he suggested, that even in such a conflict, one side would have been getting its arms and its political support from one of the main camps of the Cold War, and the other side its from the opposite camp. But the end of the Cold War had left much foreign news coverage without a major interpretive framework.

Foreign news reporting tends to involve story lines. These offer the red threads, the more enduring themes, which connect stories to one another and offer news consumers a sense of basic familiarity with times and places. Story lines are often regional. I could identify story lines for Africa, and for the Middle East, and for Japan, the places where I did the main parts of my research. But for several decades in foreign news, the Cold War had been a global story line. Like other story lines, it assimilated some events to itself—thereby perhaps transforming them—while it ignored others. Unlike the regional themes, on the other hand, it could readily cross boundaries and move between continents. When it was gone, the foreign correspondents and their editors faced more or less the same kind of challenge which had provoked Huntington, Friedman, Kaplan and others to look for the next "One Big Thing."

Among the more thoughtful of the foreign correspondents—and there are many of them—how story lines work, and their limits, and their consequences, have been a topic of enduring concern. Perhaps on the whole, in the marketplace of news, the story lines of journalists and the book-length scenarios operate according to complementary logics: the story lines allow audiences to come back to the next installment in a series of sufficiently recognizable products, while the scenarios offer a more self-contained and complete vision of proclaimed change and discontinuity. But there are interactions between scenarios and story lines; and it should be clear that the relationship is hardly one-way, but more symbiotic. On the one hand, as you check the footnotes of the scenarios, you find that their empirical evidence is often from journalism—the *New York Times*, the *Washington Post*, the *Boston Globe* (home town newspaper of Harvard faculty), *Wall Street Journal*, *Financial Times*, *The Economist*. On the other hand, scenarios can turn into story lines. And thus those key terms and formulations launched through the scenarios can often find their way to a wider circulation, with the newsmedia as gatekeepers.

So the "clash of civilizations" could seem to have turned into a substitute for the Cold War as a major story line. It came up quickly and widely after 9-11, and a few years later particularly in Scandinavian media, after the Danish newspaper *Jyllandsposten* had commissioned a set of caricatures of the Prophet Muhammad, and crowds protested in Palestine, Syria, Lebanon, Pakistan and elsewhere, burning an embassy in one city and a consulate in another, in a rather improbable *jihad* against Denmark. It might not matter all that much if commentators will go on to argue that, no, this was not really a case of a clash of civilizations, and that they do not like the notion anyway. What remains stuck at the back of the distracted reader's, listener's or viewer's mind may be that there is something called a clash of civilizations. And by then, transformed from the individual scholar's interpretive invention into a collective representation, it has certainly moved beyond what could have been Samuel Huntington's control. (In February, 2010—a little over a year after his death—*Newsweek* had as its cover story "How Bin Laden Lost The Clash of Civilizations.")

It is this kind of shift which makes the global future scenarios not only texts which are partly *about* culture, but also important cultural phenomena in their own right. They become features of our shared habitat of meaning, tools people use to think with as they face the world as it is, and wonder where it may be going. But they may not always be passively received, and uniformly accepted. It can matter where they come from, and also what people end up doing with them.

AUDIENCES EVERYWHERE

It also matters where they are headed. Returning to the book *Why America's Top Pundits are Wrong*, let us at this point go no further than the title page.

"Pundits," in English, is originally a loan word from Hindi. So it is a fairly early example of linguistic globalization. ("Guru," having made a similar but slightly later journey, may be adopted with a more ironic tinge.) Dictionary definitions tell us that pundits are authorities on one subject or other, "learned men," people who offer authoritative opinions. There might be a certain affinity between "pundits" and "public intellectuals," although they are certainly not synonymous. The contributors to *Why America's Top Pundits are Wrong*, however, cast some doubt on the authoritativeness involved. Here, to begin with, I will dwell rather on that suggested collective identity which the earlier title suggests: "*America's.*" It is not that I would deny that the pundits in question carry U.S. passports. The question is to what extent, and in what way, their punditry is all-American.

I come back here to my browsing in those dispersed airport book stalls. You can pick up at least the more commercially successful of these scenario texts next to the departure gates and runways just about anywhere in the world.

By the time Huntington got around to writing the preface to the book-length version of his argument, he could point out that in the wake of the 1993 article, he had not only become involved in innumerable meetings with academic, government and business groups across the United States. Moreover, he had had the opportunity to participate in discussions of its thesis in "many other countries, including Argentina, Belgium, China, France, Germany, Great Britain, Korea, Japan, Luxembourg, Russia, Saudi Arabia, Singapore, South Africa, Spain, Sweden, Switzerland, and Taiwan" (Huntington 1996: 13–14). Clearly there had been a very considerable interest abroad in the "clash of civilizations" scenario—judging from the list, in just about all the civilizations he had identified.

I also saw in those airport settings, nodal points of global mobility and interconnectedness, that while some of the scenario texts in question were for sale in their English-language originals, others were there in translation. In the bookshops of Berlin, Vienna or Zürich, I might find Thomas Friedman's *Die Welt ist flach*, Samuel Huntington's *Kampf der Kulturen*, Francis Fukuyama's *Das Ende der Geschichte*, Benjamin Barber's *Coca Cola und Heiliger Krieg* (since the soft drink and the hamburger are exchangeable metaphors for consumer commodity globalization in the McWorld), Robert Kaplan's *Reisen an die Grenzen der Menschheit*, Robert Kagan's *Macht und Ohnmacht*, Joseph Nye's *Das Paradox der amerikanischen Macht*, Niall Ferguson's *Das verleugnete Imperium*, and Timothy Garton Ash's *Freie Welt*. I could go into a Paris bookshop and find Huntington's *Le choc des civilizations*, Friedman's *La terre est plate*, Kagan's *La puissance et la faiblesse*, Fukuyama's *Le fin de l'histoire et le dernier home*, and Barber's *Djihad versus macworld: mondialisation et integrisme contre la democratie*. In Rome there would be Nye's *Il paradosso del potere Americano*. And so on. In Samuel Huntington's obituary in the *Daily Telegraph*, the London paper, I would learn that *The Clash of Civilizations and the Remaking of World Order* had been translated into more than three dozen languages.[19]

We will revisit the issue of language and translation in Chap. 9. In any case, it would seem that in one sense, the "One Big Thing" Quintet, and most of the other scenario writers we have taken note of here, are not only America's top pundits—they are top pundits of the world. It turns out that if they have presidents and prime ministers in their American and British readerships, there are highly placed readers in other countries as well. Benazir Bhutto (2008) of Pakistan, too, read Huntington—we come back to that in Chap. 3. When various secret cable messages from American diplomatic missions back to Washington were made public in the *Wikileaks* affair, it became known that Colonel Muammar Qaddafi, still ruler of Libya, had ordered Arabic-language summaries of books by Thomas Friedman and Fareed Zakaria, as well as by Barack Obama. And after the uprising against Qaddafi had started, in the Arab Spring of 2011, Joseph Nye and Benjamin Barber had to respond to questions about why they had earlier taken up invitations to go and visit him in Tripoli, and had offered perhaps somewhat ambiguous opinions about him.[20] In Chap. 9 we will see what Lee Kuan Yew, founding father of the nation of Singapore, had to say about the "clash of civilizations."

The global scenarists thus write about the world, and—whether they think much about this fact or not—for the world. Certainly the scenarios often show that they are primarily intended for American readers. These are stories that Americans tell themselves about themselves and their own place in the world. Even so, people in Vienna, Tokyo, Tripoli, Buenos Aires, Singapore and Stockholm read them, too—if only over the natives' shoulders, to paraphrase a well-known formulation by Clifford Geertz, that one anthropologist on the 2005 *Prospect/Foreign Policy* list of the world's top public intellectuals.[21]

If the scenarios thus travel across borders, however, some of the more interesting questions about them begin at these crossings, because their reception need not be entirely passive, smooth, and altogether predictable. That is also something we will come back to.

NOTES

1. A look at the *Prospect/Foreign Policy* list also offers another opportunity to comment on the selection of writers in the scenario genre offered in Chap. 1—there is undoubtedly something a little arbitrary about the kind of selection I have made. The individuals whose writings I dwell on here are surely part of a wider field of social, political and cultural commentary on contemporary issues. We are concerned in this book, however, with a set of writers on the present and emergent global landscape who do reach a wider audience. Some number of academics who did achieve considerable prominence in scholarly circles in the period involved do not seem to have reached quite so far outside these (or they have been more of "public intellectuals" on their national arenas, but with a more restricted global impact). I believe this is true for example of the sociologists Ulrich Beck, Manuel Castells, and Immanuel Wallerstein (perhaps most visible in a slightly earlier period); also, although this may be a more marginal case, Anthony Giddens, who unlike them is indeed on the *Prospect/Foreign Policy* list. Giddens, British sociologist, was another of Prime Minister Blair's conversation partners and eventually knighted by him, thus shifting his base from the London School of Economics to the House of Lords. Yet I think he has remained mostly of intra-academic fame. More importantly, his major intellectual contributions are not quite in the global scenario genre. Neither, I think, are those of Noam Chomsky and Naomi Klein, radical commentators on the recent era and both on the *Prospect/Foreign Policy* list, although their critical writings on world politics or the world economy certainly get a wide range of readers outside the species of *Homo academicus*. I was initially somewhat of two minds about Michael Hardt and Antonio Negri, writing together in a noteworthy radical alliance between the Italian Red Brigades and the Duke University Department of English,

and best known for their books *Empire* (2000) and *Multitude* (2004). As commentators have noted, however, their portrayal of the world is on the generalizing and abstract side, seldom touching ground anywhere in particular in the global landscape, and culture does not get much explicit attention either. Their writing may also be less user-friendly, thus hardly reaching far outside the academic world. One may note, too, that the scenario authors we focus on here hardly ever refer to Giddens, Chomsky, Klein, Beck, Wallerstein, Hardt and Negri, or Castells. Network boundaries seem quite sharply drawn here.

In *Foreign Policy*, a few years later, one article author took on the task of sketching the formula for success of scenario writers—Fukuyama, Huntington, Kagan, Nye, Zakaria—in a way which very briefly parallels the concerns of this book (Lozada 2009).

2. I have my information on scenarist ages from their Wikipedia biographies.

3. Perhaps most notably, Francis Fukuyama (2006) broke with the company of neoconservatives he had mostly been keeping until then, when he came out in opposition to the Iraq War.

4. As will be seen in Chap. 9, Fareed Zakaria, Josef Joffe and Kishore Mahbubani also fit into the same network.

5. For another instance of debate between scenarists, see the exchange between Friedman and Kaplan (2002) in the journal *Foreign Policy*, revealing in terms of content as well as style.

6. On public intellectuals, see for example Said (1994) and Small (2002).

7. Gramsci (1971) presents his view of "organic intellectuals" in the *Prison Notebooks*, written while he was in Mussolini's prisons, mostly in the early 1930s; so his understandings are embedded in Italian history and a specific political situation, but can also be adapted to other contexts.

8. Samuel Huntington worked for the National Security Council in the Carter administration, Robert Kagan was in the State Department in the Reagan Administration (and advised John McCain's presidential campaign in 2008), and Joseph Nye was in the State Department in the Carter administration and in the Defense Department in the Clinton administration. Francis Fukuyama had two periods in the State Department in the 1980s.

9. This is from "Writing Career Reflections," on Kaplan's website, *www.robertdkaplan.com*.

10. In between, Governor Mike Huckabee, candidate for the Republican presidential nomination in 2008, also identified Thomas Friedman as one of the foreign affairs thinkers who influenced him (Chafetz 2007).

11. Stratfor is the enterprise headed by George Friedman (evidently unrelated to Thomas), who himself has a couple of contributions to the scenario genre (2009, 2010); but as these tend seldom to be referred to by key

members of the cluster of authors, I do not attend to them here. Budapest-born George Friedman has a political science doctorate from Cornell University and was a college teacher for some time before starting his consultancy business.

12. The *Vanity Fair* article, titled "Wall Street Lays Another Egg," suggested that "This year we have lived through something more than a financial crisis. We have witnessed the death of a planet. Call it Planet Finance." Ferguson's role as advisor to John McCain is referred to, for one thing, in a portrait of the scholar in *The Observer*, the London Sunday paper (Skidelsky 2011). (Robert Kagan, too, advised McCain—see note 9.)

13. Huntington (1997) responded to Hassner's review by noting that a "bad review" can mean two things. In one sense, it means that the review is unfavorable, in the other sense that it is "simpleminded, superficial, irrelevant, or inaccurate." Hassner's review, in Huntington's opinion, was bad in both senses—a "bad bad review."
   For another comprehensive, critical commentary by a political scientist and Middle East specialist, see Wedeen (2003).

14. A later anthropologist commentator, Peter van der Veer (2014: 218–220), a specialist on the past and present of Asian world religions, describes Huntington's thesis as "one of the more disturbing recent theoretical applications of the concept of civilization"—"we need to avoid essentializations of civilizations without denying the deep histories of especially religious traditions and processes of state formation that connect people over vast territories."

15. I argued in note 1 that Michael Hardt and Antonio Negri were too strictly academic writers to really belong in the genre discussed in this book. Nevertheless, one could note that between *Empire* and *Multitude*, this team of authors shifted from Harvard University Press to Penguin.

16. There may have been a time when public opinion was held not to matter much in the conduct of international relations, but the view is now at least quite widespread that this is no longer true; the range of actors and interests has widened, to include for instance major NGOs and diasporas (see e g Mathews 1997, McConnell 2009). From my research on the work of foreign correspondents I recall a response by one of the best-known war reporters of the BBC, Martin Bell (1996: 138), to a comment by the British foreign secretary at the time about the impact of media images on the public view of the war in Bosnia—the latter dignitary makes it sound as if "the world would somehow be a better place if the killing continued and yet we knew nothing of it…The mandarins' objection is not just to the power but to the impertinence of the upstart medium, which challenges their monopoly of wisdom, and rushes in where the pinstripes fear to tread."

17. Among Ignatieff's books showing an affinity with the style of writing, publishing and argument of the scenario genre are *Blood and Belonging* (1993), *The Warrior's Honor* (1997), and *Empire Lite* (2003). Ignatieff was also on the *Prospect* list of public intellectuals referred to above.

18. The Rumsfeld statement occurred in a Pentagon news briefing about the Iraq conflict in 2002, and that has surely contributed to its poor reputation, even as a case of foot-in-mouth disease. Shifted to the context of viewing culture as an organization of diversity, as sketched in Chap. 6, however, it could be a formulation worth keeping in mind.

19. Note that "clash of civilizations" became *Kampf der Kulturen* in German. "Civilization" has tended not to mean quite the same thing in German as in English; in his critical review of Huntington's thesis, Hartmann (1995) also discusses translation problems. The back of a German-language edition of Huntington's book also referred to his thesis as *Kulturknalltheorie*.

20. The circumstances of Barber's and Nye's interactions with Muammar Qaddafi are somewhat murky; the contacts seem to have resulted from the active promotion of Libyan interests by the Monitor Group, an international consultancy firm in which some well-known Harvard faculty members had been deeply involved. Barber (2011) and Nye (2011a) have both responded to criticisms in American magazines; see also Wedel (2014: 208–211). Libyan transnational academic involvements were also evident on the other side of the Atlantic: for one major British university this included a controversial doctoral degree awarded to one of Muammar Qaddafi's sons. On these matters, see the illuminating account by Calhoun (2012). The message about Qaddafi's reading preferences from the United States Embassy in Tripoli, published through *Wikileaks*, appears to have been sent by the diplomat Chris Stevens, later the victim of a much-debated assassination in Benghazi, Libya's second city.

21. This is from Geertz' (1973: 452) classic interpretation of the meaning of cockfights on Bali: "The culture of a people is an ensemble of texts, themselves ensembles, which the anthropologist strains to read over the shoulders of those to whom they properly belong."

CHAPTER 3

Playing with Maps

Worlds can be made in texts, and worlds are also made on maps. Nations, too: seriously or playfully. Browsing in one of the Telegraph Avenue bookstores in Berkeley, California, one afternoon in the early 1980s, I got the message vividly from the title (and the map on the cover) of a new book named *The Nine Nations of North America* (1981). The author was a journalist, Joel Garreau, editor at the *Washington Post*. It appealed to me instantly because I have always been intrigued, as perhaps many other Europeans have not, by the internal diversity of America.[1]

Garreau claimed that the book had its origins in the period he had spent as a desk-bound editor, trying to find out from the reporters on the road what it was really like out there. A new map began to grow in his mind, resulting first in a piece for a Sunday supplement of the paper. That drew a strong response from readers, a number of other papers reprinted it, and someone persuaded him to turn rethinking North America into a book project. So he hit the road himself, and the outcome was the book where he portrayed those nine nations, with little respect for what were the conventional boundaries of the United States, Canada and Mexico. According to Garreau, San Francisco and the Bay Area would have been in Ecotopia, which stretched along the North American coast toward Alaska; south of that nation was MexAmerica, including much of the Southwest and part of Mexico. And in the southeastern corner, below Dixie, was the nation of The Islands, extending into south Florida and with Miami as its capital, but including the Caribbean and parts of the Latin American coast areas as well. Apart from these there were New England (stretching into Atlantic Canada), The Foundry (which we might now also think of as the Rustbelt), The Breadbasket (largely the Plains), The Empty Quarter (inland Northwest), and Quebec.

This, Garreau argued, was the way North America really worked in the late twentieth century. Each of the nine nations had its own capital, each a distinctive web of power and influence, each a peculiar economy. Several had readily acknowledged national poets, and many had characteristic dialects and mannerisms. These nations looked different, felt different, sounded different from one another, and each commanded a certain emotional allegiance from its citizens.

The anthropologist in me was reminded of the relatively early years of a professional American anthropology. The discipline had also been engaged with imagining North America. Before World War II, there was the age of "horse-and-buggy field work" on Indian reservations, in large part during summer vacations, and of carefully mapped trait distributions, where scholars labored to achieve an overview of the culture areas of North America.[2] They were concerned, of course, only with Native Americans. White or black Americans did not figure in their schemes. Conversely, the aboriginal inhabitants of the continent are not much visible in Garreau's.

But this also means that the temporalities of these two continent-wide geocultural mappings were different. On the whole, the pioneer anthropologists had mostly looked back to the past. And they remained in the ivory tower, arguing over matters of conceptualization and categorization only with their peers. The people in their culture areas were on the whole not in a position to talk back at them.

Garreau, in contrast, had already been amazed at the reader response to his first Sunday supplement essay—letters to the editor arriving "in torrents." What was it he had done, then? Garreau's research assistant came up with an answer. The map she helped him construct seemed to be of "the near future." It had begun with newspeople trying to get on top of events, helping them to judge, region by region, what would happen next. They wanted to stop merely reacting to events, and to start understanding and anticipating them. The nine nations were regional scenarios, emergent story lines—nine "Big Things," perhaps.

BORDERS AND FLOWS

A third of a century after his book was first published, Joel Garreau (now a university professor in Arizona) was invited to contribute to a debate in the *New York Times* on "How to Redraw the World Map." He affirmed that his "nine nations" scheme still worked very well—"One explanation for this endurance may be that those boundaries were observed by a network of dedicated amateur anthropologists all over the continent." (Garreau 2014)

Much of the time, it is true, we are neither as conscientiously reconstructing the past as those early anthropologists, nor as searchingly gazing at the emergent as Joel Garreau, assisted by his amateur correspondents. We are more inclined to take major geographical categories as given, almost part of the natural order of things.[3] But occasionally we do remind ourselves that they are not—that they are human-made, at one time or other.

The upheavals of the latter decades of the twentieth century perhaps shook our faith in "countries" as eternal entities. We might have become used to Czechoslovakia, and Yugoslavia, and the Soviet Union, and then suddenly they were no more. By now even larger-scale entities such as continents may seem most enduring, yet we are at least vaguely aware that these, too, are notions which made their appearance at some point in history, are sometimes debatable, and may change with time. "Europe" may have emerged perhaps some thirteen hundred years ago, as the Carolingian empire defended itself against the expanding Arabs; now, with the shifting boundaries and two-steps-forward, one-step-backward integration of the European Union, we are again not quite sure what sort of entity it is. "Africa" began merely as a Roman province south of Mediterranean. "America" was the name the fairly obscure German cartographer Martin Waldseemüller attached to those new lands recently discovered across the ocean from Europe, thus honoring one Florentine seafarer; and by the time he wanted to change his mind it was too late. (And until those strange ships came, the "Native Americans" had no idea what they would become.) The West Indies was fairly quickly discovered to be a misnomer; the Middle East and Far East are obviously Eurocentric categories; and "the Pacific Rim" arrived in the late twentieth century.[4]

Before that, at the beginning of World War II, those in power in Tokyo envisaged that much the same area, minus America, would be their Greater

Asia Co-Prosperity Sphere. As the Commonwealth may have become a rather too unwieldy and varied entity for some oldtimers, Britain and what had once been its white settler colonies could be thought of as the Anglosphere. And so on. Early mapmaking indeed also left some room for the imagination in the spaces between borders. Lands fundamentally unknown could be filled in with weird people and animals.

The main question of this chapter is what the global scenarios do to our maps—what divides they point to, what routes they suggest. In *The Nine Nations of North America*, Garreau's game was fundamentally one of drawing new borders, and that is also one part of the imaginative work of our scenarists. Yet they can work with old as well as new borders, and they also engage with flows.[5] Borders are sites of difference, of discontinuity in distributions. Flows involve diffusion, redistributions, passages in space, not least across borders; the new appearance of ideas, symbols, practices and people identified with one territory in another territory. In *1984*, George Orwell, with his Oceania-Eurasia-Eastasia divides, may stand out as a border thinker: the novel's archtraitor Emmanuel Goldstein, object of hate sessions, had an analysis of contested areas. Olof Rudbeck, in his *Atlantica*, was a flow man, preoccupied with flow from Sweden outward. Those twentieth century keywords of social science and debate, "modernization" and "cultural imperialism," were both terms of flow, welcome or unwelcome. Nobody may ever have been as successful in introducing a new border metaphor as Winston Churchill was with "the Iron Curtain," in his speech at Westminster College in Fulton, Missouri, in 1946.

With his "clash of civilizations" thesis, Samuel Huntington wanted to draw new attention to some very old cultural borders, the "fault lines" between civilizations, where, in his view, conflicts must develop again and again. But then some borders are rather more emergent, or may have evolved surreptitiously without everybody noticing—like supposedly those of Bat Ye'or's Eurabia. At a time, too, when some saw a drifting apart of America and Europe, Robert Kagan, borrowing from a title of popular psychology to suggest that Americans were now from Mars and Europeans from Venus, imported his border zone of disagreement and misunderstanding all the way from outer space.

Joseph Nye's writings on "soft power," mostly the spread of American values, stand as a prominent example of one variety of flow thinking. With *Jihad Vs. McWorld*, Benjamin Barber intends precisely to counterpose borders to flow, as "jihad" is made to stand for nativism, xenophobia and the like, while "McWorld" is the superexpansive market. (We will come back for another look at these terms in Chap. 5.) Thomas Friedman symbolizes much the same contrast with the olive tree and the Lexus, although the latter seems to interest him rather more, as this luxury car comes off its Japanese assembly line—and when the Electronic Herd stampedes through open spaces, flow thought gets another lively metaphor. Fukuyama's possible "end of history" would involve one major, final flow, as the market and liberal democracy take over the world. One might regard Robert Kaplan, who sees his "coming anarchy" in almost epidemiological terms, as also in a sense, and at times, a flow thinker. In later work, however, we shall see, he too seems more into border thought: the virtually timeless entities of classic geopolitical interpretations, as revisited in *The Revenge of Geography*, or the world as divided between U.S. military area commands, offering a structure to his reporting on *Imperial Grunts*.

THE COMING (AND GOING, AND RETURN)
OF THE GEOPOLITICAL

A term with a history confronts us here, so that past needs to be summarized. As it happens, the word "geopolitics" seems to have been coined in the final year of the nineteenth century by another professor at Olof Rudbeck's old university—Rudolf Kjellén, in *Ymer*, a publication of the Swedish Society for Anthropology and Geography.[6] The chair at the University of Uppsala which Kjellén occupied in the early twentieth century was very ancient, hence the unusual designation of "Eloquence and political science," but in fact this particular incumbent was well-known as a public speaker. He was a sometime Conservative member of parliament, and he also contributed frequently to newspapers. He also traveled widely—around the world, and to the United States.

Intent on distancing the study of politics from the field of law, Kjellén wanted to turn it into a more empirical science—the state should be seen as "a living organism." He launched a concept of "ethnopolitics" as well, intended to focus on the characteristics of the population (and, it seems, on the relationship between state and nation), but that never got so far. Perhaps we should be grateful for that. Rather remarkably at the time, however, he approved of nations with populations of mixed origins. As far as geopolitics was concerned, he emphasized the value of natural borders (preferably in water), and had views on the optimal shape of countries. For one thing, he felt that countries in large part made up of narrow strips of land were not a good idea (which could have been one argument against

Norway breaking away from a union with Sweden, as it was just doing at the time). Generally he favored large units—the future, he suggested, belonged to empires. Considering what would happen in the next couple of decades, one might feel that this scenario was a spectacular failure.

As Kjellén's scholarly thinking mixed with his conservative nationalist ideology and with social Darwinism, later generations have mostly found his conceptual and theoretical efforts unpalatable. In an era when Sweden was geoculturally largely an academic periphery to a German academic center, however, he was much involved intellectually with the big neighbor to the south, and politically pro-German. While none of his writings seem ever to have been translated into English, much of his work appeared in German. It was read, for example, by Karl Haushofer, an army general but also a geographer, who reputedly gave private tutorials to Adolf Hitler while the latter was in jail after a failed Munich *putsch* (and at the same time writing away on the manuscript for *Mein Kampf*).

Kjellén, for his part, had already found inspiration in the work of the German anthropologist-geographer Friedrich Ratzel, professor at Leipzig.[7] In anthropology, the *Kulturkreislehre* of Ratzel and his German contemporaries in the late nineteenth and early twentieth centuries now tends to be remembered as the nearest European counterpart to the work of those early American anthropologists on "culture areas," mentioned before; remotely academic, preoccupied with ordering the artifact collections of museums, tracing the diffusion of cultural elements in the global terrain. (As Ratzel argued that distance makes little difference, diffusion can reach from anywhere to anywhere, one may see a comical parallel with Thomas Friedman's more recent view that the spatial has been neutralized, and the world has become flat.) But wait a moment—Friedrich Ratzel's thinking was also about migration and ethnic expansion, about culture moving as people moved, and he was an active participant, as both scholar and journalist, in imperial Germany's campaign for colonial territories. This went well with his coining the later notorious concept of *Lebensraum*. So here, again, was some academic activism not entirely concerned with an opaque past, but with the geopolitics of the present and proposed future as well.

Both Ratzel and Kjellén may indeed be seen as "public intellectuals" by the standards of their time—moving across the boundary between Academia and journalism, they could remind us of the more recent scenarists. Ratzel died in 1904, Kjellén in 1922, and one cannot entirely blame them for what happened afterwards. With the kind of following some of their ideas came to attract in later years, however, the very term "geopolitics" may be taken to carry rather heavy historical baggage. (Haushofer, as scholar-ideologue, remained an influence on Hitler when this pupil had become *Führer* as well; then committed suicide by drinking arsenic in the aftermath of World War II.) But the line of thought had an early branch in the Anglophonie, too, represented particularly by Halford Mackinder—again a kind of public intellectual, a director of the London School of Economics for one period, an elected MP for a Glasgow constituency for another.[8]

Mackinder also found time to climb Mount Kenya, and from there he could look out over some of the African possessions of the Empire. But his geopolitical thinking was more concerned with other parts of the world. Observing a Great War, the tensions leading up to it and the upheavals following it, he was preoccupied with the balance of power on the European continent, argued for a buffer zone of countries between Germany and whatever would become of Russia, and worried about a decline of British sea power which could follow with new railroads across the Eurasian land mass. Whoever controlled the Heartland (Russia and most of Siberia) would command the World-Island (mainland Eurasia plus Africa), and control of the World-Island would allow control of the world as a whole. Mackinder died in 1947, the year after Haushofer. By then, another theorist of geopolitics was also dead since a few years: Nicholas Spykman, who after an early stint as a Dutch foreign correspondent migrated to the USA, dividing his academic career there between Berkeley and Yale. Spykman took a view of the world which probably matched his experience as a traveling journalist, as well as his boyhood in Amsterdam, forever marked by its history as one of the world's major port cities. As far as the Old World was concerned, the focus was on the Rimland, the maritime margins of Eurasia, stretching from Britain and northwestern Europe by way of the Middle East to South and Southeast Asia, China and Japan. In the western hemisphere, by the mid-twentieth century or so, a matching understanding had the Caribbean as "an American Mediterranean"—one single political region including North America, Mexico and Central America, the northern lands of South America, the Caribbean islands.[9] Only the rainforests to the south formed a real boundary. That kind of geographical Thinking Big, it seems, would bring The Islands, MexAmerica and more from Joel Garreau's scheme into a single entity. And in Spykman's view, that had been important for the growth of American power.

From there we leap forward some sixty years, to the more recent phase of Robert Kaplan's work. In *The Coming Anarchy* (2000: 37–43), Kaplan devoted some pages to "the lies of mapmakers," mostly on the grounds that maps which only show sharply drawn boundaries of unicolor purported nation-states often do not do justice to the complexity of ethnic distributions. But he was not entirely enthusiastic about Thomas Friedman's futurist imagery either. If the world was "flat," this sameness would be not just the end of history but the end of geography as well. So by 2012 he proposed that the time had come for *The Revenge of Geography*. A front cover blurb was from Henry Kissinger, identified inside the book, with Spykman and some others, as among those mid-twentieth century European immigrants "who brought realism to a country that had given them refuge but which they felt dangerously naïve."

While Kaplan notes the origins with Ratzel and Kjellén, his main sources of classical geopolitical inspiration are Mackinder and Spykman. So in *The Revenge of Geography* he offers a largely bird's-eye view of much of the Eurasian mainland, region by region, keeping physical and human geography together, although with an emphasis on the former, and taking deep dips into history. Mountain chains and seas can offer enduring natural borders. Flatlands do not, and so whatever borders are decided, perhaps in conference rooms and drawn across maps, in such spaces there are likely to be invasions, stretched over time or again and again, military or peaceful. Natural resources—metals, oil—are there, somewhere; although their particular importance may change between times. Occasionally the vivid story proposes stunning historical continuities—"true to the innovative imperialist traditions of its medieval and ancient past, Iran has brilliantly erected a postmodern military empire, the first of its kind" (2012: 281).

Notably erudite, while selective about sources, and mixing textual learning with personal impressions from his world-wide travels, Kaplan makes bows of appreciative recognition to some number of scholars of persuasions not really like his, and inserts a qualification here and there. In its strongest (often early) forms, geopolitics may turn into a rhetoric of inevitability, an incontrovertible logic of facts on the ground: in the famous phrasing of the real estate agent, what matters is "location, location, location." People may then look like puppets of physical geography. Kaplan is more cautious with predictions, yet points toward strong possibilities coming back to confront us—"we must never give in to geography, but must fundamentally be aware of it in our quest for a better world" (2012: 346). And so the emphasis in this book is not on questions of culture, or human agency.

CIVILIZATION AS SOCIAL CAPITAL

In *The Clash of Civilizations and the Remaking of World Order*, Samuel Huntington played with actual, printed maps in his own way—in a set of three, devoted to showing major world divides in the 1920s, 1960s and 1990s, he does not have my own country, Sweden, in the 1960s "Free World" (while apartheid South Africa, and Portugal's colonies, supposedly belonged there). Perhaps I should feel a little bit hurt; but then this is no doubt the old Cold War combatant Huntington slipping back into an earlier mindset. (Austria and Switzerland were not at that time in his free world either.)

But his civilizations Huntington takes seriously. There is no Mackinder and no Spykman, and certainly no Ratzel or Kjellén, among his references. What matters here is not physical geography, but at least in a way, culture. The geopolitical is grounded in the geocultural. What civilizations are there in the world, then? First of all, Huntington emphasizes, there is as yet no "universal civilization." That and similar recent notions are really too thin to be of much use. Most concretely it could perhaps be associated with what he calls "Davos Culture," after that selection of people who come together and mingle each year at the World Economic Forum—we will get to them in Chap. 7.

So rather than just one, there are a number of these entities dividing the world. Here Huntington offers a bricolage of example and arguments from earlier civilization theorists from different periods of the twentieth century. The selection can seem a bit alarming: Oswald Spengler, Leo Frobenius and Arnold Toynbee may all in different ways have been important and intriguing figures in public thought earlier in the century, but toward its end, citing them seemingly uncritically as sources on the rise and fall of civilizations is hardly a way of inspiring scholarly confidence, for Huntington or anyone else.[10] Anyway, Huntington finds that his predecessors have come up with somewhat different lists. Quickly enough, however, he comes down rather pragmatically in favor of the set of "seven or eight" civilizations we have identified in Chap. 1:

> It provides an easily grasped and intelligible framework for understanding the world, distinguishing what is important from what is unimportant among the multiplying conflicts, predicting future developments, and providing guidelines for policy makers. (Huntington 1996: 36)

There will be reasons to come back to various aspects of Huntington's arguments and assumptions in later chapters. They are rather tricky to summarize, because Huntington is too experienced a scholar and too wily a debater not to anticipate various counterarguments and insert qualifications which he thereafter basically disregards. Here we could just take up some issues that in a way have to do with his mapping of the major units. So again, these are Huntington's civilizations, the largest and most enduring cultural units in the world: Western, Latin American, Slavic Orthodox, Islamic, Hindu, Confucian, Japanese and…African.

Many of these coincide with world religions—but there are already some complications here. It might seem remarkable, even if it is utterly conventional, that with "Western," there is a quick shift away from religion to a mere compass direction. We sense that in the instance of the civilization which Huntington himself identifies with, that of most of Europe and North America, there already appears to be a more tricky relationship of the general culture to Christianity, which would be the religion in question. But in principle, that same question of the stamp of religion on culture could be raised about other civilizations as well. Are all the inhabitants of the Hindu civilization more Hindu than all Europeans are Christians? Are all people in the Islamic civilization more Muslim than all Europeans are Christians? Between the original journal article in *Foreign Affairs* to the book, Huntington does rename one civilization, from "Confucian" to "Sinic." Perhaps from Confucius via Mao to Deng Xiaoping, there is something other than religion to being Chinese. (But then the Koreans and the Vietnamese are supposedly also Sinic.) [11]

About Africa Huntington is somewhat uncertain. Should it count as another civilization?[12] Its world religions are imported from the outside. Christianity was present early in the northeast, as in Ethiopia and Egypt, but mostly arrived elsewhere in an occasionally complicated alliance with European colonialism, while Islam came from the north and east, through trade and occasional conquest, entering through the Sahara and from the Indian Ocean. And if elements of African religion have later spread westward across the Atlantic, this has become a component in the internal diversity of other civilizations.[13] On his map Huntington handles the problem by placing the largely Muslim areas with Islamic civilization—while the regions where Christianity has left the stronger mark are certainly not "Western" but "African." And in the long run, whatever might be the character of African civilization hardly bothers him so very much: it does not appear as a major player anyway in the future political scenarios he envisages.

Huntington's commentary on some instances which do not fit so well into his scheme is actually among the more notable. The short discussion of Ukraine's internal divide, for instance, could cast light on what would happen in that country a couple of decades later. Turkey shows different faces, in different directions, at different times; the *New York Times* editor alluded to this in that conversation with which I began Chap. 1, and the shifts continue into the twenty-first century. Nonetheless, one could argue that Huntington's mapmaking tends to give too little attention to important cleavages within civilizations, sometimes indeed having to do with those world religions. In western and central Europe, the divide between Roman Catholic and Protestant regions has been more or less noticeable for several centuries. A very long war—thirty years—was once fought over it. In the early twenty-first century economic crisis, some would argue that the divide showed up again; raising once more the question of the linkage between religion and cultural stances. (How do you argue about economics, it is asked, with a German Protestant for whom the same word stands for both "debt" and "guilt"? That happens to be the case in Swedish, too.) At a time, too, when a great many people in Europe and North America could hardly tell the difference between Shia, Sunni and Sushi, Huntington could perhaps get away with the view of a single and undivided Islam—but later on, even if many outside that civilization could not quite grasp its internal theological divisions, they would at least know that they were there, visible in major internal conflicts (and not to be confused with anything out of the Japanese cuisine). In Latin America, the difference between Brazil and everything else should not be disregarded—a major anthropologist-cultural historian, Gilberto Freyre (1956), undoubtedly one of Brazil's major twentieth-century public intellectuals but altogether ignored by Huntington, has indeed depicted the emergence of his country as a tropical civilization (with an African component) in its own right.[14]

In sum, Huntington's overview of the field of civilization studies seems rather spotty. Yet another key feature of his clash scenario may really be more important. Huntington tends to shift easily, rather unnoticeably, between terms of "culture" and "cultural identity," in such a way that the latter term may even seem redundant. However, there is a distinction to be made here.[15]

As I (and probably most anthropologists) use it, culture itself is a matter of meanings and meaningful forms—I will return to a more extensive discussion of this in Chap. 6. One might indeed argue that all identities are cultural, insofar as they are constructed from such materials. From this vantage point, it might seem rather brave, or inattentive, of Huntington to claim a long-term stability for a cultural identity, precisely in that late twentieth-century period when much argument—at least in some parts of the world, and in certain circles within these parts—would focus on the protean nature of identities, as shifting entities to be forever experimented with.

The way Huntington and many others use the term, however, cultural identity is above all a particular kind of collective identity. A connection to some particular cultural item or cluster of items is understood as the major marker of group membership—and it is the shared group membership which constitutes (in another recent vocabulary) a kind of social capital, a claim on the support of others. Contacts with other people can be resources. As a political scientist, Huntington sticks to the idea that states are the main actors in international relations, but states are inclined to be most friendly with those other states which belong to the same civilizations, and civilizations are presumably very durable entities.

Again one could discern that a certain playfulness in Huntington's view of the world here. It was the British nineteenth-century statesman Lord Palmerston who said that in international politics, "there are no permanent friends, only permanent interests." Since the "clash of civilizations" thesis basically suggests the opposite—civilizations are clusters of permanent friends—this has Huntington standing Lord Palmerston on his head. The Victorian aristocrat might not have been amused.

Anyhow, "cultural identity" here becomes primarily a fact in the realm of social (and in Huntington's case, political) organization, rather than a summarizing reference to a cultural whole. Perhaps this could seem like a matter of academic terminological nitpicking, but the implications show up in arguments about the "clash of civilizations" thesis in the public arena as well. In his book *Identity and Violence* (2006), Amartya Sen, renowned philosopher-economist of Indian origin, alludes to them already in a chapter title: "Civilizational confinement." Sen takes the appeal of civilizational analysis to lie in its invocation of "the richness of history and the apparent depth and gravity of cultural analysis." (2006: 43) But in the end it is not helpful: "Civilizational partitioning is a pervasively intrusive phenomenon in social analysis, stifling other— richer—ways of seeing people," Sen (2006: 42) suggests; it "lays the foundations for misunderstanding nearly everyone in the world." Here Sen takes a view of identity which seems more attuned to contemporary understandings. The point is that people tend to have more than one identity, more than a single characteristic which they can identify with (or for that matter, which others can identify them with). They may feel differently strongly about them, and such priorities can change over time. So very possibly, they will again and again break out of those civilizational confinements. We may sense here that if Amartya Sen were to be our mapmaker, the outcome would be something much more complicated and kaleidoscopic than what Huntington offers us.

A main point for Huntington, too—which also relates to his dismissal of the "world civilization" notion—is that "modernization" is not identical with "Westernization." In those past days when his academic generation concerned itself with modernization theory, the tendency had been strong to take the two to be synonymous. Now, in Huntington's view, it must be emphasized that people can have modernization and their own civilization, too. (In other parts of the scholarly landscape, not so much involved with a wider public, more or less related arguments have been made with notions of both "multiple modernities" or "alternative modernities." [16])

But would that necessarily leave those deep divides between them, with their potential for major conflict, intact? Another prominent Huntington critic, former Pakistani Prime Minister Benazir Bhutto (2008), did not think so. In a book published only after her assassination (during an election campaign when she was trying to stage a comeback), she devoted a chapter to a response to the "clash of civilizations" thesis, and to what she labels as "clashers" generally.[17] For one thing, she foregrounded organized attempts to develop dialogue between civilizations—one of her good people here is Mohammad Khatami, one-time reformist president of the Republic of Iran (who took the idea to the General Assembly of the United Nations in 2001). For another, she reminisced about her own college years in the United States, formative years when she engaged with ideas of democracy, freedom of speech, gender equality (books by Germaine Greer and Kate Millett were among those that mattered to her)—ideas which she would associate with modernization, take back to Pakistan, and find not so alien to Islamic thought, as she scrutinized it. So the conflict was not between civilizations, but within them, and not least in the wider Muslim Ummah, between progressives and traditionalists.

Here, then, are presumably one voice of Hindu civilization and one voice of Islamic civilization, rejecting Huntington's view of civilizations, and of their clashes. But then like Huntington, Amartya Sen has been a Harvard professor, and Benazir Bhutto was a Harvard undergraduate. In other words, these are disagreements among sometime neighbors in Cambridge, MA. Bhutto's reminiscences of campus life suggest that gender would be a dimension not to be disregarded in the view of her civilization and its contemporary debates.

But moreover, she seems to offer support to the view of yet another Harvard professor: "Our exposure to life at Harvard and life in the United States empowered us and fundamentally changed our lives" (Bhutto 2008: 271) That sounds like evidence for Joseph Nye's view of soft power.

Lands of Disorder

In the early phase of scenario writing, Robert Kaplan could start out from a war-torn corner of West Africa and see anarchy spreading from there to everywhere. At the other end of things, Francis Fukuyama could be more or less dismissive of the global outskirts, and the weird ideas that might occur there to "crackpot messiahs." If history could have seemed to take a timeout in the 1990s, however—at least to some people, in some places—it surely started again with a rush hour in the morning of September 11, 2001, when one uncertainly defined network, with a base in the mountains of Central Asia, and a leading figure with his ancestry in the mountains of Arabia, issued its dramatic challenge to the world order and to its dominant power.

In between Fukuyama and Kaplan, there have been further varieties of mapmaking, at least slightly more nuanced in placing disorder on the map, at least insofar as they contrast it to relative order reigning elsewhere. Here we find, among others, Thomas P.M. Barnett. His most-noted book, *The Pentagon's New Map* (2004), shows a world basically divided into two major sections: "the Functioning Core" and "the Non-integrating Gap." Or, for short, the Core and the Gap. As things stood at the time, the Core included North America, Brazil and the southern cone of South America, Europe excluding its Southeastern postcommunist parts, Russia, South Africa, India, East Asia, Australia and New Zealand. The Gap included the rest: Central America and the Caribbean, the parts of Europe just referred to, the Middle East, Central Asia, Southeast Asia, and most of Africa.[18] The Core consisted of the countries actively integrating into the global economy and abiding by its rules, the Gap of those which had failed to do so. Roughly speaking at least, the Core was Fukuyama country, the Gap Kaplan country.

Barnett argued that his "new map" had implications for American policy, and not least for Pentagon planning. For a machinery that had grown to keep the Cold War from turning hot, but to be prepared for that eventuality, this was a new working situation: "America was not a global cop, but at best a global fireman… not trying to make the world safe for anything; we just worked to keep these nasty little blazes under control." (Barnett 2004: 4) As he was taking his ideas around in Washington and elsewhere, Barnett found that not everybody in the defense establishment liked his ideas. But then again he had also worked closely with some circles of the financial world, even in workshops on one of the top floors of the World Trade Center, and he had found this very inspiring in forming his understandings of world connectivity. So one might describe some of the conflicts in which he became involved as another clash of civilizations, between Pentagon and Wall Street.

In *The Breaking of Nations* (2003), Robert Cooper, the British diplomat, came to a rather similar view, but complicated it a little by dividing Barnett's Core into two; and then he complicated things yet more by giving the resulting three parts of the world a sort of quasi-evolutionary labels: the present-day world was at the same time, but in different places, premodern, modern, and postmodern. By the time his book appeared he had already gone public with this vocabulary elsewhere, but in a first endnote in it he lets the reader know that "I have many times regretted the choice of the term 'postmodern', since it carries a lot of complicated baggage that I hardly understand" (Cooper 2003: 173).

Somewhat preoccupied with the politics of cultural difference, Cooper may remind us of Samuel Huntington. Yet (in line with the distinction made above) Cooper's emphasis seems to be more on culture as such, rather than cultural identity. Foreign policy would be easy if it were not for the foreigners, he writes ironically (Cooper 2003: 88), and notes that it is important to realize that the end of the Cold War brought a new situation. Until then, Western policy had mostly dealt with countries and people from cultural traditions similar to their own. In the new era problems will come from cultures little understood in the West.[19] And on identity matters, Cooper and Huntington are not altogether in agreement. Where Huntington sees a largely frozen global identity politics, Cooper is more open to process and change, looking toward diplomatic work to increase order and trust in a varied but fluid environment.

With regard to his own three parts of the world, his main argument is that identity—for the postmodern state as for the individual—is a matter of choice, and the Europe that has grown into increasing togetherness since the latter half of the twentieth century is his main case in point. In contrast, the modern world for Cooper is that of nation-states. He finds the United States still there.

While Cooper's understanding of Europe at the beginning of the 2000s may on the whole be valid—not least contrasting it with what had been there during much of the century before—we should be aware that he wrote at a time when the European Union was doing well, growing and integrating, leaving its thinkers and doers in a state of mild Europhoria, not yet so troubled by those conflicts over matters of finance and migration that would be evident a decade or so later.[20] And we will get to the geography of his split between "modern" and "post-modern" in a moment. What concerns us immediately is that supposedly "premodern" world: characterized, again in Cooper's (2003: 16) words, by "pre-state, post-imperial chaos." The premodern world belongs, he argues, "as it were, in a different time zone: here, as in the ancient world, the choice is again between empire and chaos." Which, since the imperial urge is mostly dead in the countries that might be capable of imperialism, tends to mean chaos.

For the first time in over a century, consequently, there is a *terra nullius*, a no-man's-land. Unlike in the past, however, Cooper notes that this may be a *terra nullius* with an international airport. Television teams may fly in and out, bringing back pictures of suffering, and members of crime and terrorist syndicates may fly out of there, to conduct their business both in the modern and the postmodern world. So if chaos were somehow to be in a different time zone, even a different epoch, as Cooper's terminology suggests, it would appear that people fly in and out of that airport on time machines.

But then of course we know that they do not. That airport takes ordinary aircraft (if frequently of rather old, decrepit models), and Cooper's conceptualization comes uncomfortably close to that denial of coevality which we recognize as a recurrent component in ways of dealing with, and of down-ranking, the alien contemporary.[21]

The years around the millennium change, when Barnett and Cooper developed their views, were indeed a time to worry about disorder. After 9–11 the United States had two wars in "the Gap," in the Middle East and in Central Asia. But much of the Gap was in Africa, and here it was a time for "Afro-pessimism": a *Time* magazine cover story described the continent as "a nightmarish world where chaos reigns."

Indeed it was a difficult period for the continent. But did the news media really present an entirely balanced view of it? When I engaged in my study of the work of foreign correspondents at that time, I discovered that a remarkable proportion of the world's "Africa correspondents" (reporting mostly to Europe and North America) worked out of two office buildings in a suburb of Johannesburg, many of them with the task of covering those forty-some countries south of the Sahara. They did travel out of there, but reporting journeys were expensive, and their head offices at home would not very happily pay the bills for anything but "hard news"—which tended to be bad news, of conflicts and disasters. So there would be less room and resources for feature stories of whatever might be relative normalcy and stability, or coping capacity. And insofar as scenario authors tended to take the view from afar, their overall picture was likely to become grim.[22]

Yet one could change vantage point, and possibly get a somewhat different view toward their views. This was a time when the notion of "failed states" came into increasing circulation. Huntington and Barnett, political scientists, and Cooper, diplomat, are all eventually state-centered in their perspectives; Kaplan, speaking in large part to and for American military concerns, likewise. It becomes rather obvious that this limits their understanding, perhaps their curiosity, about what is non-state. So how do they represent the inhabitants of anarchy?

"Because the demographic reality of West Africa is a countryside draining into dense slums by the coast, ultimately the region's rulers will come to reflect the values of these shantytowns," wrote Robert Kaplan about the coming anarchy in 1994. True, one may never be sure what is "ultimate." But Liberia was one of those countries with internal warfare where Kaplan saw global anarchy starting—and twenty years later, the country's president was a woman economist, winner of a Nobel Peace Prize. (The story of how she got there, and stayed there, was not altogether simple, but we knew from before that not all Nobel Peace Prizes have been awarded to saints.[23]) And the country next-door, Sierra Leone, from which Kaplan had reported directly, those two decades later had a president who was a former insurance company director, and a graduate of the local university (the oldest in West Africa). For all Kaplan's bush taxi travel along the West African coast, the only memorable personal encounter with someone local in his most famous essay is with one minister, whose eyes "were like egg yolks, an after-effect of some of the many illnesses, malaria especially, endemic in his country." During the rest of the journey, encounters seem to have been mostly with threatening, loitering youth; sick people; beggars. For Kaplan, fleeting physical presence, but human remoteness.

And this remoteness appears characteristic of much scenario depiction of the lands of disorder. There is a risk here that those regions in maps which are not really known will, as in the distant past of map-making, be filled with strange creatures.[24]

Thomas Barnett for his part offers much breezy reporting on the landscapes of strategic knowledge production along the United States East Coast, but mostly makes no real effort to match it with materials from elsewhere. He notes that one *Wall Street Journal* reporter took sufficient interest in his view of the world to travel to Kyrgyzstan, to (in the reporter's words) "check out the Gap in person." (Barnett 2004: 182)

We may remind ourselves what sort of states we find, in large part, in those lands of disorder. Many of them had come into being in the period of post-World War II decolonization which coincided with the Cold War. In that Huntington map of the 1960s, some found their place in his "Free World," a few then or later made their way to "the Communist Bloc," many stayed non-aligned. There was a pronounced tendency toward a standard formatting of state organization, in outward appearance at least supported for one thing through the United Nations machinery and other international organizations, with which they all became involved.[25] In reality, however, many of them were weak, with limited organizational or material resources. In terms of what they could deliver, their potential for becoming "failed states" was soon clear. As many of them were not *really* nation-states, but often once-upon-a-time creations at the map-drawing board of some remote conference of colonial powers, the popular support for them as somehow natural units could be weak. Regime change could most easily be accomplished through coups rather than elections. The ongoing Cold War might keep some regimes going through support from the outside rather than from below.

"A son of a bitch, but our son of a bitch": apparently the classic formulation was Franklin Roosevelt's, talking about one Central American dictator already before the Cold War. In that latter period, there were some number of them on both sides, but then as it ended, it was apparently less important to keep these S.O.B.s going, and so as some of them were overthrown, that helped in developing the Gap. Furthermore, those who wanted to keep whatever passed for order going, or wanted to overthrow it, or just keep it at a distance, could all find that there were plenty of guns to be had, since the armament industries left over after the Cold War might survive only by finding new customers.[26]

So who are these people in the Gap? How do you get to be premodern nowadays? Ranging between investigative journalism and ethnographic field studies, the reporting from those zones of more or less disorder has actually been quite rich.[27] It shows great diversity (in large part reflecting very real variations, although ideological and theoretical predilections among the reporters may be noticed as well). Some of it depicts great misery: hunger, physical violence, epidemics (like Ebola), dislocation, people trying to get by living in ruins or refugee camps. At times, on the other hand, it becomes clear that disorder is something relative. There is not really a sharp break between that and order, but rather a continuum where the situation may shift over time, not seldom back and forth.

Moreover, sometimes people may not miss the state so much, if it more or less goes away. A state apparatus may be failing in delivering anything much in the way of services, but it may insert itself into the lives of its subjects as a burden. It can be a mostly predatory state and a corruption machine, demanding taxes, tributes, bribes, occasionally exercising arbitrary physical power. Consequently, some people could just possibly greet a "coming of anarchy" with a certain pleasure, or relief. If it is the right kind of anarchy: some variety of self-organization, perhaps not perfect, but not absent. There are parts of the world, indeed, which have long practiced "the art of not being governed"—highland regions of Southeast Asia are prominent in this regard.[28]

Paul Richards (1999: 17), British anthropologist-geographer for an extended period dividing his time between the Netherlands and Sierra Leone, can reminisce about a debating encounter he had with Robert Kaplan at the Dutch Foreign Ministry, and also about talking to teenage fighters fresh from all sides of the Sierra Leone internal war about their common enemy:

> politicians too busy fishing in overseas ponds. They see their violence not as anarchic bickering over scraps, but a life-and-death struggle against a political elite pursuing global riches at the expense of domestic improvement. The well-travelled, highly-educated, yellow-eyed politician who persuaded Kaplan that Sierra Leonean youths were cultureless criminals is an embodiment of the enemy against whom they fight.

One might wonder what Richards' teenage informants would have said about the more recent incumbents of Sierra Leonean and Liberian presidencies. Moreover, this veteran observer cautions against bush taxi epistemology: "the highway in West Africa is itself a very special world.

Travel writers should be careful not to draw general conclusions from life in roadside villages." [29]

Some decades after Robert Kaplan's "The Coming Anarchy" article, and a little less after the climax of "Afro-pessimism" in the media of what Barnett had called the Core, one might perhaps tentatively conclude that African conflicts have not been continuously spreading, covering an increasingly large proportion of the continent. They occur rather as local or regional eruptions, often far from each other (Central African Republic...Burkina Faso...Burundi), variously durable, involving different equations of class, livelihood, ethnicity, religion, generation and/or gender—although when ideas, ideological complexes, and moral panics spread rapidly across borders through media and in other ways, local frames may be penetrated and become open to more globalizing interpretations.[30] A decade or so into the twenty-first century, too, some African countries have shown signs of getting closer to that Core.

Yet looking back to what Barnett and Cooper had been arguing in the think tanks of the United States and Europe, one could also reflect on the possibility that while the vocabulary might have shifted, some of their views come close to what has actually happened—again and again. Early in the century, Robert Cooper suggested (2002) that the "premodern" parts of the world could benefit from "a new kind of imperialism, one acceptable to a world of human rights and cosmopolitan values." This might not have been altogether the kind of language expected from a diplomat (although even old-style imperialism would have its new defenders, such as Niall Ferguson).[31] As the eruptions now occur, however—in Mali or in newly independent South Sudan (with the Nuer and the Dinka again fighting each other, as they already did in classic University of Oxford anthropology almost a century ago)—we do see the Core, under one national or international-organizational flag or other, often in some kind of joint arrangement with the African Union, showing up to bring peace back.[32] In Barnett's terms, again, global firemen, dealing with nasty little blazes.[33] After the conflagrations in Iraq and Afghanistan (and more distantly, but still, Vietnam), however, neither the "modern" nor the "postmodern" regions on Cooper's map are eager to remain very long with soldiers on the ground and in combat situations in distant lands.

With such military excursions, anyhow, one might be closer to the kind of mapmaking involved with "flow"—in these cases, passages of people. Yet between the Gap and the Core, not least between "premodern" and "postmodern," there were also passages, or tragically unsuccessful attempts at passages, in the opposite direction, following very specific local maps. Finding that they could not make their voices heard, or live the life they wanted, a number of good people (and probably some bad) chose to head for the exit—over the Mediterranean close to the small Italian island of Lampedusa, or at the high fence surrounding Spain's anomalous North African enclave Ceuta (hoping to make a domestic trip across the Straits of Gibraltar from there). Here was continuing personal Afro-pessimism combined with Euro-optimist dreaming. Others crossed the Indian Ocean between Indonesia and Australia, close to that dot which happened to be named Christmas Island. So at such border lines, drawn in the water, global divides between the have and have-not regions of the world were again and again most cruelly demonstrated. We have been getting some of the stories from there as well.[34]

MARS, VENUS, AND THE ATLANTIC IN BETWEEN

Men Are from Mars, Women Are from Venus by John Gray (1992), relationship counselor, was an American bestseller on gender psychology in the 1990s, selling some fifty million copies and becoming part of popular culture.[35] A *Peanuts* comic strip took off from the title. Lucy holds a book in front of her, reading the title: "Men are from Mars, women are from Venus." She tells Snoopy, sitting on the roof of his doghouse with his typewriter: "That's a good title…you should write a book like that." So Snoopy begins writing: "Dogs are from Jupiter, cats are from the Moon."

And then there was Robert Kagan, historian and political commentator, beginning his book *Paradise and Power* (2003) with the suggestion that Americans were from Mars and Europeans from Venus: "They agree on little and understand one another less and less." Here the map showed a border in the middle of the North Atlantic, although transported from somewhere in outer space.

The divide more or less coincided with Cooper's "modern"/ "postmodern" divide, however, and Kagan indeed had a blurb on the back of Cooper's *The Breaking of Nations*, proclaiming that "this brilliantly written book carries the transatlantic conversation to the next stage." At least this Martian and this Venusian had apparently found some way of reaching mutual comprehension.[36] (The back cover of *Paradise and Power*, by the way, had an endorsement by Francis Fukuyama: "Brilliant." There was no Fukuyama blurb, on the other hand, for a later [2008] book by Kagan, *The Return of History and the End of Dreams*.)

One could see a difference between them, perhaps, in Cooper's concern with grasping cultural differences. To the extent that Kagan took an interest in matters cultural, they tended to be seen as growing out of the realities of power. American "strategic culture," he argued, is the natural product of the increasing global power of the United States particularly in the latter half of the twentieth century. Europe, in coming to terms with its combined declining external power in the same period, looks more inward. Where Americans talk about foreign "threats," Europeans look at "challenges"—ethnic conflict, migration, organized crime, poverty, environmental degradation. These may be questions to be handled through negotiation and transparency, in a "postmodern" way to adopt Robert Cooper's vocabulary.

So Europeans, criticizing American ways of problem-solving, may ironically say that "when you have a hammer, all problems start to look like nails." To which Americans might reply that "when you don't have a hammer, you don't want anything to look like a nail." (Kagan 2003: 27–28) That is precisely a point where Kagan and Cooper seem to be in agreement. In *The Breaking of Nations*, Cooper (2003: 62) suggests that Europe has to realize that "in the jungle, one must use the laws of the jungle."

Cooper and Kagan were right, obviously, that much of the difference between Europe and the United States that can seem important now is a product of relatively recent world history. There would have been a long period, say in the eighteenth and nineteenth centuries, when many Asians, Africans and Native Americans would all have shaken their heads (if that could be taken as a transcultural way of expressing disbelief and/or disapproval) and said, "Christianity has bloody borders." It might have seemed an unlikely future scenario for them that the heartlands of Europe, where all that came from, would turn peacefully postmodern.

The period when Kagan and Cooper published their works in question, however, was one when the divide between the United States and much of Europe seemed particularly deep—after 9-11, the United States quickly became involved in a war in Afghanistan, and was soon on its way into another, more controversial, war in Iraq. What had for some time been major American allies were critical toward especially the latter, and were held to be disloyal. Some engaged observers would draw a map with finer distinctions: Donald Rumsfeld, viewing the world from the Pentagon at the time, saw an "Old Europe" and a "New Europe," where much of what had been west of the Iron Curtain was now "old," and a number of the states which had been east of it were labeled "new." The latter were those where the governments at the time were, Rumsfeld thought, more favorably inclined to the U.S. stance. In contrast, at least in the minds of some of those who would count as Kagan's Martians, the European "oldies" were held to be decadent and treacherous. So "French fries" would be renamed "Liberty fries" in some Washington cafeterias, and it was held against one presidential candidate at home (in a later period to become U.S. Secretary of State) that his haircut looked a bit too French. There could be counterpart hard feelings east of the Atlantic.

In his *Colossus* (2004a: 289), Niall Ferguson did not quite go along with Kagan's view of the Martians. The Americans had the power, but were reluctant to use it. His emblematic figure was Arnold Schwarzenegger, as the Terminator: "As his original program battles this contradictory command, the word ABORT flashes in bright red letters in his head, all but paralyzing him." And at much the same time, another of our authors (British like Ferguson) set forth quite another view. In *Free World* (2004), Timothy Garton Ash was not so inclined to place the peoples around the North Atlantic either on different planets or in different epochs. In his understanding of the world, the Atlantic connected rather than divided. The notion of "the West" was not just a survival from Cold War days. Neither was it, as Ash put it, a "vulgar Huntingtonism," a region defined by age-old external conflicts. Britain, his own homeland, was forever facing Janus-like in two directions. On the one hand, there was that supposed "special relationship" to America. (We have already seen that George Orwell, in *1984*, had taken that as far as to make Airstrip One, with London as its capital, a province of Oceania.) On the other hand, there was the somewhat ambivalent but nonetheless enduring involvement with Europe. Ash did not want Britain to choose. Both attachments were important, and should be maintained and developed. Yet this did not mean that Britain somehow had to keep some sort of specialized brokerage role between America and Europe for itself. The aim was rather for all of the United States to relate equally closely to all of Europe. This was now "the West." And as the European part of it was getting to be synonymous with the European Union, the latter ought to take a generous view of its blurred eastern borders, and aim at including countries like Ukraine and Turkey. Not, however, Russia, the Caucasus, or Maghreb—Russia was just too large to fit in, Caucasus and North Africa simply not Europe. But there should be close partnerships with these, for worthy purposes in shaping the world's future.

Foremost among the goals was certainly a free world—not "the" free world, as what was then the West had often described itself during the

Cold War, but freedom, that is, democracy, everywhere. That was to be cultivated, but not imposed. One would have to stay together in meeting threats of violence, of terror, but that would entail working toward a world free of poverty and hunger as well. This might involve aid, but it must involve trade: opening the markets of the West to the produce of less privileged parts of the world. Furthermore, to keep the world livable, there must be some foresight in handling the environment. Pollution, global warming and the depletion of energy sources could not be ignored.

"The West," however, Ash noted, was already becoming the post-West. Its leading role in the world was no longer to be taken for granted. Even as more parts of the world might be joining in its values and practices, it was probably wise to try and use its influence while one could realistically assume that it would still be there. So Ash's future scenario was one for the next twenty years or so. Those people in the West who shared views like his had to put pressure on their politicians to get their act together.

On his way to this conclusion, Ash also rejected Secretary Rumsfeld's European cartography. In many countries public opinion was against the Iraq war, even when the governments were not, and it would only take a closely contested election to shift a country from that "new Europe" to the "old Europe" column (or more rarely perhaps vice versa). But then certainly not all Americans could be counted among Kagan's Martians either. "Blue" Americans tended to be more like Europeans than they were like "Red" Americans.

Back momentarily, then, to some American domestic mapmaking here: Garreau may have found nine nations in North America, but Ash refers to that simpler coloring scheme which continues to puzzle the Europeans, and which would seem to be another instance of American exceptionalism—making "Red" the color of the right and "Blue" the color of the left (both relative). Incidentally, about half of Garreau's nations would seem to fall on each side. Ash's comment, however, about how an election could move a country from "new" Europe to "old" would certainly have its colorful U.S. counterpart. While rather quirky election procedures in the American system result in a blue/red binary, it is still true that about a quarter of the voters in Utah may go blue, and just over a third of those in New York may go red. So actually the states are fifty shades of purple. And Kagan's Martians and Venusians could meet and mingle in Ohio.

Again, too, as far as Rumsfeld's European mapmaking was concerned, by the time of the financial crises a little further into the twenty-first century, one could reflect that the dividing line was not so much between an Old Europe to the west and a New Europe to the east. It was back, at least as much, between the north and the south, between two Old Europes which had been there more or less since the Westphalian Peace.

AMONG THE GRUNTS

In any case, if there could be some consensus that Europeans had been fairly recent migrants to Venus, this would not necessarily mean that Americans had only arrived on Mars at about the same time. Robert Kagan has made the point in another more recent book, *Dangerous Nation* (2006), that for several complex reasons (territorial, commercial, idealistic), the United States has had an expansionist leaning from the very beginning. We can come back to Robert Kaplan here as well. *Warrior Politics* (2001a) is a deskwork exercise in popular political philosophy, drawing on Sun Tzu, Machiavelli, Winston Churchill and others, revolving around the idea that optimism and good intentions can have disastrous consequences.

The Martian leanings may be clear, but *Warrior Politics* is not otherwise a book of real interest here. Kaplan's two reports on his excursions embedded with US soldiers, *Imperial Grunts* (2005) and *Hog Pilots, Blue Water Grunts* (2007) do more with maps. This is Kaplan with boots on the ground again, when they are not crossing seas or in the air. "Embedded reporting" could be described as an approximation in journalism to what "participant observation" means to anthropologists, spending an extended period sharing the life of a group under study. The term came into more general use during the Iraq War of 2003, and the practice became controversial as critics argued that it would make journalists too dependent on the military units they were with, and less likely to live up to newswork ideals of autonomy and impartiality.[37] In *Imperial Grunts*, Kaplan (2005: 259) responds with his own class analysis to such critique:

> ...the charge that embedded journalists had lost their objectivity was itself a sign of class prejudice. Even with the embed phenomenon, the media maintained a more incestuous relationship with academics, politicians, businesspeople, international diplomats, and relief charities (among other non-governmental organizations) than it did with the military. The common denominator among all of these groups, save for the military, is that they spring from the same elevated social and economic strata of their respective societies.

In any case, Kaplan does his own embedded work, as resulting in the two books, more under what would pass for peace-time conditions, in large part in what with Thomas Barnett's terminology would be categorized as the Gap. There are brief historical overviews of regions, whether they are now in the lands covered by CENTCOM, PACOM or SOUTHCOM (together, the five such area commands, also including EUCOM and NORTHCOM, encompassed the globe), and vivid portrayals of scenery: Timbuktu! Lamu! Bagram! Andaman Sea! Zamboanga![38] But since he spends his time and his words almost entirely with American soldiers, whether on or off base, or on ships or in aircrafts, this also tends to become like what is now described as "anthropology at home": with one's compatriots, although in this case they are a sort of expatriates, in a special kind of diaspora. The Grunts—soldiers, mostly not so high-ranking—are his tribe, and he offers intriguing ethnography. There are differences between branches of the military services of which most member of the public, including academics, are little aware. Here, too, Kaplan gets closer to the live human beings he encounters than he does in his travels, say, along the roads of coastal West Africa. He does not miss opportunities to identify the soldiers by name, rank, and home town in the United States. And it might seem as if he never met an American soldier he did not like.

About a master sergeant from Mississippi, in the Philippines: "He made snap cultural judgments of the kind that would burn an academic's reputation, but which in the field prove right seven out of ten times." (2005: 160)

And about the language of the Grunts: "Soldiers talked in clichés. It is the emotion and look in their faces—sweaty and gummed with dust—that matters more than the words. After all, a cliché is something that only the elite recognizes as such." (2005: 57)

All in all, Kaplan argues, "Militaries are the ultimate reflections of national cultural achievement, or the lack thereof." (2005: 53) Probably Robert Cooper's "postmoderns" would not all agree with that, but then in the judgment of a combat pilot on the Guam base who is a final informant voice in *Hog Pilots, Blue Water Grunts* (2007: 368), that would be an expression of decadence. Kaplan also points to some facts, however, which relate more directly to our concerns in this chapter. When he is not with U.S. troops abroad, he visits them on some of their bases at home; and he notes that these are mostly in the South, the Midwest, and the Great Plains.[39] Some of the origin myths of the American military, he suggests, are not from the world wars of the twentieth century, but from

Injun Country: fighting the Cheyennes, the Flatheads, the Comanches (Kaplan 2005: 8–11). (One might wonder, even if Kaplan apparently does not, whether the myths have not kept interacting with Hollywood products as well.) And then Injun Country, "the badlands," may bear a certain resemblance to twenty-first century lands of disorder.

Intriguingly, this view of the past could appear to connect with the classic frontier theory in American history writing, as set forth in the late nineteenth century by Frederick Jackson Turner (1893). Pointing in a slightly different direction, Kaplan (2005: 56, 260–261) emphasizes that the people he meets, whether at Fort Bragg, North Carolina, or at stationings spread out overseas, are not really a cross-section of the people of the United States. If he comes across a soldier from the Northeast, it is likely to be someone of working-class Irish background, or someone African-American or Hispanic. Yet much more often he encounters Southerners. The southern "bent toward militarism" is nothing new; Kaplan refers here to Samuel Huntington's 1950s work on military matters. In a way, however, this again takes us back to where this chapter started. Of Garreau's *Nine Nations of North America*, Dixie would seem to have the largest army.

NOTES

1. As one example of a certain unwillingness to make finer distinctions from a distance, one might see the fact that the Thomas Frank's U.S. bestseller *What's the Matter With Kansas?* (2004) was retitled *What's the Matter With America?* in the British edition.

2. Alfred Kroeber (1939) offers an overview of those efforts—we will come back to him in another context in Chap. 7. Interestingly, in his major book *Europe and the People without History* (1982: 6), published the year after Garreau's, the anthropologist Eric Wolf notes rather offhandedly that "there could have arisen a polyglot Floridian Republic, a Francophone Mississippian America, a Hispanic New Biscay, a Republic of the Great Lakes, a Columbia— comprising the present Oregon, Washington, and British Columbia." That comes to five nations of North America, but still leaves a fair amount of the continent outside. It is also a variety of counterfactual history, something we will turn to in Chap. 5.

3. Malkki's (1992) essay on the naturalization of nation concepts has become a classic in anthropology. On methodological nationalism, see Wimmer and Glick Schiller (2002) and Beck (2005).

4. For critical views of the "Pacific Rim" concept, see Dirlik (1998).

5. Flow concepts gathered new academic strength in the late twentieth century, although they have a longer history. When the new journal Public Culture, interdisciplinary but perhaps with anthropology at its center of gravity, appeared in 1988, the editors could declare that they wanted "to create an intellectual forum for interaction among those concerned with global cultural flows." And Scott Lash and John Urry (1994: 4, 12), social theorists, suggest that late twentieth-century societies are characterized by flows of capital, labor, commodities, information, and images; thus economists, demographers, media researchers, geographers and others can all engage with flows. For discussions of the recent use of flow concepts in anthropology, see Heyman and Campbell (2009) and Rockefeller (2011). I have discussed the notion more fully elsewhere (Hannerz 1992a, 1997).

6. The Swedish term Kjellén invented, in his 1899 article on Sweden's boundaries, was *geopolitik*, which would also be the form in German. The publication *Ymer*, still appearing, has its name from pre-Christian Nordic mythology, in which "Ymer" was a giant; to make a long story short, after his assassination, the world was created from his body. Strictly speaking, Kjellén was then not yet a professor at Uppsala University, where he had been awarded his doctorate; in between, he held positions at a newer and less prestigious academic institution in Gothenburg. For further considerations of his life and work, see Holdar (1992) and Tunander (2001).

7. Woodruff Smith (1991: 219–240), American historian of ideas, places Friedrich Ratzel in the context of linkages between German politics and academic views of culture in the late nineteenth and early twentieth centuries. "Significance in human studies meant, to Ratzel, the big picture." (1991: 220)

8. Kearns (2009) offers a view of Mackinder's ideas relating them to current geopolitical thought.

9. By the time Kaplan got to the later book *Asia's Cauldron* (2014: 44–50), he could return to Spykman's idea, with a striking comparison: the South China Sea was "an Asian Mediterranean," as important for China's power as that "American Mediterranean" had once been for the expansive United States.

10. Oswald Spengler, marginal academic, was catapulted into fame as his *The Decline of the West* appeared at the end of World War I, and showed a perfect fit with a widespread public mood, in Germany and elsewhere. Arnold Toynbee's *A Study of History* was a comparable success, not least as the twelve-volume set was abridged to a single volume (1947), at which time his portrait was on the cover of *Time* magazine. This, too, was writing in the shadow of war; while a professor at the London School of Economics, Toynbee was also active in foreign policy intelligence work. Both Spengler and Toynbee met with Adolf Hitler; at the time Toynbee was evidently more impressed. Leo Frobenius, German Africanist scholar-explorer (briefly a junior colleague of Friedrich Ratzel's) for his part had a fan in ex-Kaiser

Wilhelm II, and others among the Francophone African intellectuals who drew on him in developing Negritude. We have seen in the Prologue that in the seventeenth century, Olof Rudbeck the Elder placed the vanished Atlantis outside Uppsala, Sweden; Frobenius had it among the Yoruba people of southwestern Nigeria.

For a view of more recent scholarship on civilizations by specialists from several disciplines, see Melko and Scott (1987) and Sanderson (1995).

11. See Chap. 5, note 4, on Jacques' (2009) view of China as a civilization-state, rather than a nation-state.

12. There have been attempts to identify the characteristics of African civilization, from different scholarly or ideological points of view, but these have apparently not been in Huntington's library. But perhaps he could have consulted with Kwame Anthony Appiah, a polymath of African background, who had just published a book on "Africa in the philosophy of culture," and who was a professor at Harvard at the time (Appiah 1992). We come back to Appiah in Chap. 7. With regard to the idea that states within a civilization will tend to come together in international politics, we may remind ourselves that visions of Pan-Africanism have been there, although mostly with limited practical effects, since before the end of the colonial era.

13. On African religion in the Americas, see for example Bastide (1971) and Matory (2005).

14. Huntington likewise seems unaware of another Brazilian public intellectual, anthropologist-politician Darcy Ribeiro, whose *The Americas and Civilization* (1971) offers an original comprehensive perspective toward the lands of the Western hemisphere.

15. My reasoning draws on the view which has been established in anthropology particularly since Fredrik Barth (1969) argued for a clear analytical distinction between ethnicity and culture, the former being a matter of collective identity, drawing on culture as meanings and practices, but in complicated and selective ways.

16. The notion of "multiple modernities" is particularly associated with Eisenstadt (e.g. 2000). On alternative modernities, see Gaonkar (2001).

17. Benazir Bhutto's (2008) book is somewhat ghostwritten; the back cover of the paperback edition has a Fareed Zakaria blurb.

18. As Paul Kennedy, historian in the original "One Big Thing" quintet, and his collaborators at about the same time identified nine "pivotal states," with their futures at critical turning points, they listed Indonesia, Pakistan, Turkey, Egypt, Algeria, Brazil, Mexico, India and South Africa among these (Chase et al. 1999). So the four latter were perhaps not quite so safely in Barnett's Core. One could note, too, as we did in Chap. 1, that since then, the recent history of those pivotal countries has continued to have its times and places of turbulence.

19. More about Cooper's views on this in Chap. 6.

20. There were observers taking a more critical and nuanced view even at this stage; see e.g. a study by the anthropologist Cris Shore (2000).

21. The pioneering anthropological critique of the use of temporality in "Othering" is Fabian's (1983).

22. More from the *Time* story: "The usual images are painted in the darkest colors. At the end of the 20th century, we are repeatedly reminded, Africa is a nightmarish world where chaos reigns. Nothing works. Poverty and corruption rule. War, famine and pestilence pay repeated calls. The land, air, water are raped, fouled, polluted. Chronic instability gives way to lifelong dictatorship. Every nation's hand is out, begging aid from distrustful donors. Endlessly disappointed, 740 million people sink into hopelessness." (McGeary and Michaels 1998).

    On the concentration of Africa correspondents in Johannesburg, see Hannerz (2004a: 61). For more debate over Afro-Pessimism, see Gordon and Wolpe (1998) and Rieff (1998). James Ferguson's (1999: 236) discussion of "abjection," in the context of an ethnography of urban Zambia in the same period, provides a nuanced view of local sentiments revolving around decline, and their sources. The historian Achille Mbembe's (2001) interpretation of the postcolonial African state is also illuminating in this context.

23. At the time of the 2014 Ebola epidemic in Liberia and neighboring countries, Epstein (2014) reported highly critically on the implications of President Ellen Johnson Sirleaf's rule.

24. Philip Gourevitch (1996), specialist on Africa reporting and renowned for his writings on Rwanda, subtitles an extended critical review of several scenario texts (by Huntington, Barber and Kaplan) in the *New Yorker* "In a new trend, Hell is other peoples." Of Robert Kaplan's *The Ends of the Earth*, following the approach of anarchy, he concludes that the author now "has included much of the rest of the non-Western world in his zone of incomprehension." And as Kaplan muses that "We are the world and the world is us," Gourevitch responds that this is "a notion that reduces the gravity of the violent social and political transformations of our times to a vacuous inanity."

25. The sociologist John W. Meyer and his collaborators (e.g. Meyer et al. 1997; Meyer 1999) have argued that as "nation-states" have become a globally dominant mode of political organization, and as notions of modernity and rationality diffuse among these states, their formal structures tend to become quite similar.

26. After Colonel Ghaddafi's fall in 2011, and with the chaotic conditions in Libya thereafter, arms spread through the Sahara, to Mali and elsewhere, leading to further political and military upheavals. Here, then, anarchy did not emanate in West Africa—considering the part Europe and the United States had in the struggle against Ghaddafi, perhaps one could borrow Robert Cooper's term to suggest that in this case, the postmodern and the modern world got together to create premodernity?

27. See for example Richards (1996, 2005), Nordstrom (1997, 2004), Trefon (2004), Roitman (2005), Finnström (2008), Knörr and Trajano Filho (2010), Hoffman (2011) and McGovern (2011).

28. The Dutch anthropologist Willem van Schendel has introduced the name "Zomia" for this region, which has drawn much anthropological interest over the years. James C. Scott's monograph *The Art of Not Being Governed* (2009) offers a comprehensive view of it.

29. More of Kaplan's West African travel (Guinea, Sierra Leone, Liberia, Ivory Coast, Ghana, Togo) is covered in *The Ends of the Earth* (1996). Richards' own monograph *Fighting for the Rain Forest* (1996) takes Kaplan's original "coming anarchy" as its point of departure, and is a full-scale critique of its kind of argument, based on deep familiarity with Sierra Leone and its youth.

30. Gender may be included in the list of conflict factors as the more active combatants have usually been male. One could note, too, that one of the co-winners of the Nobel Peace Prize in 2011, with the female president of Liberia, was a woman political activist from the same country whose movement, among a range of other tactics, saw scandal as a mode of pressure, using a threat to undress publicly as they protested the lack of progress in peace negotiations.

    In 2014 the abduction of several hundred Nigerian schoolgirls by the Islamist terrorist movement Boko Haram drew global attention.

31. In the 2002 article on "the postmodern state," Cooper argues that "it is precisely because of the death of imperialism that we are seeing the emergence of the pre-modern world." He goes on to note that under postmodernity, "empire" and "imperialism" have become terms of abuse; both the supply and the demand for imperialism have dried up. "And yet the weak still need the strong and the strong still need an orderly world."

    With regard to the old kind of imperialism, see Niall Ferguson (2003) on the British Empire in its heyday as a major force of modernization in the world.

32. In the academic division of labor within colonial anthropology, Sudan (including what is now South Sudan) was largely Oxford University turf. Evans-Pritchard's *The Nuer* (1940) remains one of the classics of anthropology. At a later point, when it was argued, on the basis of an attempt at historical reconstruction, that the Nuer had actually started out as Dinka (Newcomer 1972), it provoked some rather subtle academic controversy. One might wonder what such identity work could do to current conflicts; most likely very little. For a more recent example of the continuous anthropological concern with the area, see Hutchinson and Pendle (2015).

33. As I first wrote this, I could hear on the morning news that Sweden was about to contribute by sending a small troop, specializing in telecommunications and intelligence, to Timbuktu, as part of a United Nations mission in Mali.

34. On the refugee traffic between North Africa and Europe, see ethnographic studies by Lucht (2011) and Andersson (2014). For a global overview of

the multifaceted "migration industry," see Gammeltoft-Hansen and Nyberg Sörensen (2013).

35. This John Gray should certainly not be confused with the British political philosopher John Gray, whose critique of global capitalism in *False Dawn* (1998a) is in a way closer to the topic of this book. The latter John Gray (1998b) has also commented on Fukuyama and Huntington.

36. In a later portrait of Kagan and his family life in the *New York Times*, we learn that "Mr. Kagan, who often works in a book-lined studio of his cedar home here in the Washington suburbs, exudes a Cocoa-Puffs-pouring, stay-at-home-dad charm." (Horowitz 2014) This does not seem very Martian. At about that time, however, Victoria Nuland, Kagan's spouse and an Assistant Secretary of State, was in the news when, visiting a Ukraine in political upheaval, she made the suggestion to "f**k the EU" in a telephone conversation with another American diplomat. At a precise point in time when it was widely understood that great powers listened and looked into just about all each other's communications, on telephone and the Internet, this was seen as not so professionally diplomatic. For one thing, Angela Merkel, German *Bundeskanzler*, was reportedly not amused. Perhaps it suggests, anyhow, that views of the US-EU relationship in the Nuland-Kagan household had not changed so much over time.

37. The resort to embedded war correspondents in the 2003 war had its prehistory. In the Vietnam War, journalists had been on the war scene, although in large part operating rather independently, and the result was a kind of critical reporting which created its own heroes and heroines among the practitioners, and had a large part in turning domestic opinion gradually against the war. Then in the 1991 Gulf War, the strategy was to keep journalists away from the front, on reservations where they could attend the press conferences organized for their benefit by the military. As this caused considerable dissatisfaction, "embedding" followed.

38. Kaplan (2005: 4) notes that the map of U.S. area commands strikingly resembles one drawn in 1931 by Karl Haushofer, the German geopolitics proponent. It may be added here that Kaplan does not dwell very much in these books on the effects of American military bases on the life of surrounding areas, or on the understandings of host populations of their presence. One gets a view of such matters from an edited volume by Catherine Lutz (2009).
See also Chap. 8, especially note 6, on the mark the soft power of the American occupation left on Tokyo.

39. Kaplan takes the same view in an earlier book, *An Empire Wilderness: Travels into America's Future* (1998), which I do not deal with here; its first chapter is devoted to Fort Leavenworth, Kansas.

CHAPTER 4

Side Shows: Eurabia, MexAmerica

The cover of *The Economist* (June 24, 2006), the newsweekly with a considerable transatlantic if not global circulation, showed the Eiffel Tower at dusk, with a crescent on top. And the big rubric next to it said, "Eurabia." Was this a new continent, perhaps hybrid continent, coming into being? And across the Atlantic there seemed to be a similar, although not quite so strikingly publicized, development. So perhaps by now both the Martians of the United States and the Venusians of Europe, in Robert Kagan's version of interplanetary migration, would have to worry. According to some views, what had become their homelands were being invaded once more, this time from nearby. Compared to more complete global visions, as I noted in Chap. 1, these could be mere sideshows. But they are scenarios for one continent, and one very large country, which have for some time enjoyed a great deal of attention. Again there is some playing with maps, some dramatic geocultural imagination, and now some inventive name-calling.

INVASION ALARMS I: EURABIAN STORIES

With that cover story in *The Economist*, a neologism which until then mostly had a rather obscure existence may have had its public breakthrough. Whether she had discovered it or not, a writer named Bat Ye'or did much to promote it, with the book *Eurabia* (2005). In Hebrew, "Bat Ye'or" means "daughter of the Nile"—this was the pseudonym of

81

Giselle Littman, later apparently mobile in Europe but originally from the old Jewish community in Egypt, of pre-Nasserite times. Before *Eurabia* she had another book named *Islam and Dhimmitude* (2001), subtitled "Where Civilizations Collide."

Who, or what, was actually invading? There is a certain fuzziness in the cluster of alarmist statements we encounter here. Sometimes "Arab" and "Islamic" (or "Muslim") tend to be used more or less exchangeably. Yet of course, Muslim migration streams to Europe after World War II have been quite different in their distributions. Past imperial connections have largely taken North Africans to France and Pakistanis to Great Britain. Turks have gone to Germany in large part for reasons of geography. Other countries have their own mixes. But the Turks and the Pakistanis are not Arabs.

Bat Ye'or, for her part, perhaps for her own biographical reasons, emphasizes the Arab facet of the complex; and her Eurabia is first of all a top-down construct. She finds its origins in the post-World War II period, as an anti-American strategy promoted by European politicians, not least by General, later President, de Gaulle. Anti-Semitic politicians of the Nazi-collaborationist Vichy regime were kept in important positions, and according to Ye'or, de Gaulle was also lenient toward the Mufti of Jerusalem, despite his pro-Nazi past. Then this Euro-Arab axis, she argues, just grew and grew, through publications, organizations, conferences, and policies of collaboration and appeasement; anti-American, Judaeophobic, pro-Palestinian. And its end result will be that Europe turns into a land of "dhimmitude," inhabited by peoples who may be allowed to remain non-Muslim, but who are subordinate to Muslim power. The political history of Islam offers models of this.

Again, however, the idea of "Eurabia" would not remain Bat Ye'or's intellectual property. At some point, she and Oriana Fallaci, Italian star journalist, discovered one another, and thereafter consistently showed their mutual appreciation. Fallaci was a more prominent figure than Bat Ye'or. Even as a child, in Tuscany, she had participated in the Italian anti-fascist resistance. During her almost half-century long career as a journalist and author, she made her fame as a war correspondent and interviewer, conversing in agonistic style with, among others, a pope, an ayatollah, and Henry Kissinger. (The latter would reminisce that his interview with Fallaci was "the single most disastrous conversation [he] ever had with a member of the press.") Fallaci loved freedom, and was suspicious of power. By the beginning of the twenty-first century, however, she was in her seventies and seriously ill, and it was clear that she was approaching the end of her life. The events of 9-11 made her spend her remaining years concentrating on a campaign against Islam. Her book *The Force of Reason* (2006) appeared in English the year of her death.

Both Bat Ye'or and Oriana Fallaci roam freely through the centuries, collapsing history so that jihadi strategy remains forever the same. Perhaps they follow the Orwellian dictum from *1984*: "who controls the past controls the future…" They relate to the present, on the other hand, rather differently. Fallaci (2006: 138–139) draws on Bat Ye'or for "extraordinary research"—indeed, Ye'or is a footnotes person. With Fallaci herself, one gets a sense of a writer with considerable imagination, who writes whatever enters her mind—and then possibly ends up believing it all. In a remarkable portrait and interview in the *New Yorker*, published a few months before her death, Fallaci could make her working philosophy entirely explicit:

> You have this respectability that is given to you, more or less. But you don't give a damn. It is the ne plus ultra of freedom. And things that I didn't use to say before—you know, there is in each of us a form of timidity, of cautiousness—now I open my big mouth. I say, 'What are you going to do to me? You go fuck yourself—I say what I want.' (Talbot 2006)

So Fallaci could begin her last book with the story of a medieval heretic in her home province of Tuscany, whose world view was incompatible with the reigning orthodoxy, and who was therefore tortured, sentenced to death, and burned alive…And she predicted that her own fate would be similar. Around midway through *The Force of Reason*, she notes that her Swedish publisher had declined to take on her previous book—"on the contrary, texts singing the praises of Islam fill the bookshops like sardines in a can of sardines. Where Swedish citizenship is granted to anybody who whispers Allah-akbar" (Fallaci 2006: 79).

Well, not really. And in the country just south of Sweden: "for the last decade the Danes have been converting in droves" (2006: 79) No, I do not think so either. (And when Francis Fukuyama in his later writings seeks for "the road to Denmark," he does not have that kind of country in mind.)

Another commentator on Eurabia is Mark Steyn, Canadian-born syndicated columnist writing mostly for North American publications.

The back cover blurb of Steyn's book *America Alone*—again a 2006 publication—describes him as "hilarious, provocative and brilliant." (The front cover announces: "Soon to be banned in Canada" but also "New York Times Bestseller") So evidently his Eurabian tales should not be taken too seriously—although there may be a certain risk that some of his readers do. Interpretations of selected statistics are inserted among stories of encounters between clever crypto-jihadists and gullible political, academic or ecclesiastical natives, where the former make their moves toward a final takeover. Steyn makes brief mention of some heroes and heroines, like Bat Ye'or and Oriana Fallaci, but mostly, when writing about people or nations, his strategy seems to be "When you cannot ridicule them, demonize them (if you cannot do both)." It is not very clear if Steyn has had his boots on the ground in Europe, or Eurabia, very much. The book's acknowledgments says: "Above all, I am grateful to readers in America, Canada, Britain, Europe, the Middle East, Africa, Asia, Australia, New Zealand, and elsewhere for many useful insights and anecdotes into our fast-changing world." So perhaps most of the time, Steyn has been in New Hampshire.

Bruce Bawer published his *While Europe Slept* in 2006, too—a strong year for predictions of the decline and fall of a continent. This begins as the somewhat typical account of an American expatriate arriving in a charming old European city: at first enthusiastic, then disenchanted. Bawer enjoys the easy-going life of Amsterdam, walking along the canals… But then he notes an inclination toward comfortable mediocrity rather than American-style striving, and toward conformity and political correctness, and toward staying encapsulated within one's group. It is also a central fact that he is gay, and he and his partner learn that the Muslim, mostly Moroccan, migrants who are a very conspicuously there in the streets and neighborhoods of Amsterdam can react violently to visible signs of homosexuality. When the two move on to Oslo, where they can marry, they find that this is in some ways a very different city, and yet in other ways much like Amsterdam. The Muslims here are more likely to be Pakistanis, but they are no more tolerant, and they seem to exploit the advantages of the welfare state without trying hard to fit in. Alienated, Bawer evidently takes to gathering materials on the dark sides of the Muslim presence all over Europe—the subtitle of his book is "How Radical Islam is Destroying the West from Within." Here his exposition partly parallels Bat Ye'or (whose *Eurabia* he lauds as "sensational"), partly gets more anecdotal, similar to Steyn's. But then he does not really stick to the proclaimed topic: much of the time he really spends discussing Europe more generally; and it seems to be mostly awake, although not in ways he approves of. So here again we are back in that period when American-European relationships seemed to be at a low point, where as Kagan had it, the peoples of Mars and Venus "agree on little and understand one another less and less." Intentionally or not, Bruce Bawer offers evidence for both.

Christopher Caldwell's *Reflections on the Revolution in Europe* is from slightly later, in 2009. Caldwell was a senior editor of *Weekly Standard*, a conservative American magazine, and a columnist for the *Financial Times*. This is a book rather different in tone from those of Bat Ye'or, Fallaci, Steyn and Bawer: less strident, more skeptical. "Eurabia" is not really part of his vocabulary, so if he is identified here together with these other four, it is because his line of argument belongs with theirs. But Fallaci—"the late Italian polemicist," with "one of her more rabid tirades against Islam"—becomes a case rather than a colleague. The other three are not mentioned.

Caldwell is well-read, although selectively so, at least in what he refers to. He offers an overview of major issues, incidents and personalities which have drawn public attention to the problematics of Muslim presence in Europe over the post-World War II period, setting it also in a wider context of European politics and transnational migration. Some of the personalities of politics and organized religion whom he introduces are probably not so widely known, and he has a sharp eye for inconsistencies and contradictions in the policies of European governments. For a reader seeking an overall critique of the implications of an acceptance of large-scale Muslim immigration to Europe, Caldwell may be a guide to turn to, even if one is not ready to follow all his directions. Nor may one want to accept his concluding statement about the encounter of Europe with Islam:

> When an insecure, malleable, relativistic culture meets a culture that is anchored, confident, and strengthened by common doctrines, it is generally the former that changes to suit the latter. (Caldwell 2009: 286)

Finally, we reach *Londonistan*, with Melanie Phillips (2006), prominent British journalist, as our guide. The book's beginning scene is from the London Underground, on July 7, 2005, when three bombs go off in trains, while a fourth blows up a double-decker bus in a street.

"Londonistan" is playing with maps again. As a world city, the British capital lends itself to that. As Russian oligarchs go west, one journalist notes, it has also earned nicknames like "Londongrad" and "Moscow-on-Thames" (Cowell 2006). "-istan," in Phillips' case, could conceivably stand just for a general remoteness, and wild countries, but it is hardly a coincidence that it also goes with countries like Pakistan, or Afghanistan. Phillips is not much concerned with those major migrant streams arriving in Britain from a variety of other places over the years, such as those who began coming in larger numbers from the Caribbean after World War II (symbolically linked with the passage of the ship *Empire Windrush* from Jamaica to London, in 1947). Her critical focus is on the Muslims, and in that way she connects to the general Eurabia theme; on this she refers to Bruce Bawer. She is not so narrowly preoccupied with London either, but with Britain more generally. Yet London was also special—long before those bombs exploded,

> Incredibly, London had become the hub of the European terror networks. Its large and fluid Muslim and Arab population fostered the growth of myriad radical Islamist publications spitting hatred of the West, and its banks were used for fund-raising accounts funnelling money into extremist and terrorist organizations. Terrorists wanted in other countries were given safe haven in the United Kingdom and left free to foment hatred against the West. (Phillips 2006: 12)

A considerable part of *Londonistan* is devoted, then, to documenting the presence of dangerous Islamism in Britain. Yet the book also becomes a partisan account of an internal culture war among the British, where the author proposes that it is the secular, rationalist, egalitarian ethos of the British political and educational elite, with its deficient pride in British culture and history, which has rendered the country defenseless against creeping Islamization. Even the Prince of Wales, heir to the throne with its special link to the established church, had tried out the idea that as king, he would no longer be Defender of the Faith, but "defender of faith." (2006: 118) Remarkably, Phillips goes as far as to refer to "decolonization as catastrophic loss of influence"—this would seem to have her disagreeing with about half a century of both Labour and Tory policy, and placing her, with regard to the global arena, in the pro-Empire camp. Surprising perhaps for a George Orwell Prize winner, in 1996, but since then Melanie Phillips has clearly been politically mobile.

Much of the ideological goods which Phillips finds largely destructive in the British encounter with Londonistan is imported, she suggests, from America—but in the USA, there has also been a counteroffensive which she can approve of (2006:27). Although her own book seems aimed at a British audience, it is striking that much of the other writing about Eurabia and related matters has an American orientation. Both Bruce Bawer and Christopher Caldwell are Americans. Bat Ye'or's *Eurabia* was published by a rather marginal American university press. Even Oriana Fallaci had a Manhattan town house, although she went home to Tuscany to die. And clearly Mark Steyn's *America Alone* was in the end about the presumed fact that as that oldest allied region across the Atlantic was falling apart, or conquered by the enemy, there was only America left. While Steyn sees Islam eating its way into American life as well (although I have not come across any reference to an Amerabia yet), Europe Eurabizing would be among the grounds for a cultural, social and political divorce.[1]

WAR CORRESPONDENCE: WORLD WAR IV

Under such circumstances, it was inevitable that images of a changing Europe also had ramifying connections to other notions and arguments in early twenty-first century public culture. The spread of anti-Americanism—"Why do they hate us?" (Or don't they?)—was among these. Another was that struggle against "Islamofascism" which some commentators numbered as World War IV.[2] (World War III, of course, had been the Cold War.) I will make a slight detour here on the latter notion, as I think it is interesting to see how a scenario makes its way across borders.

"World War IV" was launched as buzz term by the political scientist Eliot Cohen in an op-ed piece in the *Wall Street Journal* in November 2001, a few months after the 9-11 events, to argue for the necessity of "regime change" in hostile, Islamic countries in the Middle East—the war in question, in his view, was already on. While he did not get the military attack on Iran that he wanted, he went on to support the Iraq War strongly, and at the time had strong official Washington connections. (So here was one more person straddling the boundaries between Academia, media and politics.) Later the term was picked up by the long-time New York neoconservative publicist Norman Podhoretz, not least for his book *World War IV: The Long Struggle Against Islamofascism* (2007). Endorsements at the beginning of the book were by various notables, including radio show host Rush Limbaugh and New York ex-mayor and occasional presidential candidate Rudy Giuliani; the subtitle caused some argument, as some commentators would hold that among those distant adversaries, those who were most "Islamo" were not really fascists, and those who were most "fascist" perhaps wore their Islamic persuasion somewhat lightly. (By the time of the Islamic State movement, emerging as a military force in Syria and Iraq in 2014, and becoming an erratic global force thereafter, Islamofascism would seem to have become more of a reality; see e.g. Napoleoni 2014 for one early account.) But in any case, Podhoretz' real adversaries could seem to be more nearby, the people to the left of him on Manhattan and along the United States East Coast. He actually did devote much of his book to them.

By the time that book appeared, however, I could witness how "World War IV" had made it across the Atlantic, and across the Mediterranean as well. In early 2005, I heard Bernard Lewis, the renowned Orientalist (who had once coined the term "clash of civilizations") give a public lecture at Tel Aviv University, where he was a frequent visitor. One of the largest halls on campus was full, although much of the audience was elderly, obviously from off-campus. Aged 88 at the time, Lewis was a remarkably clear, rhetorically skilled speaker. So Bernard Lewis had been born just before the fall of the Ottoman Empire in that part of the world he had spent his life his studying. This evening, however, he hardly offered any new facts. The point was rather to place what was familiar into a firm framework, attractive to the audience at hand. Not a critical word about Israeli politics, nothing to complicate the picture of good against evil. The war in Iraq was at its height. And so now the topic was "World War IV." What was the war against? It was useless, Lewis argued, to describe it as a war against terror, as terror was merely a method. Obviously it had to do with Islam, but here his emphases became a bit shifting. Osama bin Laden had a major part, but he also enumerated the several places where Islam was involved in violent conflicts—Islam with its "bloody borders." Kosovo, Kashmir, Chechnya... So why does Palestine get most of the attention? The major reason, Lewis suggested, was that "Jews are news"—the audience clearly enjoyed the joke.

There were, he acknowledged, peaceful varieties of Islam as well, such as Sufism. Wahhabism, on the other hand, with its Saudi center and its global missionizing, among Muslims in Europe as well, was a much more dangerous influence. For Osama bin Laden, the collapse of the Soviet Union had been the first big victory of World War IV, and he had expected that thereafter Americans would turn out to be a nation of weaklings.

Arabic culture being a warrior culture, repeated defeat at the hands of Israel, a mere statelet, had been very humiliating. It did not help either that women were beginning to make their voices heard at home. But then there was also Iran. For Lewis, the Iranian revolution of 1979 was as important in defining a new phase of world history as the French and the Russian revolutions had been in their time. And so, juggling past and present with habitual dexterity, he could offer a couple of startling histori-cal comparisons. Now, in the early 2000s, he suggested, the revolution in question had reached its Stalinist phase. And Islam, which began in the 600s with its Prophet, had now reached its 1400s—and "you all know," he could admit, "what kinds of things we did in the West when we were at that point."

MY HOME TOWN: A CORNER OF EURABIA?

Back to Europe, however, and the Eurabia scenario texts. The book you are reading now is one which is mostly about other books, less about the societies which these books are about. But under the circumstances, par-ticularly in the case of these books about Europe and its future, I feel a certain need to confront them with my own sense of what are some major features of current history. So let me fairly concretely focus on one corner of Europe which I believe I know something about.

One Swedish city, Malmö, with a third of a million inhabitants or so, is mentioned with some frequency as one of the centers of Eurabia—both Bat Ye'or and Bruce Bawer refer to it, and Christopher Caldwell in some-what different terms. It has had a virtual existence on the Internet, where I have seen that it is well on its way to a Muslim majority according to some rather obscure web sites, and already has one according to others. As it happens, Malmö is where I was born. So this is a native speaking back.

Malmö is at the southwestern corner of Sweden. Nowadays there is a longish bridge connecting it to Copenhagen, but at the time when I spent my very first years there, one would not cross over to Denmark at all, as that country was occupied by Nazi Germany. (On the other hand, a little further up the coast, there was a period when fleeing Danish Jews arrived in small boats; to a friendlier welcome than those boat people tended to get who arrived on European shores some seventy years later.) Since then, Malmö has been through a period of industrial decline, and a rather diversified revival including some high-tech business, services, and higher education. The city's own web site (*www.malmo.se*) notes that there are residents from 177 countries. By 2012, Iraqis, Syrians, Afghans, and Turks were among the fastest growing immigrant groups; and Iraqis had become the largest group—but the second largest group was still the Danes, many of whom presumably commuted across the bridge. About a third of the population was foreign-born.

If one adds to that the children of the foreign-born, we might estimate that perhaps half the population of Malmö is now of something other than old-style Swedish background. Malmö was the second Swedish urban center in recent times to build a mosque. Over the years, a fact that has probably contributed to the sizable settlement of newcomers is that this is simply the first larger city one gets to if one arrives in Sweden by ferry from the south, or over that bridge. But then of these 177 nationalities, a sizeable number may be represented by people who are not Muslims; perhaps not much more culturally different than those Danes from the other side of the bridge. And while many of the most recent arrivals have been from Muslim countries, reflecting major political upheavals, one should also note that Christian minorities in these countries have been strongly represented among the people who leave from there, as they have been particularly vulnerable in local conflicts.

The former mayor (to translate the official leadership position somewhat loosely) of Malmö, who served for a long time, had come to Sweden as a one-year old, in a small open boat across the Baltic Sea, a refugee from what was Soviet-occupied Estonia; his successor, fairly young and recently promoted to the office, was born in Malmö in a Swedish family and was a political science student at a nearby university, but her married last name is West African. At the dominant local newspaper, the political editor is a transnational migrant, with her origins in the Swedish-speaking minority in Finland. Its cultural editor is Swedish-born, a member of a Syrian Orthodox ("Assyrian") family. (In her younger years, she was the leader of the youth section of the Swedish Liberal Party in her home town.) So if all of these are of a Christian, or more likely post-Christian secular, rather than Muslim background, they may suggest that even some Malmö elite circles reflect the variety of national backgrounds. The rather new university is sensitive to the fact that many of its undergraduates have a non-Swedish background, and are likely to be first-generation academics.

Nonetheless, particularly one of Malmö's suburbs has acquired not only local but national ill-repute, and would offer the key to its place in Eurabian imagery. "Suburb" may mostly mean something different in

Europe than it does in the United States.[3] In recent times, it has referred to an outlying, low-income area of more or less high-rise housing, in large part built rather hurriedly in the latter half of the twentieth century. The French term tends to be *banlieues*, in England "tower blocks" would typically involve this kind of area. Frequently, these areas have a large proportion of transnational migrant inhabitants.

The Malmö suburb in question, Rosengård, with a population of around 30,000, has a very high proportion of people of "foreign background," as the vocabulary has it: foreign-born or children of two foreign-born parents.[4] In one particular neighborhood there are hardly any indigenous Swedes at all, and overall they are not more than about 10 percent. There are considerably more children and youth than the national average, and the area has Sweden's highest proportion of youth with a criminal record, about 15 percent. People tend to move in and out of the area rather rapidly, so that it is hard to build a real sense of neighborhood, but there are many associations, often based on nationality or ethnicity. The main Malmö mosque is at some distance from Rosengård, but there are various small basement mosques, and it was when an Islamic cultural association running one of these was evicted, late in 2008, that a riot broke out, with mostly young protesters. There were no serious injuries, but some small fires were set, and fireworks and stones were hurled at the police. Things calmed down when neighborhood adults came out to make their voices heard. Various other incidents have occurred over the years, and the local police have not been very gentle in dealing with such matters. There has been some evidence of racist and xenophobic attitudes in the force, and a lack of skill in dealing with strangers. In the case of the 2008 riot, however, it seems that an escalation was due to the sudden presence of outsider participants from an extreme leftist group, without any real connection to Rosengård, or to any religion. In later years, local internecine violence seems to have more to do with the beginnings of an organized crime scene, not much with Islam or Islamism.

The main mosque, for its part, has been set afire once, and there have been a couple of minor acts of sabotage there. Moreover, Malmö has had its own lone gunman, aiming at what were to him undesirable dark aliens, killing two, failing in several more cases. (He was Swedish, although he had spent a part of his youth in the United States, where he seems to have moved in rather gun-happy circles.) On the other hand, the Jewish community in Malmö has recently felt ill at ease, and some of its members have chosen to move elsewhere (which in turn becomes a threat to the infrastructure of community life). There has been harassment in the streets, and some anti-Semitic graffiti. There are men who have stopped wearing their skullcaps in public, and when there was a tennis game between Swedish and Israeli national teams in Malmö, after disorderly protest at the stadium, the game had to be played without any spectators allowed in. That Estonian-born mayor, still in office at the time, got himself into an amount of controversy when in his public comment on this affair he seemed to get anti-Semitism mixed up with critical stances toward Israeli policies relating to Palestine. That, it would seem, is a confusion which is not his alone. Anyway, the circumstances have drawn enough attention for President Obama's emissary on Jewish affairs to come to Malmö to look into the situation. When the president came on official visit to Sweden in 2013, however, he also took the opportunity to meet the young Malmö man, son of Iranian exiles, who had taken upon himself to organize "Muslims Against Anti-Semitism," and who had taken some young Muslims from his town on a study tour of Auschwitz.

Perhaps surprisingly, an internationally successful women's soccer team, regularly the best in Sweden, is named after Rosengård, although it appears to have a wider local base in Malmö.

EUROPE, AGAIN: A CONTEMPORARY MACRO-ANTHROPOLOGICAL SKETCH

Enough about Malmö—but in some ways Europe seems to be Malmö writ large. Again, alarms about Eurabia are a mere global sideshow. But what, if anything, have the major scenarists had to say about Eurabia?

Niall Ferguson has a blurb, as does Bruce Bawer, on the back cover of Bat Ye'or's book: "Future historians will one day regard her coinage of the term 'Eurabia' as prophetic." And Ferguson contributes to the circulation of the term with a column in the *New York Times*, where he reflects on the model of a minaret to be built in Oxford, and is reminded of Edward Gibbon's *Decline and Fall of the Roman Empire* (Ferguson 2004b). Others are less favorable toward the notion. In an online magazine, Francis Fukuyama (2006) is somewhat ambivalent, but his article is subtitled "Alarmist Americans have mostly bad advice for Europeans." In his book of essays, *Facts Are Subversive* (2009: 172), Timothy Garton Ash notes that "Europe's difficulties with its Muslims are also the subject of hysterical oversimplification, especially in the United States, where stereotypes of a spineless, anti-American, anti-Semitic 'Eurabia', increasingly in thrall to Arab/Islamic domination, seem to be gaining strength." And then he adds in a note that despite all this, with that *The Economist* cover story, the word "Eurabia" had gained "the ultimate seal of transatlantic respectability."

But what did that cover story actually say? It was skeptical: the full cover rubric, next to that Eiffel Tower with a crescent, was "Eurabia: The myth and reality of Islam in Europe."[5] And the conclusion of its lead article was: "for the moment at least, the prospect of Eurabia looks like scaremongering."

By September, 2011, the Paris-based *Financial Times* columnist Simon Kuper announced the end of Eurabia. Particularly since "the Arab Spring" earlier that year, and all the upheavals that followed it, it involved a stretch of imagination to believe in a top-down conception of Arab despots dominating European politicians and media enterprises, and forcing European indigenes into dhimmitude.

So it appears that Eurabia as a mapmaking innovation lasted less than a decade. But what remains, then, of the complex of issues involving Europe's relations to its local Muslim populations that it none-too-clearly referred to? I will try a sort of rough, historically medium-term, macro-anthropological unEurabia sketch.[6]

There is first of all the fact that in a great many European countries, a number of people are somehow of Muslim background. Exact figures are often not available, as official statistics are inconsistent. And "background" is a suitably vague metaphor, covering a great deal of diversity. They are from countries ranging from Morocco to Bangladesh and Indonesia, so many of them are not Arabs. Timothy Garton Ash was among the commentators who objected to Eurabist claims on such grounds. There are also the differences which already Benazir Bhutto emphasized in her critique of Huntington, between what she described as progressives and traditionalists. This is probably hardly so much a divide as a continuum, between more secular and more religious. To many Europeans "of Muslim background," that may mean having some familiarity with, and attachment to, a somewhat fuzzy set of religious ideas, symbols and practices—much like those many Europeans do who are now occasionally referred to as "post-Christian." Secondly, there are the varieties of Islam where the distinction between Sunni and Shia is only the best-known starting point of mapmaking. (I could insert here that the reason why the Malmö central mosque was not the first in Sweden is that some years earlier, there was already an Ahmadiyya mosque elsewhere—but then many Muslims would not recognize the Ahmadiyya movement as part of Islam.) Finally, with regard to distinctions that need to be made, there is clearly that which tends to employ the labels "Muslims" and "Islamists," where the latter term (not altogether universally accepted either) is used to refer to more politically activist forms. This is a distinction which the Eurabist writers frequently fail to make, and it seems that their scenario often rests on this failure.

What is on the other side, as it were? Even a more measured critic like Christopher Caldwell concludes that the European mainstream—indigenous, post-Christian, perhaps in Robert Cooper's terms postmodern—has lost its nerve, is uncertain about its own identity, and so forth. And this is why it is losing. I doubt that this is true, and believe that this is where Caldwell's cultural conservatism comes clearly through. I think rather that this mainstream—always a rather loose notion—is on the whole fairly self-confident, with a certain sense that it can afford to be self-critical, and accept and even appreciate, in a somewhat distractedly cosmopolitan way, a measure of internal and external diversity. (There will be more about both "mainstream" and "cosmopolitanism" in Chap. 7.) This may range from xenophilia, as a mostly mild and benign form of prejudice, to everyday indifference, and is at the bottom of a certain ecumenical acceptance of the presence of whatever may be the religions of various newcomer groupings, many of which are Muslim—or of Muslim background. To the question of Caldwell's subtitle, "Can Europe Be the Same With Different People In It?" a great many Europeans might respond, "Well, no, but that's OK." And for that matter, they would not *all* be "different people"—most of them would be much the same as before, and Europe would hardly be entirely unrecognizable either.

There are, however, certain key ideas which have come to be central to the public culture of this European mainstream. A number of them belong in what Timothy Garton Ash, in his *Free World*, delineated as his "The West," so they are not uniquely European. Among them, in any case, is the bundle of things referred to as "human rights," with subdivisions. Here one reaches the limits of tolerance. And in that bundle, many involve gender issues: women's rights, gay and lesbian rights.

Some number of particular practices, and certain widely publicized incidents, cannot be identified with all Muslims, or people of Muslim background (many of whom feel as strongly about them as other Europeans, or even more), but they come to be thought of as Islam-related, even as their actual historical relationship to religion may be contestable: rigid honor codes and even honor crimes, arranged marriages for very young women, veiling in its several forms, female genital mutilation, homophobia.[7] Around such matters more quotidian forms of anti-Muslim opinion may usually grow. Another key word in this cluster of negative associations may be "Sharia law," rather diffusely understood. That cluster, moreover, can also incorporate a range of other impressions of practices and events which may originate in other parts of the world, but have for some time had a public impact in Europe, and the West, in large part through the media: ranging from the 1980s film *Not Without My Daughter*, via the fatwa against Salman Rushdie after the publication of his *Satanic Verses*, to the Saudi Arabian ban on women's driving.

The focus on particular human rights issues such as gender rights is evident in the way particular activists become associated with anti-Muslim opinions and campaigns. Among the Eurabist writers, Bruce Bawer can be mentioned in this context again, but perhaps the fact that there are several women among these authors can also be seen against this background, even as they do not focus on gender issues. There are also other star figures here, like the Somalia-born feminist Ayaan Hirsi Ali (now married to Niall Ferguson), who eventually, for somewhat complicated reasons, moved from the Netherlands to the United States; and the gay Dutch politician Pim Fortuyn who broke away to form his own party before he was murdered (not by a Muslim, but by an environmental activist).

Then, too, we should remember how the mayor in Malmö somehow found himself in hot water with some misspoken words after a Sweden-Israel tennis game. For protagonists of whatever is Israeli policy on Palestine, it may at times be convenient to see any criticism of such policy as an expression of anti-Semitism; for anti-Semites, keeping the dividing line blurred could also serve a purpose. It is clear that for Eurabia writers, particularly Bat Ye'or, Arab-Jewish conflict is one significant motivating factor underlying their scenario.

In a more overall view, there seem to have been some second thoughts about what became, in the late twentieth century, a European mainstream stance toward the organization of diversity. Leading European politicians have described what has been referred to as "multiculturalism" (or a bit contemptuously as "*multi-kulti*") as a failure, resulting in the growth of "parallel societies."[8] The aim, instead, must be "integration."

One can say many things about this, but briefly, all three key concepts are problematic. To begin with, probably many users do not see a difference between cultural diversity, as a widespread fact especially of urban life, and multiculturalism as a kind of ideology and policy, sometimes propagated by organized migrant and minority groups from below—reacting in self-defense to a situation where relative cultural uniformity has simply been taken for granted—but often, and for a period, in a mostly well-intentioned top-down manner by national or local governments. No doubt this has had some beneficial effects, but because it is a rather static, large-scale, administrative approach, it does not fit very well with the actual small-scale, internally diverse negotiation of cultural process in everyday social life. It may also maintain or even create power relationships within groups, supporting leaderships which some members might rather want to be without; at least such multiculturalism also needs an exit alternative.

It is this official multiculturalism which has not worked so well. For one thing, it risks contributing to the development of those "parallel societies," keeping members of minority groups apart from other people. "Integration" indeed seems like the more desirable alternative—but then in public discourse, it is a weasel word. Many people probably think of it as simply a synonym of assimilation, doing away with cultural diversity, requiring people not belonging to whatever is thought of as mainstream to abandon any ideas or practices that have been distinctively theirs. This would seem to be a step backward from the acceptance of diversity which had emerged earlier.

The real issue would seem to be how much cultural diversity is possible, and what kind of cultural sharing is needed for a desirable kind of integration. In German debate, the term "*Leitkultur*" has played a part here, suggesting a need for one "guiding culture."[9] But it has turned out to be ambiguous. Is it merely another term for cultural hegemony, or can it mean something else? The point that needs to be made here is that culture is in large part a matter of human beings interacting. What would seem useful are shared standards for everyday contacts and co-presences, in more or less public spaces, to avoid those minor frictions which hardly amount to clashes of civilizations. And beyond that, probably an acceptance of those standards which in different ways involve human rights.

With regard to that notion of parallel societies, again, one might feel that it is to a degree a matter of choice whether one wants to spend one's time with people much like oneself or mingling with Others. Yet can the visual imagery be misleading here? "Parallel" perhaps leads us to think of societies standing upright, side by side, largely without touching. But these social entities in Europe are not arranged like that. The proponents of Eurabia scenarios tend not to offer a clear view of how group identifications based on religion, nationality or ethnicity interrelate with class:

with social inequality. Those parallel societies which disturb politicians are, in fact, subaltern societies, or societies of the excluded. We do not hear their voices so much through the Eurabia writings, or in public arguments over multiculturalism and parallel societies.

Consider places like Rosengård in Malmö, and other *banlieues*, or "tower blocks," again. The housing is frequently poorly maintained. Social as well as commercial services are often bad. Quite a large number of the inhabitants are in fact likely to have jobs, and offer such stability and social cohesion as may be there, but those who are really successful are likely to move out. And there are more people unemployed or under-employed than elsewhere in the city, especially among the young. When there is unrest, even turning to collective violence, it seems often to be local adults who come out into the streets to calm things down, telling rioters and others to go home, as happened in Rosengård. In contrast, what are supposed to be the forces for order are often understood to be forces of oppression.

The French (now U.S.-based) anthropologist Didier Fassin (2013) conducted a field study of the police in such an area in the Paris region precisely in the period when Eurabia stories were being published; inter-estingly, he found very little mention of religion or Islam at all among the policemen. Racism, aimed at black Africans, Arabs and Roma, was on the other hand widespread. As Fassin points out, there are individual dif-ferences among the policemen in this regard, differences in opinion and temperament; but he also notes that the formal rules of demonstrating effectiveness in patrolling can promote more or less systematic discrimi-nation. I would suspect, moreover, that (as in Rosengård) the youngish policemen engaged in patrolling the *banlieues* of Europe are often not recruited in circles who have already acquired some street wisdom of a cosmopolitan kind—and by the time they have done so, they may be pro-moted to office work.

The result is rather likely to be the growth of an adversary culture in such areas—often an adversary youth culture, among people who are struggling to make their way into adulthood, and who are also very pos-sibly to some degree in conflict with their own elders, who as late-arriving immigrants are frequently less knowledgeable about local circumstances than the younger generation is. As such social conditions intersect with an available array of cultural identities, moreover, these people may be attracted to whatever is present as a reasonably developed and coherent conflict idiom. In some places and at some points in history, more secular political ideologies of the extreme left or right may have been most readily at hand. At present, for people of some non-European backgrounds in the *banlieues* of the continent, Islamism has been there as organization-ideology-symbolism all in one package. So what takes shape is a blend of a local protest response of outsiders and underdogs with a world religion with its roots and center in the Middle East.[10] It may be another ingredient in the blend, too, that as local basement mosques can ill afford much personnel financed from its own resources, what could be on offer from the outside are a kind of parachutist imams recruited from more or less Islamist inclinations, possibly supported from wealthier Arab countries, and with little understanding of their new wider surroundings.[11]

In the extreme case of such identity politics, the result may even be terrorism. Notably, converts from non-Muslim backgrounds, although often from other ethnic minorities, recruited in the street or in prison, actually seem overrepresented among terrorists. This includes one of the young men involved in the London bombings in the opening scene of Melanie Phillips' book, who was born in Jamaica of an evangelical Christian family.[12] One should not disregard such diversity of backgrounds as there is among jihadists, and terrorists. It is true that some number of them have turned out to be well-educated, and not suspected of such inclinations before they actually struck. Then of course there may have been other disappointments, in careers or elsewhere, generating deep bitterness. And some may indeed simply be extremely intellectually committed.

One more factor in Eurabist thought remains to be attended to here. It is basically demographic: Muslim populations in Europe, it is suggested, will just grow, and grow, and grow.

Obviously they could do so in different ways. One would involve increasing numbers of people changing religion. This does not seem very likely. Actual conversion of European Christians or post-Christians to Islam is at least at this point probably numerically fairly negligible. (Perhaps there may have been about as many who have turned to Buddhism?) Another possibility would involve continued immigration on a large, even increasing scale. One comes back here to a sort of *Lebensraum* argument—although not so much in the way Friedrich Ratzel had it, more than a century ago. What is now involved has less to do with sheer space, as could be the case when populations made their living more directly from the land, but more with finding a livelihood in a functioning economy. What kind of openings there will be, in quantitative and qualitative terms, in the industrial, postindustrial and service economies of the European present and future would seem like rather an open question. One cannot say that Europe in recent times has seemed particularly welcoming to newcomers from the outside, but with an aging and possibly shrinking population, Europe will need more immigrants to keep going.

Then lastly, there is the possibility that the Muslim population already present will keep growing quickly, in absolute and relative terms, while other European groups grow slowly or not at all. Yet some commentators expect that as time goes by, birth rates will go down among Muslim Europeans as well.[13] Moreover, apart from local concentrations in some cities, Muslims would have a long way to go to become anything like a majority. Demography, it seems, does not fully support a near-future Eurabia scenario either.

So this sketch can perhaps stand as a reasonably durable alternative to the Eurabist view of Europe. To make the map, if not complete and detailed, a least more even in its coverage, however, it is also necessary to have a glance at what has recently been there on the other side of the politico-cultural spectrum. In many parts of Europe, there have been those recent parties and movements on the arena of organized politics which are often described as forms of "right-wing populism." That is at least sometimes possibly not quite adequate, as their positioning on a right-left scale is not always so firm. (At times they appear to be warmly in favor of the welfare state, although with welfare only for the natives.) I prefer the term "neo-nationalist," where "neo" refers to a relatively recent origin, and where "nationalist" may involve a certain celebratory stance toward a national heritage, but is above all anti-immigration, anti-immigrant, to one degree or other xenophobic (see Gingrich and Banks 2006; Wodak et al. 2013).

Such groupings can have varied origins in the past—sometimes their roots are in tax protest, of the old French Poujadist type, sometimes they are direct or indirect descendants of Nazi or post-Nazi entities. It is a kind of politics which has had its celebrities over the last few decades, such as Marine LePen (and before that, her father Jean-Marie) in France, Jörg Haider in Austria, Geert Wilders in the Netherlands. By now their agendas tend to be based on a combination of economic chauvinism and cultural pessimism: they claim that immigrants take jobs from natives and somehow at the same time make too large claims on public welfare, and are also a threat to national culture. Their appeal tends to be greatest in groups and local communities to which the presence of transnational labor migrants and refugees has been a rather sudden experience, even a mild form of what used to be called "culture shock." Perhaps an early phase was a response to that greater mobility within the European Union which showed itself in some local influx of strangers; "the Polish Plumber," for one, entered the West European imaginary. In another phase, there were the refugee streams internal to Europe, resulting from 1990s Balkan conflicts; and then only after that did "Islam" become a focal concern. Insofar as this all involved a sense of powerlessness among the affected local people, there would also be more generally anti-establishment components in the package.

While the Eurabia writers have mostly had little to say about the neo-nationalist strains in European politics, they are in large part with them on the same track, especially with regard to ideas about Islam. Retrieving Antonio Gramsci's notion again, one might indeed view the Eurabists as organic intellectuals of neo-nationalism. It is here, too, one may find politicians depicting a future Europe gone even beyond "dhimmitude"—Christian majorities forced to convert to Islam, European school children facing Mecca in their obligatory prayers.

Then, however, there are variations along a continuum here as well. As some groupings of this type meet with a degree of success in the democratic political marketplace and establish a foothold in parliaments and local councils, they may struggle to appear more respectable in the eyes of at least some groups in the electorate, often ostentatiously packaging other appealing items together with their anti-migrant stances, so as to increase their future vote; and thus they distance themselves from some of the more blatant expressions of xenophobia and racism, or find euphemisms to describe such sentiments.[14] But in the spaces they thus vacate, there is then room for other outlier groups—some of them perhaps with more taste for street fighting than for electoral procedure. And at the extreme end of the continuum (certainly as a major embarrassment to softer neo-nationalist politics), there are the isolated terrorists. To repeat, Malmö had one of these; but the most notable instance has been Norway's Anders Behring Breivik, who committed mass murder at a summer camp in 2012, among young people he saw as traitors to the nation and representatives of multicultural society.

We come back to Breivik briefly in Chap. 7. Here I would add that before he went into murderous action, he published a very long manifesto on Internet, detailing the readings on which he based his views. When Simon Kuper, the *Financial Times* columnist, announced the end of Eurabia, he commented on the Eurabist writers that "I once reviewed their books for the *FT.* It wasn't much fun: jointly with the autobiography of the footballer Ashley Cole, Ye'or's *Eurabia* is the worst book I've ever read." (Kuper 2011)[15] But he had also found that he had shared his reading matter with Breivik, whose references included Bruce Bawer, Bat Ye'or and Melanie Phillips.

2015: A TROUBLED CONTINENT

The end of Eurabia, then, perhaps—but not the end of history. In relation to the medium-term understanding of Europe, it seems necessary to consider the dramatic events of 2015.

This was an *annus horribilis.* Perhaps it could even have seemed that the batch of Eurabia books published in 2006 came nearly a decade too early? In the terms used somewhat questionably by Robert Cooper, as referred to in Chap. 3, it took the continent uncomfortably back from postmodernity toward modernity, to opacity and distrust, and strengthened borders (sometimes with new barbed wire)—yet struggling heroically, here and there and on critical occasions, to maintain achieved forms of civilization.

The year began with three young Parisian Muslims—two of North African background, one West African—engaging in massacres at the *Charlie Hebdo* satirical magazine (which habitually made fun of expressions of Islam) and a kosher food store. Close to its end, in November, there was another mass killing, again in Paris but locally dispersed over several sites, of 130 people. The sense of imminent danger spread, through much of Europe, but not least in the *banlieues* where the ensuing hunt for the terrorists was concentrated. Over these events was the shadow of the Islamic State, with its unpredictable, shape-shifting reach. In between, accelerating in late summer, there had been the massive migrant streams, in large part from war-torn Syria but also from other points east, as far away as Afghanistan, making it (although with considerable loss of lives) mostly by way of Turkey to Greece, and then onwards overland. The refugees, singles or families, congregated around major railroad stations, but also continued in striking numbers on foot, from southeastern Europe toward the north and west.

Here were old geopolitical verities in a new version. For Europe, what for centuries had been a mostly favorable location as a largish, well-endowed peninsula at the western end of Eurasia turned into the vulnerability of having lands of acute disorder nearby to the southeast (and just a small, rather easily crossed sea to the south). The reactions to the newcomers in need varied, and suggested that local and regional histories could have a part in shaping current sentiments and actions. A brief glance backward would remind us that in the Balkans, and as far into the continent as Vienna, some lands had their own collective memory of encounters and confrontations with a powerful Ottoman Empire. This could have some lingering effect. Further north, other more recent circumstances might play a part. In late 2014 and early 2015 already, before the influx of refugees reached its greatest height, a new grouping of the neo-nationalist type, named Pegida, showed up in Germany, more specifically in the city of Dresden, to protest against what its leaders felt was a deluge of strangers. Dresden, for its part, located for much of the twentieth century behind the Iron Curtain, deep in East Germany, and after that in a depressed region of the reunited country, was perhaps in the early decades of the following century not altogether tuned in to the everyday cosmopolitanism that had grown elsewhere in middle and western Europe.

But in Dresden, too, Pegida marchers met with large numbers of counterdemonstrators. And when the leaders tried to bring their public activities to other cities, even other countries, the success was very limited. As Pegida reached Malmö, in February 2015, there were between fifty and one hundred sympathizers, and about 5000 adversaries, in the city's main square.

A half a year or so later, as large numbers of refugees began arriving at the Malmö central railroad station (having crossed that bridge from Denmark), they were also met by a very considerable crowd of volunteers, spontaneously coming to welcome them and offer assistance. Yet here, too, practical and organizational capabilities were eventually stretched thin. Even offering the many refugees a roof over their heads, somewhere in Sweden, became acutely problematic. So the doors to this country, earlier remarkably open, also began to shut, or became more closely guarded, as in much of Europe. As elsewhere, too, with events like those in Paris in mind, it became a matter of concern that young militant Islamists from the dreary suburbs could be drawn to the armed conflicts in the Arab World, not least to the Islamic State, and then return home from these equipped with new and dangerous knowledge.[16]

The Paris events of 2015 also brought into sharp focus one more issue which has recurrently generated conflict between at least some Muslims and parts of the surrounding society in Europe: the question of freedom of expression. We noted in Chap. 2, as an example of the uses of the "clash of civilizations" notion in public commentary, the widespread protests occasioned by a set of Prophet Muhammad caricatures in one Danish newspaper. The killings of staff members of *Charlie Hebdo* were similarly a consequence of a sense of deep humiliation among members of Muslim communities. The massive, globalizing memorial march between Place de la Nation and Place de la Republique some days after the murders showed a deep and broad commitment to the principle of freedom of speech—and in this case, the freedom to caricature. Yet somewhat muted, in the aftermath of the terrorist attacks and the protest against them, questions were also surfacing about the possible misuses of the freedom of expression.

If it is purposely used in a way to denigrate the deeply held sense of self of some group of human beings, without really contributing to any rational debate, should this freedom still be defended, even celebrated? To raise this question does not justify violence, and does not necessarily constitute an argument for formally instituted censorship. It suggests rather that an amount of self-censorship, so as to avoid unnecessarily insulting and provoking other people, is the highest, wisest, most effective form of censorship: a part of civil, cosmopolitan common sense in a culturally diverse society. In the commentary after the *Charlie Hebdo* affair, that sometimes seemed better understood in the United States than in Europe.[17]

Almost simultaneously with the *Charlie Hebdo* events, too, in early 2015, the French novelist Michel Houellebecq's book *Soumission* was published, drawing widespread commentary and soon to be translated into numerous languages; in English as *Submission* within the year. Houellebecq's story was itself a future scenario (somewhat Orwellesque, perhaps): a middle-aged Parisian professor, in the doldrums of local academic life, promiscuous but lonely and rather lazy, witnesses France going Muslim in 2022, with much of Europe soon following after. But as depicted, this is not so much a conquest from the outside as a consequence of the mediocrity of mainstream political leadership.[18] A Muslim Brotherhood comes to power through skillful maneuvering by way of elections and alliances; funding flows in from the Gulf states, and the anti-hero's university becomes the Islamic University of Paris-Sorbonne. Yet even if possibly the Eiffel Tower would come to have a crescent on top (Houellebecq does not pick up that image), the political power center does not really move. It remains in place, in what turns into a Muslim Europe resembling an updated Roman Empire. In a fleeting reference, not so much as mentioning Eurabia by name, it is pointed out that this is where Bat Ye'or was still mistaken.

INVASION ALARMS II: BACK TO MEXAMERICA

The European problems, and Islamist terrorism, of 2015 left their mark on American public life as well. The foreign news of the refugee streams moving through Europe coincided with the beginnings of a presidential election campaign. Soon, too, there were the reactions to the November terrorist shootings in Paris, and in the same month an Islamist couple went berserk in a gathering of work mates in San Bernardino, California. The "clash of civilizations" was indeed back in some presidential candidate rhetoric. The notion that "the Muslims are coming" could remind old-timers of "the Russians are coming" sentiments at the height of the Cold War, and in the routine scaremongering, some ideas of how to handle Muslims as potential enemy aliens would also show some unfortunate resemblance to the treatment of Japanese-Americans during World War II, after Pearl Harbor.

Yet the more enduring American militant nativism still looked south, rather than across the Atlantic. Around Florida there have also been those small vessels of poor but hopeful, or desperate, people trying to cross borderlines in the sea, much like those at Lampedusa, Ceuta or Christmas Island. But more often, in North America, such irregular crossings occur through deserts.

Many years after I found Garreau's *The Nine Nations of North America* in that Berkeley bookstore, I was driving south on Interstate 5 through California, between Los Angeles and San Diego.[19] Suddenly signs warned that there may be pedestrians crossing the road. Who would be so fool-hardy, or so desperate, as to try and cross eight lanes of dense, fast-moving traffic? Hardly anybody just heading for a nice nearby beach on the Pacific. More likely newcomers from the south, who had not come through at the regular border crossing at San Ysidro to show their passports.

On Garreau's map, however, there is not really a border at San Ysidro. The borders of his nation of MexAmerica are further south, inside Mexico, and further north, leaving much of southwestern United States inside that nation. All of MexAmerica could really be seen as borderlands, and probably no borderlands anywhere in history have drawn as much attention as these: in scholarship, journalism, or fiction.[20]

Yet although Garreau's mapmaking term may not be so frequently used in such a manner, a notion of "MexAmerica" could also apply to a preoccupation more analogous to "Eurabia": a sense that the entire United States is threatened from the south.[21] A leading proponent of this view

has been Patrick Buchanan, speechwriter for President Nixon, twice candidate in Republican presidential primaries, for a period an active political
commentator, with a new book every two years or so. In 2002, there was
*The Death of the West: How Dying Populations and Immigrant Invasions
Imperil Our Country and Civilization*. But the book more relevant here
would be his *State of Emergency: The Third World Invasion and Conquest
of America* (2006). One might sense that the subtitle was a map-making
device intended to maximize alarmism, as "Third World" might have
another ring to an intended Buchanan readership than it did to those
European writers on the Left who set the term into circulation a half-
century or so ago—and who by 2006 had probably abandoned it. In any
case, the Third World in question was basically Mexico. (Although one
chapter is devoted to the Eurabian parallel.)

But we will leave Buchanan aside here, and focus on that other contributor to this scenario, the member of the original "One Big Thing
Quintet": again, Samuel Huntington.

In the journal *Foreign Affairs*, one of Huntington's critical reviewers
suggests that "*Who Are We?* is Patrick Buchanan with footnotes." (Wolfe
2004:121) One might be tempted to conclude that Huntington is to
Buchanan as Ye'or is to Fallaci, but this would hardly be fair. Huntington
is more subtle, not hysterical, not so much of a conspiracy theorist. As *Who
Are We?* (2004), too, is the last book of a veteran scholar, he has an overview of what has gone before, and remembers past answers. Clearly this
is another phase in an enduring, and yet shifting, American debate over
the shaping of a national culture with a more or less continuous influx of
newcomers. Late in the twentieth century, there were the "culture wars,"
over multiculturalist proposals.[22] His "clash of civilizations" writings were
already in part acts of soldiering in those. Now Huntington (2004: 129)
recollects past preferred blend metaphors of melting pot and salad bowl,
but seems to prefer a tomato soup—"an Anglo-Protestant tomato soup to
which immigration adds celery, croutons, spices, parsley, and other ingre-
dients that enrich and diversify the taste, but which are absorbed into what
remains fundamentally tomato soup."

This turns out to be some especially unfortunate imagery for Huntington's
purposes: another of his critics, Claudio Lomnitz (2005), anthropologist
with his own Mexican roots, points out that *tomatl* is an Aztec word. The
tomato is itself from somewhere south of the border. But in any case, even
if the Pilgrims had brought the tomato on the *Mayflower*, Anglo-Protestant
tomato soup is not the kind of recipe for American culture which all its

stakeholders could readily agree on. It is true that Huntington struggles to make clear, in this book and in later debate, that he was making a point about culture, not ethnicity: even people who were not of old Anglo-Protestant stock (perhaps what used to be called WASPs) could join what was basically the Anglo-Protestant cultural tradition, adding some spice of their own. Even so, this sounded too much like old-style cultural hegemony for many—comparing it to European debate, it might remind us of the German notion of *Leitkultur*, as understood at least by some.

Furthermore, Huntington seems to get himself into some trouble with regard to his understanding of both the two groups with which he engages in a kind of simultaneous battle.

On the one hand, there is his critique of cosmopolitan elites which made an earlier appearance in *The Clash of Civilizations and the Remaking of World Order* (for one thing as "Davos Culture"). It has its counterparts on the other side of the Atlantic in Eurabia scenarios, for example in Melanie Phillips' *Londonistan*. Yet the particular trouble here, it would seem, is that in the American instance, it is often enough these elites, failing in their patriotic duties, who are the more direct descendants of Huntington's cherished Anglo-Protestantism.

On the other hand, the Mexicans arriving, one way or other, to settle in the United States, do not seem to be quite as different from earlier immigrant groups as Huntington claims. His line of argument is that they do not identify with the United States, stay among themselves, and speak only Spanish. And since there are so many more of them than of other immigrant groups, they are a threat to the national social fabric.

To this view there are objections from various points on the political spectrum, some from familiar interlocutors. David Brooks (2004), *New York Times'* certified (although somewhat idiosyncratic) conservative columnist, points to the diversity of the Mexican-American group, and suggests moreover that what Americans share is not so much a past as a faith in the future. Francis Fukuyama (2004), reviewing *Who Are We?* for the online magazine *Slate*, argues that Mexican-Americans have traditional family values, intermarry with other groups, and are hardly lacking in work ethic. But they may be corrupted by *American* practices; their youths, for example, risk being absorbed into the underclass culture of American inner cities (what would have been *banlieues* on the other side of the Atlantic). So, concludes Huntington's old student Fukuyama, "the more serious threat to American culture comes perhaps from its own internal contradictions than from foreigners." The political scientist

Andrew Hacker (2004: 29), in a review in the *New York Review of Books*, adds that Huntington seems unaware of recent research showing, for one thing, that just about all the Mexican-Americans born in the United States speak English well, and notes that:

> What is even more troubling is that Huntington gives no sign that he has actually come to know any Hispanics well or has been willing to visit their families and hear their views about patriotism or any other subject. He seems to have little close knowledge of the people he writes about; perhaps that is why there seems an undercurrent of fear in his treatment of them.

There have not, I believe, been as many European commentators on MexAmerica as there have been Americans ready to issue warnings about Eurabia. But on this point, briefly, there is one harsh voice: that of Bernard-Henri Lévy, fairly controversial French public intellectual-philosopher (more about him in Chap. 9), whose travelogue *American Vertigo* (2006: 105) from the early twenty-first century, suggests that there are two current patterns of immigration to the USA.[23] One is that of Koreans, Armenians, Iranians and Chinese, establishing themselves in "economic and cultural cocoons." The other is that of the Hispanics, in a situation structurally similar to that of immigrants long ago. Back then, it was "First papers, then sweat." Now it is "First sweat, and later on, if all goes well, papers." Yet the structure, in Lévy's opinion, is an invariant circumstance of becoming American, "complicated, painful, caught in the patience and frenzy of things." So this observer, describing his own journey as "in the footsteps of Tocqueville," disagrees with Huntington. Indeed, before proceeding to a critique of the clash of civilizations thesis, he dismisses *Who Are We?* as "that xenophobic book that...casts thirty million Hispanics, Mexicans especially, into the outer darkness of a nameless barbarism." (Lévy 2006: 259)

One more time we return to the indefatigable traveler, and interpreter of geopolitics, Robert Kaplan—often enough one of Samuel Huntington's sympathizers, but not quite this time. Kaplan (2000: 56) already refers to Joel Garreau's "nine nations" book in *The Coming Anarchy*, viewing it rather darkly as accurately forecasting a regionalization of the North American subcontinent. Now, toward the end of *The Revenge of Geography* (2012), he offers a somewhat more developed future map of America. Earlier in the book, he has noted Nicolas Spykman's geopolitical conception of a connected Rimland stretching all around the Caribbean.

By now, some seventy years after Spykman, Kaplan draws enough on this to focus on a turn in American geography, from an east-west to a north-south orientation, with a twenty-first century "Polynesian-cum-mestizo civilization"—a multiracial assemblage of sprawling suburban city-states, with their own contacts with global trading networks. This will be "the globe's preeminent duty-free hot zone for business transactions, a favorite place of residence for the global elite." (Kaplan 2012: 339) But the "organic connection" between Mexico and America—geographical, historical, demographic—must be an integral part of this order. And so "a certain measure of cosmopolitanism, Huntington to the contrary, is inevitable and not to be disparaged."

So here MexAmerica is made to fit into another map for the future, of a "Polynesian-cum-mestizo civilization." Whatever that may be, playing even with civilizations this way probably would not have met with Huntington's approval either.

Anyhow, this chapter and the last have largely been about what scenarios can do with borders: Eurabia, civilizations with or without bloody borders, the Core and the Gap, CENTCOM, Dixie, MexAmerica... But maps are about flows as well. True, new borders may be created by flows, really or in the imagination—flows of Muslims into Eurabia, flows of Mexicans into MexAmerica. In other scenarios there are other flows, however; to come back to in later chapters.

NOTES

1. On the whole, it now tends to be understood not only that Muslim immigrant communities in the United States face another kind of receiving society, but that various background factors are also differently distributed among Muslim migrants to North America and to Europe. So in the United States, Islam tends to become one more American faith (see e.g. Bilici 2012). See also, however, Bayoumi (2015), and some further comments below, relating to 2015 events.

2. On "Islamofascism" and World War IV, see especially Podhoretz (2007). For a set of varied perspectives on early twenty-first century anti-Americanism, see Hertsgaard (2002), Sardar and Davies (2002), Ross and Ross (2004), and Krastev and McPherson (2007).
   Beeman (2005) offers a detailed and subtle analysis of "how the United States and Iran demonize each other." We touch briefly on the contemporary historian Mark LeVine's (2005) critique of American notions of anti-Americanism in Chap. 7.

3. Somewhat paradoxically, "suburbs" like banlieues may have had their nearest American political/economic/cultural/ethnic counterpart in the notion of "inner-city." But with the gentrification of at least some U.S. cities, some inner cities may be turning fashionable and prosperous, while some suburbs become increasingly like banlieues.

4. In his book on Scandinavia, *The Almost Nearly Perfect People*, the British, mostly Copenhagen-based journalist Michael Booth (2015: 322) also devotes a chapter to Rosengård: "If you believe the rumours, it is a crime-ridden hellhole, a sink-estate-of-no-hope where the country herds its Somali, Iraqi and Afghani immigrants, denying them any hope of a decent life or income." Yet walking away, he seems to have found it more dreary than dangerous.

5. There was a *Newsweek* cover story as well: "The Myth of Eurabia: The False Fears of a Muslim Takeover" (Underhill 2009). And by 2010, the journal *Foreign Policy* had an article titled "Eurabian Follies: the shoddy and just plain wrong genre that refuses to die." (Vaïsse 2010).

6. For a more extensive, detailed discussion, see for example Klausen (2005). Since that study, of course, there have been further changes due not least to the Arab world upheavals since 2011, and particularly to the civil war in Syria, leading to the major exodus of refugees referred to below. Moreover, just as there are differences between countries with respect to where their Muslim immigrants come from, there are differences in receiving conditions between countries, partly depending on histories and traditions. France, for one thing, is still not far away from the troubled decolonization of its North African possessions, and also faces the particular problems of combining a dominant secularist tradition with the active commitments to Islam of minority populations. We come back to this below, but see also Amselle (2003) on multiculturalism the French way, and two books by John Bowen (2007, 2010).

7. The Norwegian anthropologist Unni Wikan (2002) has taken a strong stand on these matters, and has also offered a sensitive account of one very widely noted honor killing in Sweden, where the young Kurdish woman Fadime Sahindal was murdered by her father (Wikan 2008). For a different view of gender issues in contemporary Muslim life, see Abu-Lughod (2013).

8. See on this Vertovec and Wessendorf (2009).

9. Pautz (2005), in a critical account of the *Leitkultur* debate in in German politics, sees the notion as relating to a "clash of civilizations" perspective toward the relationship between immigrants and native Germans.

10. When I was doing ethnographic research in an African-American low-income neighborhood in Washington, D.C., in the mid-1960s (Hannerz [1969]2004), I could discern that the Nation of Islam to a degree stood out as such a protest alternative. At the time, however, as the people involved

had little knowledge of, or contact with, Islam anywhere else in the world, this as an organized religion became something rather like the Protestant Christianity they were familiar with, with an emphasis on respectability and orderly family life.

11. In all fairness, it should be recognized that parachutist rabbis can cause some unease, too, although usually on a more modest scale.

12. The British sociologist and cultural studies scholar Paul Gilroy (2005: 125 ff.) discusses similar examples of terrorists evidently less rooted in Islam than in metropolitan adversary cultures, and notes that at one time Rastafarianism could have provided another, more benign alternative for those in one way or other of African descent.

13. See on this Courbage and Todd (2011)—certainly with some polemical intent, they title their brief book *A Convergence of Civilizations*. On Emmanuel Todd, see also Chap. 9.

14. 14. The Sweden Democrats, a party that has greatly increased its voter support in recent elections and now has some 14 % of the national vote (more in some later opinion polls), is another example of neo-nationalism. Speaking in the 2014 national election campaign, its current leader, Jimmie Åkesson, referred to Huntington's clash of civilizations thesis as if it were an established fact—another instance of its global spread and public uses. (The Sweden Democrats have also sought support for their views in the writings of Rudolf Kjellén, the inventor of geopolitics.) This party, however, is one of those neo-nationalist groupings which has to a degree sought to redefine itself and move somewhat away from more extremist origins; yet its new label as "social conservative" has been one of the causes of internal conflicts, as not least the youth wing has been more inclined to "cultural nationalism" of a fundamentalist kind.

15. It is not that Simon Kuper disapproves of all soccer books. As a soccer specialist, Kuper (2013) could even be enthusiastic about *I am Zlatan Ibrahimovic*, the ghost-written memoirs of one Swedish soccer star, who has played for a variety of top European teams after growing up in Rosengård, in Malmö (Ibrahimovic 2013). Ibrahimovic and I were born in the same parish.

16. When the Islamic State achieved media notoriety in 2014, displaying French Muslims engaged in beheadings in Iraq and Syria, there were indications that one of these was a convert from a Roman-Catholic Portuguese immigrant family, and one a Frenchman from a small town in Normandie, who had converted to Islam as a teenager.

17. In an article published only a few months after the *Charlie Hebdo* murders and the demonstrations against them, Fassin (2015) shows how overt disagreement with the protests, particularly among Muslims, could be subjected to legal punishment as "vindication of terrorism"; Fassin also offers

an overview of other Muslim grievances against the only partially secular French state apparatus.
Away from France, but soon after the *Charlie Hebdo* affair, there was a set of similar killings in Copenhagen, receiving less international attention. These occurred at a synagogue, in connection with a wedding, and at an art event. The perpetrator was again a disaffected Muslim youth from the suburbs; the apparently intended victim (who escaped unhurt) at the latter event was a marginal Swedish artist, who had arrived at a fame of sorts with a published sketch of a caricature of the Prophet.

18. See on this, for example, the early review by Mark Lilla (2015).
19. I have used this example elsewhere, in a general discussion of anthropological understandings of borders (Hannerz 1997).
20. In anthropology I come to think of an overview article by Alvarez (1995), and the different perspectives of Rosaldo (1988) and Kearney (1991). In full-length journalism, Conover (1987) has described border-crossings, Vulliamy (2010) the cross-border war on drugs, and Tobar (2005) the Hispanic-American society developing North of the Border. But there is certainly much more.
21. "Aztlán," understood as the place of origin of the pre-Columbian civilization in Mexico, is also a term used by some Mexican-American nationalists to refer to some variously defined, wider North American homeland.
22. *The Disuniting of America* (1992) by Arthur Schlesinger, historian and known as a White House advisor of President Kennedy's, and *Is America Breaking Apart?* (1999), by sociologist John Hall and anthropologist Charles Lindholm, were among the more notable writings of this period, representing different points of view.
23. Perhaps Bernard-Henri Lévy has lately been most noted for his advice pushing French president Sarkozy into military intervention in Libya in 2011.

CHAPTER 5

Reporting from the Future

"I have seen the future, and it works," wrote Lincoln Steffens, early twentieth century American muckraker journalist and social critic, in 1919. About the young Soviet Union. So, did that future work? Well, perhaps more or less, for some time. But then the aging Soviet Union declined, and fell apart. (Not very many foresaw this.) Nonetheless, when that happened, and the Cold War ended, there were again all the commentators trying to see the future—the authors of "One Big Thing" stories, and others.

Those scenarists who are still in business may not be inclined to spend much effort revisiting their past visions—they move on.[1] By now, however, some time has passed since the first of these global scenarios appeared, and we can have some sense of how well they did. The end of history? No, not really. A coming anarchy? Well, it may have come to some places, at least for some time, but it hardly established itself on a global basis. *Hot, Flat, and Crowded* (to choose one of Thomas Friedman's more straightforward titles)?

Global warming: yes, so it indeed seems. More recently, "the Anthropocene" has appeared as a new keyword for that very long geological period in which *Homo sapiens* has had a significant impact on the ecosystems of Planet Earth, and global warming emerges as one of its main references. That, of course, provides this future with even more of a past. Flat: well, in global competition, the playing field is surely more level in some places than in others, where the game may seem more like a rollercoaster ride. Crowded: obviously, "crowded" is now hardly so much a matter of a population/space ratio. In the days when the world was largely the home of hunters and gatherers, peasants and pastoralists, that could be what Friedrich Ratzel's notion of *Lebensraum* could mean, but now crowding is more a matter of what the local economies, and the global economy, can take. Moreover, population growth is far from even. In parts of Europe and East Asia, populations are most likely to shrink in the relatively near future; the Chinese one-child policy pushed this tendency along. But what happens outside the island of Lampedusa in the Mediterranean, or at the Mexico-United States border, shows the sometimes desperate face of population economics.

And what about the clash of civilizations? No, it has not happened on the scale and with the entities Samuel Huntington primarily had in mind. For one thing, his main interest was in wars between states, and that is hardly the way wars are fought any more.[2] A decade or two into the twenty-first century, moreover, the civilization (if one could call it that) which seems to have the bloodiest borders is the Post-Soviet one, involving "the near abroad" of Russia (Chechnya, Georgia, Ukraine), and drawing on political revanchism, Russian nationalism, and oligarch kleptocracy.[3] But twenty years earlier, Huntington mostly saw that region simply remaining under Moscow influence. Here one might find Robert Kaplan's retrieval, in *The Revenge of Geography*, of Halford Mackinder's World War I geopolitics more to the point, with its concern for European buffer zones between greater powers.

For that matter, Eurabia seems now to be a lost continent.

But strictly speaking, should we take the scenarios to be predictions? What kind of writing do you do when you report on the future? Of course there was some hyperbole in Steffens' claim—he had not really flown into the future on a time machine and returned to share the experience with his audience. Reporting on the future is necessarily a matter of writing fiction. Scenarios involve a suggestion that fiction can turn into fact, somewhat like Orwell's *1984*. But they are not pure fantasy either—they draw on a selection of facts to make the fiction seem credible. Perhaps they are best placed in that field which has earned increasing recognition as "creative non-fiction." But then it is another question whether the authors actually want to see their scenarios realized.

In recent times, in large part after the global scenario genre had already gathered speed, doubts about our capacity of predicting future developments have become increasingly widespread, public, and popular. There have been bestsellers such as *The Black Swan: The Impact of the Highly Improbable* (2007) by Nassim Nicholas Taleb, identified for one thing as Professor in the Sciences of Uncertainty at the University of Massachusetts; and *The Age of the Unthinkable: Why the New World Disorder Constantly Surprises Us and What We Can Do About It* (2009), by Joshua Cooper Ramo, former foreign editor of *Time* magazine, later managing director at Kissinger Associates, and dividing his time, the back flap of the book tells us, between Beijing and New York. And Malcolm Gladwell launched a career writing more or less on this theme with *The Tipping Point: How Little Things Can Make a Big Difference* (2000). As such works take their place on the display tables of airport bookstalls, they may share space there with the most recent global scenarios. We find, too, that in his book *The Signal and the Noise* (2012), Nate Silver, the one person who has recently reached fame for his expertise in prediction (not least in the 2012 U.S. elections), does not mention any of the scenarists. However, we can also note that Francis Fukuyama, pioneering scenarist, has taken time out to edit a volume named *Blindside: How to Anticipate Forcing Events and Wild Cards in Global Politics* (2007). So he by now seems concerned with the problem. Thomas Friedman (2014b), for his part, has reported from an environmentalist-conservationist conference that he came across a new phrase there—a "black elephant" is a cross between that unexpected black swan and "an elephant in the room," the conspicuous presence of which nobody wants to acknowledge.

Anyway, scenarios can be good to think with, as long as we do so critically. Apparently we had better give some more attention to what goes into scenarios, to their forms, and to their passages through public life. What can happen to them on their way toward the future? And if one cannot be sure that they will come true, what can scenarists do to make them seem credible, or at least interesting? Such are the questions we confront in this chapter.

Michael Schudson (1987: 106–108), leading scholar of media, journalism, and advertising, may have coined the term "subjunctive reporting," for a variety of journalism which speaks of what may happen if certain trends continue. His examples were American domestic news stories, feature stories from the *Los Angeles Times*. One was about the kind of life that might arrive when it would be possible to stay home and do your work there, by telecommuting, instead of spending more than an hour per day commuting to work by car. Another story was about toxic waste in local water supplies, and what could eventually happen if governments at all levels would continue to ignore the problem.

The global future scenarios would seem to be very large-scale examples of reporting in this subjunctive mood. Subjunctive forms involve "what could be," "what could come to be," "what could have been" rather than what is, what will be, what has been. They are representations of hypothesis and possibility. This mood has its own range of cultural and textual forms. Victor Turner (e.g. 1977: 71), mid-twentieth century British anthropologist transplanted to American Academia, who moved on from an interest in Central African rituals to a wider preoccupation with the cultural forms of representing flux and uncertainty, has referred to his classic notion of liminality as subjunctive, a world of "as if." In the rituals he had in mind, you depart momentarily from ordinary, "real" life, into a phase of little or no structure, or an alternative structure, before returning to the more or less stable everyday again. Humanity finds many uses for the subjunctive in allowing some room for the imagination.

VARIETIES OF THE SUBJUNCTIVE MOOD

For one thing, predicting what will happen in human society is very difficult because the latter is at any time quite complex. But it also becomes more so because so many members of the species *Homo sapiens* can read, and shake their heads. That is a problem natural scientists will mostly not have. The scenarists do not put together their texts and then file them away, in a top drawer of their desks as it were, to see later on if their forecasts did come true. They are public intellectuals; as noted in Chap. 2, at times even organic intellectuals, integrated into a power elite. The scenarios are out there on the arenas of opinion-making, intended to influence their audiences, at least as likely to be prescriptive as predictive.

One way this can work, for better or for worse, intentionally or unintentionally, is through self-fulfilling prophecies. In the case of Samuel Huntington's clash of civilizations scenario, this was a possibility raised by some number of commentators: if actors, particularly political leaders, found reason to mistrust counterparts across civilizational borders, the risk could increase that things would go wrong, and the borders would indeed turn bloody. In her critique of the Huntington thesis referred to in Chap. 3, Benazir Bhutto was among those who noted such a risk.[4]

Probably more often than they are self-fulfilling, however, scenarios may be self-destructive prophecies, or may at least be so intended. The futures they outline are frequently dystopic; the scenarios are supposed to serve as early warnings, attempts at consciousness-raising.

Robert Kaplan did not wish anarchy upon the world; Samuel Huntington wanted wise statesmen to conduct their *Realpolitik* so as to forestall major conflicts. To the extent that the scenarios have actually been attended to, and acted upon (or at least played some part, modest or not, in pushing public and strategic consciousness in a desirable direction), one may see them as successes rather than failures. But they are not all alike in this respect. Francis Fukuyama's "end of history" may not have been so much a scenario of warning (although again, not entirely celebrationist). And Thomas Friedman was evidently more inclined to accept the coming of "the Electronic Herd," and the need to don that Golden Straitjacket.

If the scenarios have not been realized, however, one could see that they have moved within the wider family of subjunctive forms—from "what could come to be" to "what could have been." It may be useful to take more of an overall look at this family of possibilities. In more or less the same period as our scenario authors have been active, there was a book by Martin Jacques named *When China Rules the World* (2009), and another by Oscar Guardiola-Rivera named *What if Latin America Ruled the World?* (2010) These may sound rather similar (even if the contents may be worlds apart). Yet there is a difference between "When" and "What if." The China book seems to make its way into the future scenario genre as we have seen it. The Latin America book more likely belongs in another variety of imagination.[5]

There is another large class of subjunctive forms which shows some affinity with scenarios: counterfactuals. *What if Latin America Ruled the World?* seems rather to belong there, challenging us to think of alternatives to what is really at hand. One set of texts appearing over the years has offered imagined subtractions. The most radical of such texts would seem to be Alan Weisman's *The World Without Us* (2007), about what the human species would leave behind if it disappeared from the Earth, and what would then happen.

In *A World Without Jews* (2014), Alan Confino describes the stories which the Nazis told themselves, which led to the Holocaust. In *A World Without Islam* (2010), Graham Fuller suggests that even if Prophet Mohammed had not been there, and the religion he founded so successful, tensions between the Middle East and the West could have been there anyway. The oppositional role that Islam came to take on might have belonged, for one thing, to Eastern Orthodox Christianity instead. So this book, too, is in large part an argument against the Huntington thesis. In a later book, too, Robert Kagan (2012: 3) seems to have played with the idea of writing a "world without…"—it would have been nice "to see what the world would have looked like had the United States not been the preeminent power shaping it for the past six decades." But then he takes another path, and the book becomes *The World America Made.*[6]

VELOCITIES OF HISTORY

Historians have their own noteworthy subjunctive specialty in counter-factual history, the analysis of what might have happened if something had first happened that did not actually happen, or if something had not happened that in fact happened. In the extreme form the focus is on how some apparently minor mistake, misunderstanding or accident made a difference: "For want of a nail the shoe was lost, for want of a shoe the horse was lost, for want of a horse the rider was lost, for want of a rider the message was lost, for want of a message the battle was lost, for want of a battle the kingdom was lost, and all for the want of a horseshoe nail."

And so, if Richard III had not lost that late fifteenth-century battle, what would have been the history of England? (Some six hundred years later, the remains of Richard III were discovered buried under a car park, and were properly reburied in Leicester in 2015; this is not counterfactual.)

But as a somewhat controversial practice in the historical discipline now, counterfactual history seems more inclined to take on more complex and better-documented uncertainties. As it happens, someone recurrently present in these pages, Niall Ferguson, took on the challenge of both scrutinizing and advocating counterfactual history fairly early in his academic career. In his first major book, *The Pity of War* (1998), we remember, he considered the possibility that Britain might have been wiser to stay out of World War I. Even before that, however, he had edited *Virtual History* (1997), with contributors on a number of "what if…" questions: if there had been no American Revolution, if Hitler had conquered Britain, if President Kennedy had not been murdered. After these he had his own highly imaginative afterword, covering the period from 1646 to 1996: in the twentieth century, the Anglo-American Empire finally disintegrated in the 1990s (1776 had been just one of these forgettable years), and before that, the Georgian ex-seminary student Josef Djugashvili never took the name Stalin but took over much of Russia leading a militant religious revival movement, eventually becoming czar and founding a new dynasty. (If I may add my own counterfactual to that: imagine that the Stockholm police had found reason to arrest the exile V.I. Lenin at Hotel Regina, on his way back to the old country in 1917. Then he might never have reached the Finland Station, in that city which would never be renamed after him, he would not have led any revolution, and Lincoln Steffens might never have seen the future.)

Anyhow, before these retrospective fireworks, Ferguson's more sober and thoughtful introduction reviewed the potentials and limitations of counterfactuality, and also revealed some of his own sympathies and antipathies in the craft of history. On the whole he takes a dim view here of "historical determinism," and in this context he criticizes one major historian who shows up in the work of at least two of our scenarists. At this point, it seems useful to reflect a little on the uses of the past in their imagined futures. Fernand Braudel was one of the leading figures of the twentieth-century *Annales* school of French historians (so named after the journal in which they tended to publish). In a classic statement (1980: 25 ff., but first published in 1958), Braudel, a specialist on the Mediterranean region, distinguished between three typical time spans in history writing— three velocities, as it were: event history, conjunctural history, and the history of the *longue durée*, which was his own preference and specialty. Conjunctural history is a medium-term history, covering a decade or two, or at most a half-century.

The *longue durée* is a matter of things not seeming to change much at all—it bears some resemblance to the old anthropological notion of an "ethnographic present," of time frozen. It pays much attention to matters of geography, climate and the like, mostly quite stable. So this is where Niall Ferguson finds Braudel too determinist. Yet for our purposes, Braudel's gross classification of the three kinds of history seems illuminating.[7]

At the time when he wrote, Braudel identified event history as the strongly preferred time span of most historians, and he also compared it to journalism. I see the point—in my meetings with foreign correspondents reminiscing about their coverage of hard news stories, I found that the notion of "writing the first draft of history" had widespread appeal among them.[8] Yet I also learned that at times they felt a need to draw attention to some important, but more drawn-out process: the trick then was to find a "peg," some new event on which they could hang their reporting and interpretation. So the "peg" would seem to be where event history and conjunctural history could meet.

One might see, too, that dramatic year of 2015 as packed with event history generated for some time in conjunctural history.

It would seem to be event history that goes best with counterfactual history, even if the events involved tend to be decisions, decision-making processes and negotiations, with identifiable human agents, rather than sheer accidents. But what about the uses of history among the scenarists? Indeed it is drawn upon to provide persuasive materials for views of what will come. (Although one may suspect that it can also be used to construct the Maginot Lines of future scenarios.) But they use it in different ways. Back in the seventeenth century, Olof Rudbeck the Elder was eclectic in his historical tastes as he turned Atlantis into Sweden. More recently, we have seen, thinking about his own country in a more pessimistic mood, Robert Kaplan returned to Gibbon's *History of the Decline and Fall of the Roman Empire*. And as another member of our "One Big Thing" quintet, Paul Kennedy, chronicled the careers of great powers between 1500 and 2000, he may in each case have done something most resembling conjunctural history, but more importantly this was comparative history. As he begins his *Preparing for the Twenty-first Century* (1993), too, it is with a look back, for comparative purposes: to a point in time two hundred years earlier, when Thomas Malthus took his bleak view of explosive population growth, and before large-scale migration, the agricultural revolution and the industrial revolution really got underway. "We should see the demographic and economic conditions of the late eighteenth century as a metaphor for the challenges facing our present global society," he proposes (1993: 11), as he takes on the task of trying to anticipate major changes again. It is Samuel Huntington and Robert Kaplan who to different degrees identify Braudel as a source of inspiration. Huntington has Braudel in his extensive list of writers on civilizations, and describes the latter as the most enduring of human associations, "realities of the extreme *longue durée*" (1996: 43), but otherwise does not do very much with him. In Kaplan, with his interest in mapping the lasting material bases of geopolitics, Braudel has a greater fan: "…he is more than a geographer or strategist. He is a historian whose narrative has a godlike quality in which every detail of human existence is painted against the canvas of natural forces." (Kaplan 2012: 323) One can discern here a difference between Kaplan and Ferguson, who otherwise tend to place themselves similarly on the political left-right scale.

The main implication of drawing on the *longue durée* for scenarios, however, would seem to be "more of the same." (In their view of jihadism, Bat Ye'or and Oriana Fallaci also lean toward this kind of long-term history.) In contrast, event history tends not to be good news for scenario making—when something unexpected happens it may ruin longer-range forecasts. It is better for breeding those black swans. What future scenarios seem to need is mostly conjunctural history, a sense of trends, a grounding of their views forward in a relatively recent past. Scenarists are not always particularly clear about the time frames they have in mind, but in *Preparing for the Twenty-first Century*, as we have noted, when Paul Kennedy looks forward, he declares that he will be discussing primarily the next thirty years—demographic projections mostly work within that range. Timothy Garton Ash, considering what the West can do for the world, thinks about the next couple of decades. And on a quite different basis, when, in *The Lexus and the Olive Tree* (1999), Thomas Friedman identifies hedge fund managers as among his preferred informants (being people, he argues, with particular skills in pulling together diverse kinds of information), that also seems to place him among those leaning toward conjunctural history.

WAYS WITH WORDS

The varieties of subjunctive imagination shade into each other, but now we can certainly see that they tend not to be a matter of pure fantasy. Scenarios are made plausible in large part through a more or less skillful handling of facts out of the past and the present—even when they begin as works of imagination not really with the projection from what has gone before into what may come later, but already in the selection of what is to stand as relevant current or historical reality. That is how we can get these several different "one big things." Yet with the element of uncertainty, and also freedom, necessarily involved in the subjunctive, it may be a good idea to pay some special attention also to other features of its genres which can be employed to make works more persuasive, more worthy of attention.

Again, there are those paradoxes and counterintuitives in several book titles, convertible into oneliners, soundbites and catch phrases for more general use. Perhaps even *The Revenge of Geography* has some of this, insofar as it locates fateful agency where we do not usually expect it. And those bad-news scenarios for Europe carried such an element of surprise as well, shifting from routine to surprise between one syllable and the next: Eur… abia, London…istan.

Occasionally title-making may involve some risk, inviting misunderstandings or ridicule, and there may have been times when the authors wished they had thought of something else. Benjamin Barber's *Jihad vs. McWorld* offers striking imagery, but the title (which had been tried out first on an article in *The Atlantic Monthly*, 1992) does not really stand up well to closer inspection. "Jihad" is made a metaphor for "the grim prospect of a retribalization of large swaths of humankind":

> culture is pitted against culture, people against people, tribe against tribe, a Jihad in the name of a hundred narrowly conceived faiths against every kind of interdependence, every kind of artificial social cooperation and mutuality: against technology, against pop culture, and against integrated markets; against modernity itself as well as the future in which modernity issues. (Barber 1996: 4)

According to such a metaphorical usage, of course, not only Muslims participate in jihad, but xenophobes, fundamentalists and antimodernists from everywhere. Perhaps it was difficult to find another equally vibrant term to cover such militant particularism. Yet it was probably not only Muslims who felt that this writer made Muslims carry too much of the burden. So in the later paperback edition Barber added a new afterword where he apologized.[9] But then one could further argue that jihad, as a movement with global aspirations, does not really stand well as a marker for the kind of local isolationism he had in mind—any more than "crusade" would. Real jihad is more a matter of flow than of borders, to come back to a distinction from Chap. 3.

And then, if one enjoys nitpicking, one could perhaps argue that his other key image, "McWorld," carries its own ambiguity. It does not refer to a global Scotlandization, after which everyone will wear kilts, play bagpipes and eat haggis.[10] The intended reference is to the small California hamburger business which Ray Kroc took over from the founder brothers, Maurice and Richard McDonald, and built into a fast food chain which brought "the golden arches" to most corners of the world.[11] If one insists on sticking to the original Macs, however, the ancient feuding of clans like the MacLeods and the MacDonalds might seem to come closer to the "tribe against tribe" situations which Barber called "jihad." So this kind of critical scrutiny may leave Barber standing on his head.

But no matter. It is a measure of their success in reaching out to a wider imagination (if not their precision) that these titles become words to be played with. As the authors comment on one another, or as other thinkers and writers comment on them, their conceptions and key terms are taken apart and put into play in further multiplying forms and combinations.

With an ironic nod toward Fukuyama, Robert Kagan has an article titled "End of Dreams, Return to History" (2007) as well as a book, *The Return of History and the End of Dreams* (2008). At a time when conflicts in the Middle East were occurring on a variety of scales, a couple of decades after Huntington launched his key idea, Thomas Friedman (2014c) could suggest, perhaps somewhat facetiously, to his *New York Times* readers that "the Israeli-Palestinian conflict is to the wider East-West clash of civilizations what Off Broadway is to Broadway."

Niall Ferguson (2004a: 106) describes the Middle East as a "civilization of clashes."[12] Another historian, Timothy Mitchell (2002: 3), describes the involvement of transnational capitalism with conservative Islam as— "if one wants to use these unfortunate labels"— a "McJihad." An Israeli scholar writes about the Americanization of his home country, and the title becomes "McIsrael" (Azaryahu 2000).[13] Having lent his support to the notion of "Eurabia," Ferguson shows his taste for word play with a fistful of similar new constructs: "Anglobalization" as well as "Tory-entalism" in his book *Empire*, then at some point in the early 2000s "Chimerica." But the life of that continent becomes even briefer than that of "Eurabia": in a *New York Times* op-ed piece (with the economist Moritz Schularick, 2009) he notes that for a period the combination of Chinese and U.S. economies had been the key driver of the global economy, but it had all the time been a chimera, "a monstrous hybrid like the part-lion, part-goat, part-snake of legend."[14]

Thus the scenarists and their readers build a dense network of images, allusions and intertextual references—sometimes by inverting titles, sometimes by creating paradoxical hybrids. Robert Kagan, again, had his comical twist on this with the Americans from Mars and the Europeans from Venus. The Eurabists brought other variations: Bruce Bawer with *While Europe Slept*, Christopher Caldwell with *Reflections on the Revolution in Europe*. Both of them obviously picked titles to allude to rather better-known earlier texts, thus borrowing some extra historical weight to their themes: Winston Churchill's book on sleepy Britain as Hitler prepared for war, and Edmund Burke's thoughts on the meaning of the French revolution.[15]

Such appropriations may be used to suggest similar heroic insight, or foresight. But that may be accomplished by more independent means of dramatic imagery as well. As far as titles go, Thomas Friedman's first major excursion into the scenario genre, *The Lexus and the Olive Tree*, was perhaps rather a rhetorical failure—neither the car model nor that small Mediterranean tree was a really striking summarizing image. *The World is Flat* was more successful, and here the magic moment, the revelation, comes when Friedman returns home to Bethesda, Maryland, from Bangalore and whispers to his wife: "honey, I think the world is flat." (Friedman 2005: 5) At that point, if this had been what really happened, one might expect Mrs. Friedman to worry that Tom, far away from home on his journey, had gone mad. But actually, it turns out a few pages later that he had already told his spouse in a long-distance phone call about the great title he had come up with to summarize a complex story. Robert Kaplan, for his part, evidently takes some pride in being ahead of stories. For him, on the night when the Berlin Wall fell (at least figuratively), "the future was in Kosovo," where he was (Kaplan 2000: 57). And when Yitzhak Rabin and Yasser Arafat shook hands in front of the White House, "the real news" was in Bamako, Mali, down there among the corrugated-zinc shacks at the edge of the desert, below the flight which Kaplan was on. The future, and the real news, was in the coming anarchy.

The scenarists do seem to have a knack for memorable (perhaps sometimes just too memorable) formulations, a way with words, in their titles and in their texts. With some of them, particularly the professional journalists, this may be what we expect. Thomas Friedman needs a steady stream of eye-catching headings for his *New York Times* columns, so he gets a lot of practice. But as he is profiled in the *New Yorker*, under the title "The Bright Side: The Relentless Optimism of Thomas Friedman," it seems to become a personal rather than a merely professional talent, and inclination:

> By temperament or by training, Friedman is a phrasemaker, and a friend of phrasemakers; and he seems unusually receptive to marketing in any form. He is the person who wants to hear the story that a tour guide wants to tell. (Parker 2008: 52)

We could note also that Robert Kaplan has not confined himself to political writing. There has been other travel writing as well, such as *Mediterranean Winter* (2004), about his journeys in Greece, Sicily, and Tunisia, and dwelling on archaeology.

What is more noteworthy are the varieties of dealings with words that several of the academics have had, apart from their scenario productions. Both Benjamin Barber and Joseph Nye have also written novels. Most political science professors do not.[16] That may be a sign of an inclination toward expressive experimentation. Barber, it turns out, is the son of the-ater people, and the Wikipedia tells us that he has also been active as a playwright, lyricist, and film-maker. In an op-ed piece in the *New York Times* at the time his novel came out, but reminiscing about his past State Department experiences, Nye (2005) explained that his academic writings could not fully describe what went on as people tried to shape policy deci-sions in the midst of uncertainty. In contrast,

> In fiction, I could elaborate the dreams and nightmares involved in such situations, and describe the struggles for power, the effects they have on friendships, and the problems of sorting out moral obligations to policy, to the president, to foreigners.

For such reasons, Nye also noted, he often recommended his students to supplement their academic readings with films and novels. (Away from Academia, Robert Kaplan [2000: 143] expresses a related view: "The reli-gious and social backgrounds of officials are inseparable from their opin-ions. Policy making, like lovemaking, is an intensely human activity." That may sound a bit like The Revenge of Psychology.)

As for Niall Ferguson, already his taste for counterfactual history could suggest a leaning toward fiction. When he faced the choice between study-ing history or English at the university, he has said, it was Leo Tolstoy, and *War and Peace*, that took him to history. But even before that, it had been his journalist maternal grandfather who had encouraged him to write.

AGAINST ACADEMIC WRITING

Discussing one of one of Niall Ferguson's books (in a review I have already referred to before), Paul Kennedy (2006b) mentions Ferguson's com-mentary in newspapers and magazines on both sides of the Atlantic, and notes that this, "plus his carefully cultivated public persona, drives more traditional members of the academy in Britain quite nuts."

The scenario genre may indeed be one arena for the display of endur-ing tensions between two kinds of crafts of writing and knowledge pro-duction: journalism and academic work. In both there are tendencies of celebrating one's own characteristics (at least as one claims them) and den-igrating those of the other. Journalists may see themselves as close to the action—again, "writing the first draft of history"—streetwise, parachut-ists at least metaphorically, as they make their way to the world's danger spots. When I was doing my study of newsmedia foreign correspondents, and comments turned to one of their colleagues who was seen as more inclined to lean back, stay at his desk and do think pieces, he was referred to as a "thumbsucker."

So academics may risk being seen in a similar light, maneuvering with ideas, a bit remote from realities; moreover, not good at reaching out, too inclined to stay within the compartments of their disciplines with their specialties and fashions. The *New York Times* columnist Nicholas Kristof (2014) places one critique of the inclination of academics not to bother with public outreach under the rubric "Professors, We Need You!"[17] Occasionally, the journalist finds an exception, and makes note of it. In *The Lexus and the Olive Tree*, Thomas Friedman (1999: 20–24) cites with approval an article co-authored by Paul Kennedy on the need to train a new generation of strategists to be globalists, not particularists. And he goes on to quote a Nobel laureate in physics:

> Unfortunately, in a great many places in our society, including academia and most bureaucracies, prestige accrues principally to those who study carefully some [narrow] aspect of a problem, a trade, a technology, or a culture, while discussion of the big picture is relegated to cocktail party conversation. That is crazy.

So, "on to my cocktail party," says Friedman. And again, from his perspective toward knowledge production and synthesis, his conversations with the hedge fund managers are time well spent.

For Robert Kaplan, we may already have noticed, Academia is a foreign country, and he prefers to keep the border well guarded (although he himself makes the occasional visit across it). One of his reviewers notes in the *New York Times* that "Kaplan merges literature and analysis, storytelling and philosophy, observation and history in a way that few writers even dare nowadays." (Garfinkle 2000: 27) Unfortunately, Kaplan does not himself find comparable versatility common on the university campus, and has his strong doubts about the grounding of the expertise displayed there. In *Imperial Grunts* (2005: 56), he points out that "the world of the military is not like the world of social science, in which one can be an academic superstar without having a day's experience inside the crucible of government, with its humbling crises." And among those educated in that latter world, "the sheer accumulation of texts produces people conditioned to jargon and arcane monographs, yet increasingly ignorant of great philosophy."

(Kaplan 2000: 183) When the anthropologist Paul Richards (1999) confronts Kaplan over the facts on the ground in Sierra Leone, proclaimed starting point of "the coming anarchy," as referred to in Chap. 3, Kaplan changes the subject and responds by accusing him of academic babble. But now and then, he can make an exception: in Henry Kissinger's style (and we saw already in Chap. 1 that he is a Kissinger fan) Kaplan finds "elegance, thickness of meaning, and narrative ability." (Kaplan 2000: 142?)[18]

A few exceptions like Kissinger apart, then, are members of the campus tribes all thumbsuckers? To the extent that anthropologists stick to the central practice of field study (as Richards has certainly done), one might sense that they actually come closer to the knowledge-producing habits of journalists than most of their academic neighbors. (I know of at least three anthropological textbooks with the title *Being There*.[19])Yet for reasons of career structures not least, they, too, may show an inclination toward inward-turning: in one fairly recent book scrutinizing the U.S. university, Louis Menand (2010:118), a Harvard professor of English and a regular contributor to the *New Yorker*, notes that if one asks anthropologists what their discipline is about, you would now be likely to get two types of answer. One answer is that anthropology is the study of its own assumptions. The other answer is that anthropology is whatever people in anthropology departments do.

The gap in writing styles, it seems, is in large part between journalism and Academia—but it is not quite as simple as that. Even with their own origins or a current home in the professoriate, some among our scenarists, and their commentators, can show a certain impatience with styles of work they see as favored in the ivory tower. Paul Kennedy, again, is himself one of the less adventurous wordsmiths among our scenarists. Yet as he responded to a critical review of his own *The Rise and Fall of the Great Powers* by W.W. Rostow, prominent American economist and political theorist of an earlier generation, he had this to say:

> Interpreting the larger tendencies and broader patterns of world history is, by its very nature, an intellectually risky business. The mere fact of generalizing across centuries and continents disturbs the orthodox professionals, whose own focus upon a single decade or region probably represents over 99 percent of all historical studies. (Kennedy 1988: 1108)

In a *Wall Street Journal* obituary for Samuel Huntington, Fouad Ajami (2008), Middle East specialist, reflects: "We don't have his likes in the academy today. Political science, the field he devoted his working life to, has been in the main commandeered by a new generation. They are 'rational choice' people who work with models and numbers and write arid, impenetrable jargon."[20]

Writing on the web site of the School of Advanced International Studies of Johns Hopkins University during his period there, Francis Fukuyama (2003) takes a similar view, although he then seems to point in another direction with his critique—he complains that the typical article nowadays appearing in the *American Political Science Review* contains much complex-looking mathematics, the sole function of which is often to formalize a behavioral rule that everyone with common sense understands must be true. "What is missing," he argues, "is any deep knowledge about the subtleties and nuances of how foreign societies work, knowledge that would help us better predict the behavior of political actors, friendly and hostile, in the broader world." And so "most of what is truly useful for policy is context-specific, culture bound and non-generalizable."

In these cases, the academics among the scenarists aim their criticisms at the disciplines they know best: history in Kennedy's case, political science in Fukuyama's.[21] And in a way they point in different directions: one wanting more of the Big Picture, the other more of a close-up view. If Fukuyama once rose to scenarist stardom with nearly the ultimate in Big Pictures, he distances himself considerably from that here. But they seem to agree more on what they do not much like.

Yet then as we have seen, the scenario writers themselves often roam rather freely in a contact zone between scholarship, media and politics, and they seem to reach audiences where they are likely to want them. It is interesting that when the journal *Foreign Policy* reported on a study of ratings of "most influential scholar," among American scholars in the international relations field and among American foreign policy makers, these two groups came up with rather different lists (Avey and Desch 2014). At the top of theirs, the academics had people whose names will appear nowhere in this book; Joseph Nye showed up in sixth place. On the list of the policy makers, Nye was first; Samuel Huntington second; Henry Kissinger third; Francis Fukuyama fourth. (Further down the list, there was Bernard Lewis as well.)

So policy makers do seem to pay attention to academics with scenarios. True, they may not be everybody's most desirable audience. If and when they move off-campus, scholars could want to find a yet wider public than that. Some, with sensitive local knowledge about some part of the world, of the kind Fukuyama describes, may also just shudder to think what could be done with their knowledge in the hands and minds of the wrong policy makers.[22]

Yet could we foresee changes in the landscape of knowledge production, and knowledge circulation? The question was already raised in Chap. 2: will perhaps the distance between the edifices of Randolph Hearst and Leland Stanford soon not be what it used to be? With the revolution which started in Silicon Valley, both university worlds and media worlds are trying out, and taking on, new shapes. Some old newspapers and magazines just lie down and die. Journalists may find that the news business increasingly becomes precisely a business. An elderly foreign correspondent I talked to in Jerusalem shook his head and said he could hear "the accountants cracking their whips." But other media organizations expand from print into a variety of electronic costumes. And "longform journalism," a rather essay-like kind of writing which surely has many happy consumers among academics as well, thrives in venerable publications such as *The Atlantic*, *Harper's*, and the *New Yorker*, and at least in magazine sections of some dailies, but also on the Web. (It seems to be rather an American specialty.)

As far as Academia is concerned, tendencies seem rather contradictory. On the one hand, there are the pressures of auditing and ranking which keep scholars writing mostly for each other, inside the gated community of professorial peers and captive audiences of graduate and undergraduate students. These pressures mostly strengthen the inward-turning tendencies we hear Kaplan, Kennedy, Ajami and Fukuyama complaining about.

Yet perhaps if media people engaged in a little more outreach of their own, they might just find some of those academic writings not so entirely opaque, and if they even take a field trip to the campus, they could discover the occasional office door left ajar. And then there is the rise of the MOOC, "Massive Open Online Courses." Focusing on these, *The American Interest*—the journal devoted to politics, policy and culture, initiated by Francis Fukuyama—has devoted one cover story to "The End of the University as We Know It" (Harden 2013). When the teaching of star faculty from globally leading institutions becomes electronically available everywhere, we are told, it is not so clear what will happen to the university as familiar from the twentieth century: a campus territory with lecture halls and seminar rooms, large libraries with stacks full of printed books and journals, and quite possibly housing, food and entertainment facilities, and sports arenas as well.

Once more, what will really happen is another of those things which appear hard to predict. It seems unlikely that the campuses of Stanford University, or Harvard, Princeton, Yale and a number of others, in the United States and elsewhere, will turn into ghost towns any time soon.[23] But in the new landscape, the new market place of knowledge and ideas, global as well as local, the border between media organizations and academic organizations could possibly turn more blurred. And both institutions and individuals may just want to rethink their brands and their publics; changing styles and repertoires, dividing their efforts in other ways between monographs, flagship journals, op-ed pieces, blogs or whatever. There is room for a scenario or two that will take on reporting from this future.

NOTES

1. One exception is Francis Fukuyama's (1995b) essay, reflecting on the reception of his "end of history" thesis five years after it appeared.
2. The point here is that what may recently have been identified as wars are mostly asymmetrical—there may be one or more states on one side, but on the other there is some non-state variety of violence drawing on warfare, terrorism, and often organized crime. The British political scientist Mary Kaldor (1999) had a pioneering analysis of this a few years after Huntington's book appeared; we may be reminded here of Barnett's "The Gap" and Cooper's "premodernity," as discussed in Chap. 3. See also the closeup anthropological reporting by Carolyn Nordstrom (2004) and in a volume edited by Paul Richards (2005).
3. See a little more on this in Chap. 9.
4. Among those who quickly responded to Huntington's thesis in Foreign Affairs, both Ikenberry (1997) and Smith (1997) also pointed to this possibility. For a more elaborate view of the thesis as an example of political myth, see Bottici and Challand (2006).
5. Both these books relate to the genre discussed in the present book, but despite their titles they are not quite global scenarios—not about the way China or Latin America would rule, say, Sweden, or Russia, or Australia. In a way they could belong among the "Scenarios from everywhere" discussed in Chap. 9—but at the time of writing, at least, both authors were based in London. Guardiola-Rivera offers a vision from the left of the development of more radical perspectives in Latin America, as a "view from the South," with possible implications for foreign as well as domestic policy in the United States. Jacques—who remarkably has back cover blurbs by both Niall Ferguson and Eric Hobsbawm—emphasizes China's scale, complexity, and historical consciousness. This is not a nation-state, but a civilization-state.

And in contrast with that European model for relationships between states which came out of the Westphalian Peace, China offers a history-based model for a tributary system between a very large, powerful state and its smaller, weaker partners.

6. Barma et al. (2007), political scientists, sketch "a world without the West": "This world rests on a rapid deepening of interconnectivity within the developing world—in flows of goods, money, people and ideas—that is surprisingly autonomous from Western control, resulting in the development of a new, parallel international system, with its own distinctive set of rules, institutions and currencies of power. This system empowers those within it to take what they need from the West while routing around American-led world order."

7. Guldi and Armitage (2014) offer an up-to-date overview of the handling of temporalities in academic history, with a preference of their own for the long term. No mention here of Niall Ferguson.

8. Thomas Friedman has commented on the tendency in a column titled "What is News?" (2014b), contrasting his recent event reporting from Ukraine and the Middle East with his valiant attempt to cover the continuing decline of biodiversity in Madagascar: "...where we in the news media fall down is in covering big trends—trends that on any given day don't amount to much but over time could be vastly more significant than we can now imagine." Elsewhere I have developed a point of view toward the place of events and "the first draft of history" in the social sciences (Hannerz 2010a).

9. Barber's apology: "While extremist groups like Islamic Jihad have themselves associated the word with armed struggle against modernizing, secular infidels, I can appreciate that the great majority of devout Muslims who harbor no more sympathy for Islamic Jihad than devout Christians feel for the Ku Klux Klan or the Montana Militia might feel unfairly burdened by my title. I owe them an apology, and hope they will find their way past the book's cover to the substantive reasoning that makes clear how little my argument has to do with Islam as a religion or with resistance to McWorld as the singular property of Muslims." (in *Jihad vs. McWorld*, paperback afterword, 1996.)

10. To Scottish friends: my apologies. Indulging in these stereotypes just seemed to be an effective way to make a point.

11. George Ritzer (1993, 1998), American sociologist, has been using the term "McDonaldization" more broadly to refer to a mode of standardization of production in contemporary life. The spread of the fast-food chain keeps challenging the imagination of scenarists—Thomas Friedman (1999: 195) has launched the Golden Arches Theory of Conflict Prevention: "No two countries that both had McDonald's had fought a war against each other

since each got its McDonald's." For a set of ethnographic studies of how McDonald's restaurants are integrated into local life in China, Taiwan, South Korea and Japan, see Watson (1997). "CocaColonization" occasionally offers an alternative as a term for global Americanization through consumer culture— again, the title of Barber's *Jihad vs. McWorld* in German translation is *Coca Cola und Heiliger Krieg*. In a way this works better: for reasons of climate and kitchen technology, soft drinks may reach where standardized hamburgers do not.

12. A prominent German scholar in peace and conflict studies, Dieter Senghaas, also has a book with the title *The Clash Within Civilizations* (1998).

13. Azaryahu's article on Israel does not actually refer to Barber's writings, so the McDonald's allusion can come up in more than one author's mind—but then it can be another measure of success that explicit footnotes and references are no longer necessary.

14. If one wants more such geohybrids, "Chinafrica" might be a candidate, to denote the growing, multifaceted presence of China and the Chinese in Africa; see on this e.g. French (2014).

15. Then a very young John F. Kennedy also made his Churchill connection with *Why England Slept* (1940), originally a Harvard undergraduate thesis. A more recent check on the title *While America Sleeps* on Amazon.com offered four books, with these subtitles and authors: "Self-Delusion, Military Weakness, and the Threat to Peace Today" (2001) by Donald and Frederick W. Kagan (father and brother of Robert Kagan, who figures more often as a scenarist in this book); "How Islam, Immigration and Indoctrination are Destroying America from Within" (2007) by Wells Earl Draughon; "An FBI Whistleblower's Story" (2009) by John M. Cole; and "A Wake-up Call for the Post-9/11 Era" (2012) by Russ Feingold, former Senator from Wisconsin. With so much going on during such an extended nap, it might indeed seem like a good idea for the country to rub its eyes.

16. Benjamin Barber's novel is *Marriage Voices* (1981). Joseph Nye's novel is *The Power Game* (2006).

17. Nicholas Kristof has a past as a foreign correspondent, especially in China and Japan; he and his colleague and wife Sheryl WuDunn have more recently been at the outskirts of the global scenario genre with books on human rights issues, especially focusing on the situations of women and children (Kristof and WuDunn 2009, 2014). For the view of ways of addressing a wider audience by an anthropology professor who has been eminently successful at it, see Eriksen (2006).

18. In his own way, Kaplan (2005: 290–291) also extends his approval to the sociologist Donald LeVine's classic study of Ethiopia, *Wax and Gold* (1965): it shows "a practical, old-fashioned common sensibility rare in contemporary academic circles."

19. See Bradburd (1998), Watson (1999) and Borneman and Hammoudi (2009).
20. Ajami, who died in 2014, was professor of Middle East Studies at The Johns Hopkins University, School of Advanced International Studies, and also affiliated with the Hoover Institution (Martin 2014). Of Iranian and Arab background himself, he reputedly was someone the U.S. government listened to as it formed its Middle Eastern policy (and its plans for the Iraq invasion) in the early 2000s. While he had been a critic of Huntington's clash of civilizations thesis in the early set of comments in *Foreign Affairs*, Ajami notes in the obituary that he later came to feel that Huntington had been right. For Huntington's less friendly view of Ajami before the latter changed his mind, see one mention in Chap. 7.
21. A critical comment on a decline of international studies in the United States by Charles King (2015), professor of government at Georgetown University, is also to the point here. King describes uncertainties of funding, decreasing interest in foreign language studies, notes that "an iron law of Academia holds that, with time, all disciplines bore even themselves" and concludes that doctoral programs "do a criminally poor job of teaching young scholars to write and speak in multiple registers." Also according to King, more than half of the American respondents to a survey of international relations scholars state that the rarely or never cite sources in any other language than English in their work.
22. One example is the popularity of the book *The Arab Mind* by Rafael Patai, a marginal and certainly outdated scholar, in neoconservative policy circles before the 2003 Iraq War, as described by Seymour Hersh (2004), investigative journalist; see also Hannerz (2010b: 110–112).
23. See for example the value attached to major U.S. universities by the Singaporean scenario author Kishore Mahbubani, as described in Chap. 9.

CHAPTER 6

Contemporary Habitats of Meaning

When the journal *Foreign Affairs*, where Samuel Huntington's "clash of civilizations" thesis was first launched, later devoted a section to responses to it, one of the commentators, Bruce Nussbaum (1997: 165), was among the unenthusiastic:

> His argument is weak, first and foremost, because it is built on the concept of "culture," which has about as much concrete definition as a snowflake in June.

And Nussbaum went on to conclude that:

> It might provide pseudo-intellectual ammunition to nativists everywhere seeking justification for ugly thought and uglier deeds. (Nussbaum 1997: 165)

Nussbaum was identified as an editor at the magazine *Business Week*.

Eight years later, the political scientist Mahmood Mamdani (2005: 148)—from Uganda, now U.S.-based—reviewing new books on political Islam for *Foreign Affairs*, began as follows:

> The debate over why the attacks of September 11, 2001, occurred has been dominated by different versions of "culture talk," the notion that culture is the most reliable clue to people's politics. Their differences notwithstanding, public intellectuals such as Samuel Huntington and Bernard Lewis agree

135

that religion drives both Islamic culture and politics and that the motivation for Islamist violence is religious fundamentalism. Ascribing the violence of one's adversaries to their culture is self-serving: it goes a long way toward absolving oneself of any responsibility.

Along lines somewhat related to Mamdani's, the veteran political commentator William Pfaff (1997: 96), writing in *World Policy Journal*, had already suggested that there is a streak of fatalism in Huntington's scenario:

> His argument that wars in the future will be conflicts of civilization shifts the responsibility for those wars from the realm of human volition and political decision to that of cultural predestination.

"As much concrete definition as a snowflake in June"? Perhaps we need not take a *Business Week* editor as an authority on the culture concept. Mamdani's skepticism toward "culture talk" in political debate still suggests that culture remains what has been called an "essentially contested concept," and Pfaff's claim that volition here stands against predestination makes the relationship between culture and human agency one important issue.

There are other commentators on the past and present world scene, with implications for the future, who are not impressed with arguments about culture as a determining influence either. The book *Why Nations Fail* (2012) by Daron Acemoglu, M.I.T. economist, and James A. Robinson, Harvard political scientist, drew much favorable attention as it appeared. It does not quite belong in our scenario genre, but is close enough—for one thing, it has blurbs by Francis Fukuyama and Niall Ferguson. Early in the book, Acemoglu and Robinson hurry through "theories that don't work" in explaining national failures, and "the culture hypothesis" is one of them, getting a few pages. In their concluding bibliographic essay, they state that "Views about culture are widely spread throughout the academic literature but have never been brought together in one work." (2012: 466) The nearest thing to it they seem to know of is an article in the *Journal of Economic Perspectives*.[1] So they go on choosing some examples to demonstrate the deficiencies of claims about culture. One focuses on religion, with a bow to Max Weber and the Protestant ethic—but no, Middle Eastern countries are poor (unless they have oil) not because they are Muslim, but because after the dissolution of the Ottoman empire, through Western colonial as well as postcolonial periods, they got bad political regimes. In another case, the question is raised whether a good national culture can make a difference. Again, no: both Canada and Sierra Leone were British colonies, but the cultural legacy they shared seems not to have put them on the same track.

One might feel it is a remarkable idea that Canadian and Sierra Leonean national cultures would be very similar, due to a British heritage. (That would presumably then also include Zimbabwe, Cyprus, Belize, Hong Kong, and a fair number of others.) In both cases, furthermore, one could indeed problematize the notion of a "national culture." Getting to their own point, Acemoglu and Robinson devote their book to arguing for institutional understandings of power, prosperity and poverty. That seems useful enough: but one senses that they briefly introduce "the culture hypothesis" mostly as a straw man, without feeling any pressure to go beyond common sense understandings, or avoid circulating misunderstandings of their own making.

CULTURESPEAK IN THE SCENARIOS

Of the scenario writers we focus on in this book Huntington may indeed have been the most emphatic in his foregrounding a conception of culture. Others do more or less with the concept itself, explicitly –with what Mamdani we could refer to as "culture talk," or with a more Orwellian slant, culturespeak—even when matters they discuss could have lent themselves to it.

Thomas Friedman, detailing the experiences which led him to the multiple factors coming together in the view of globalization he presents in *The Lexus and the Olive Tree* (politics, culture, national security, financial markets, communication technology, environmental change), points out that he began his career as a foreign correspondent, in Beirut and Jerusalem, with a two-dimensional news site. In the Middle East it was all about culture and politics, with people's culture basically defining their politics: "the world for me was all about watching people clinging to their own roots and uprooting their neighbors' roots." (Friedman 1999: 16) This takes him on to the olive tree as, indeed, a root metaphor.[2] Yet one senses that he is inclined to shift his interest, like Huntington, from culture itself to cultural identity. And in any case, he has more to say about the Lexus, the Japanese car in a world of market competition.

In *Jihad vs. McWorld*, Benjamin Barber does not dwell very much on the culture concept as such, and we have already noted that his basic divide is not so different from Friedman's. Mostly he places culture on the side of deeply conflictive group identity; but then he also notes that his McWorld is "about culture as commodity" (1996: 17), so altogether his idea of culture becomes more pluralistic. We will come back to that. Joseph Nye's concept of soft power involves culture very centrally. That will be the topic of Chap. 8.

The diplomat Robert Cooper takes considerable and straightforward interest in cultural matters in *The Breaking of Nations* (2003)—that book where he also rather dubiously maps those three worlds in one: premodern, modern, and postmodern. Professionally, Cooper is concerned with cultural difference primarily as a source of misunderstanding. Again, foreign policy would be easy if it were not for the foreigners. He points to some fateful misunderstandings in history: the British misunderstanding the Arabs as they joined together in defeating the Ottoman Empire, Chamberlain and then Stalin misunderstanding Hitler, Roosevelt in his turn misunderstanding Stalin. European countries could only be brought together after centuries of war, and then it could after all be done against a background of common history and culture. "The problems of the new era will come from cultures that are little understood in the West. The effort required to understand them and the risks of not doing so are alarmingly great." (2003: 86) Furthermore, Cooper makes his point that "foreigners are different" by listing concretely some of the channels and influences through which they are made so:

> They have been brought up differently; their thoughts are structured differently by the different language they speak and the different books they have read; their habits have been influenced by different schools, different social customs, different national heroes, different churches, mosques and temples; they may sometimes watch the same TV sitcoms, but the TV news still comes from a different studio and from a different point of view; their ideas of justice and legitimacy may be quite different from ours. (2003: 94)

The big, strong and powerful may have some special difficulty understanding the outside world, Cooper notes. With such advantages to start with, they may not care to be bothered with the tedious, time-consuming business of trying to understand and even persuade others.

What is often needed are people with some special knowledge of difference: Cooper points to instances when diplomats with decades of experience in particular regions could exercise some real influence on the conduct of policy toward them. He also contrasts the American failure to understand its adversaries in the Vietnam War with "the approach to Japan after the Second World War, when the Pentagon commissioned one of America's greatest anthropologists to write a study for them on Japanese society." (2003: 94)[3]

Robert Kagan's use of culturespeak, as in *Paradise and Power* he finds people on different sides of the North Atlantic originating on different planets, is limited to the notion of "strategic culture," but his warning against the dangers of misunderstandings is in line with Cooper's view: again, Americans and Europeans "agree on little and understand one another less and less" (2003: 3). While he spends a paragraph on acknowledging internal differences on both sides of the Atlantic, the next paragraph begins, "Nevertheless...," and then Kagan proceeds to underline the transatlantic divide, without returning much to that internal complexity. The actors are simply "the Americans" and "the Europeans."

His "strategic culture" concept would thus seem to homogenize political outlooks at a continental level, and also to emphasize durability. It thus defines what was in the beginning years of the twenty-first century the American neoconservative position in foreign policy as a more general national outlook, and deemphasizes its conjunctural character. "The reasons for the transatlantic divide are deep, long in development, and likely to endure." (2003: 4) It is true that Kagan does not make these strategic cultures entirely timeless and unchangeable: it would appear that Europeans had been rather more Martian until after World War II, and turned Venusian after that—rejecting its past divides, and painstakingly building its new integrative structures. On the other hand, it is Kagan's opinion that American strategic culture has been more consistently and dominantly Martian through history than many have recognized. This line of thought is more fully worked out and documented in one of his later books, *Dangerous Nation* (2006).[4]

Kagan never in *Paradise and Power* makes an explicit case for his use of culturespeak. "Culture" and "strategic culture" are recurrently in quotation marks, which suggests some ambiguity in their use, perhaps some hesitation or ambivalence. Actually he comes fairly close to the way a rhetoric of culture—"the culture of" this, "a culture of" that—is often employed merely to suggest something pervasive, enduring, and rather fuzzy. Culturespeak often does not get much further.

Apart from this, however, his argument also draws notably on practical insight into the uses of specific cultural imagery. The difference between

Americans and Europeans is underlined by references to popular culture, rather more from the western than from the eastern side of the Atlantic. So if the title of that original bestseller was *Women are from Venus, Men are from Mars* (Gray 1992), it would appear to follow from this intertextual allusion that in Kagan's view Europeans are like women, and Americans are like men.[5] Indeed he finds that this corresponds to a certain European opinion: "the European caricature at its most extreme depicts an America dominated by a 'culture of death,' its warlike temperament the natural product of a violent society where every man has a gun and the death penalty reigns." (Kagan 2003: 4) Moreover, he finds that in the European imagery, Americans are cowboys. On this theme he then elaborates himself: the West turns into the Wild West, where the United States becomes the sheriff (although possibly self-appointed) in a lawless world, while Europe is more like the saloonkeeper. And "from the saloonkeeper's point of view, the sheriff trying to impose order by force can sometimes be more threatening than the outlaws, who, at least for the time being, may just want a drink" (Kagan 2003: 36) The identification of the part of the European in the Wild West scenery seems a bit arbitrary, but one might suspect that a saloonkeeper is more shortsighted, more corrupted by business interests, than the brusque but honest sheriff. And this Western motif comes back once more: "...Americans can still sometimes see themselves in heroic terms—as Gary Cooper at high noon. They will defend the townspeople, whether the townspeople want them to or not." (2003: 95)

THE MEANINGFUL LIFE OF *HOMO SAPIENS*

What shall we do with culture, and culturespeak? Perhaps we might turn to a classic authority on word use, Humpty Dumpty. When Alice encounters Humpty Dumpty in Lewis Carroll's *Through the Looking-glass*, they have their famous exchange about the meaning of words. "When I use a word," Humpty Dumpty says, "It means just what I choose it to mean, neither more nor less." And then a little further along in the conversation, as Alice remarks that Humpty Dumpty makes one single word mean a great deal, Humpty Dumpty responds that "when I make a word do a lot of work like that, I always pay it extra."

"Culture" seems to be a word we would have to pay extra. ("Power" might be another.) I noted in the Prologue that the notion of culture has been central to anthropologists. The trouble is, of course, that they, alone or with other academics, cannot claim ownership of the concept. By 2014,

Merriam-Webster, the dictionary company, declared it the most important word of the year, as more people looked up its definition online than any other word (Dressler 2015). So this is not like "governmentality," or "rhizomes," or "actor-network theory," something that has its time in the seminar rooms and the library stacks for a while without too many in the society outside noticing it.

Even so, there may be some wider public recognition that culture is something anthropologists speak about with a measure of authority. They may not altogether agree with each other, or with people in general, on how to use the concept—a once widely-cited critical review by two prominent mid-twentieth century anthropologists (Alfred Kroeber and Clyde Kluckhohn, both of whom we will encounter again in the next chapter) could already cover some hundreds of definitions of it, in and out of the discipline—but they have developed a certain expertise on what it may mean and what it should not be taken to mean.[6] I do not believe too many anthropologists would now insist on the superiority of some purely cultural*ist* interpretation of the world, in the face of which all other analytical apparatus would crumble or shrink. It cannot offer another "theory of everything." More likely they would try to suggest what kinds of understandings of culture seem most intellectually viable, and also to identify what may be their limitations, what qualifications need to be made, what is the nature of the interplay between the cultural and whatever may be noncultural. This may leave the culture concept with less of the explanatory and predictive power than has sometimes been attributed to it, but may in the end offer us something more useful in understanding how people make and use culture together, and how cultural differences sometimes draw them apart.

So that is my agenda in this chapter. Again, it would be foolish to claim to speak for the entire discipline, and I will certainly be leaving loose threads hanging out. Yet my way of charting the territory may at least help show where the global future scenarios as we have encountered them fit into a view of contemporary world culture.

To begin with, I think we must understand that not all important keywords can serve well as sharp analytical tools. The very fact that they are widely used, in different contexts, by a variety of people, in itself makes this rather unlikely. But we also have a use for words which, in all their flexibility, can sensitize to certain kinds of issues, make us ask certain kinds of questions. "Culture" is one of these.

To begin to get a handle on what the issues are in this case, I will go back about two and a half centuries, beyond Humpty Dumpty, to my countryman Carolus Linnaeus—as it happens, a professor at the University of Uppsala, like Olof Rudbeck the Elder, nation-branding pioneer, and Rudolf Kjellén, the geopolitics inventor. In publishing his overarching biological nomenclature in *Systema naturae* in 1758, Linnaeus attached the name *Homo sapiens* to that species of animal to which he belonged himself—thus generously sharing that epithet "wise man" with all his species mates. And why were they wiser than all other species?

Presumably because of their special capacity for learning.

Linnaeus was not right about everything (in fact some of his ideas were, by twenty-first century standards, bizarre), and it may be that the line he drew between humans and other species has become a bit more blurred, as we have learned more about the intelligence and organizational capabilities of various animals. We hear more these days about intraspecies and interspecies communication, and we are said to be in a posthuman era. We are becoming more wary of speciesism.

Nonetheless, dolphins have not written the Koran (or any more aquatic counterpart), ants have not built the Taj Mahal, baboons did not form the United Nations, Fox News is not by foxes, for foxes.

Here, then, is what makes all members of the species *Homo sapiens* cultural animals. They come into the world quite incomplete, and pick up what they need to know, and more, by learning from life, and in very large part from one another. As at the same time social animals (and for them the social and the cultural go together, inseparably), they deal with life and with each other in large part by way of interpreting and making signs, managing meaning. And this is what culture is about: meanings and meaningful forms, more or less organized into wider complexes. In an oft-cited passage, Clifford Geertz (1973: 5), one of anthropology's most prominent wordsmiths, concluded that "man is an animal suspended in webs of significance he himself has spun." The abstractness of that formulation, however, risks making it a bit misleading. There is not just a single, solitary spider in that web, but a great many—by current estimates, over seven billion of them.

Moreover, they do not all inhabit the web in the same way. The fact that people are open to learning from their experience in the world also means that they do not necessarily all learn the same things. That is a major reason why there is so much diversity in humanity. Now the culture concept can be taken in two contrasting directions here. Frequently the emphasis has been on the fact that when people learn from each other, they may come to share a great deal. Here culture is taken to involve a replication of uniformity, within some unit often simply described as "a culture." But that view tends to have its limits. People are also usually more or less aware that other people they know of have learned other things, think differently, and conduct themselves differently. And they take this understanding into account in their own actions. So culture becomes an organization of diversity.[7] Both these conceptions, of the replication of uniformity and of the organization of diversity, have their uses, but often the former has prevailed in culturespeak, and I often find the latter more productive, so it will get rather more attention here.

Culture is in part in people's minds, but it is also out there in forms accessible to the senses. Some of these forms may be human-made, like languages, or the Taj Mahal or Fox News. Others are nature-made, like stars or a tsunami, although people can still attach meaning to them. Whatever people think about it and call it and say to each other about it, however, a tsunami is a tsunami, and has to be dealt with as a natural phenomenon. So culture is open to nature, and to an extent constrained by it, although through culture people may work to modify it. One way that culture is open to nature, obviously, is through the fact that humans are also biological creatures—aging and health, for example, are there to be handled.

Among themselves, furthermore, some people have more power than others, and much as they may all argue about this and give it various cultural forms, in the end such people can demonstrate their power through force. Thus nature and power are among the kinds of things that cannot just be reduced to culture, even though learned meanings and meaningful forms are there as people engage with them.

Culturespeak, again, tends to suggest that culture is stable, enduring. We are better off making the relationship of culture to time a matter of systematic inquiry. As forever cultural, information-handling animals, human beings are in principle engaged in life-long learning. They may be more open to new experiences at certain times, and some information may be stored in such a way as to have more enduring weight. Yet there is hardly a time, except perhaps in states of extreme illness or dementia, when they stop taking in information, and making use of it for their own purposes. We can remember from previous chapters that Paul Richards, veteran scholar in Sierra Leone studies, reported on his confrontation with Robert Kaplan about the supposedly approaching anarchy, and about academic language. Debating with Kaplan, he noted that "modern anthropologists treat culture as a label for values and commitments generated in the process of making social life happen. We produce culture as we go. Change the social process and culture changes." (Richards 1999: 17) ("We," here should be understood to refer to human beings, not just anthropologists.) That represents current thinking among his colleagues quite well.[8] On the whole, people are capable of assessing circumstances and pursuing but also changing objectives; there is agency involved.

The notion referred to before, as expressed for example by William Pfaff, that culture involves predestination, and stands opposed to volition and decision-making, is clearly out of place here. It used to be assumed that culture is something "handed down from generation to generation." That is now more likely understood as no more than a partial truth. Even when we deal with durable meanings and forms, and with culture which stays in place, we must be aware that they can only be durable by being in a way constantly in process. To keep culture going, people as actors and networks of actors have to invent culture, practice it, experiment with it, reflect on it, remember it (or store it in some other way), and pass it on. And along the way, they may just debate it, and change their minds.

But Pfaff may not have been entirely wrong about the implications of Huntington's conception of culture. Again, Huntington was really more preoccupied with cultural identity than with culture itself, and he quickly reduced that identity to a matter, mostly, of an encompassing identification with one world religion or other. He did not engage much with a scrutiny of meanings or meaningful forms in their own right. Nor did he give much attention to the kinds of complexity of meaning management that his critics Amartya Sen and Benazir Bhutto soon pointed to, as we saw in Chap. 3. Yet his certainty that religious identifications are central and durable, indeed matters of *longue durée*, seem to take us some distance toward the assumption that human beings are rigidly unchanging.[9] There appears to be no real sense here that the conditions of cultural continuity need attention in themselves. Nussbaum's and Mamdani's critiques of the political uses of "clash of civilizations" arguments seem to allude to this taken-for-granted stability in difference. It is difficult to imagine a particularly useful dialogue between radically differently preprogrammed robots.

About the time when Huntington first went public with his thesis, the Barcelona anthropologist Verena Stolcke (1995) described a complex of understandings comprising what she called "cultural fundamentalism"—human beings are by nature culture bearers; cultures are distinct and incommensurable; relations between bearers of different cultures are intrinsically conflictive; it is in human nature to be xenophobic.[10] Such cultural fundamentalism, Stolcke noted, differs from traditional racism in that it does not necessarily carry with it assumptions of hierarchy. It may well proclaim a sort of cultural relativism, but then each culture should stay in its place. As they are incommensurable, they must be spatially segregated. Cultural fundamentalism has thus come to serve, not least in neo-nationalist European politics, as a discourse of exclusion. It has seemed to me that "the Huntington thesis" has been rather like a high-status variant of cultural fundamentalism, taken into world politics.

On the whole, one might also discern that within the confines of a world religion or a nation, both Samuel Huntington and Robert Kagan import into their varieties of culturespeak the assumption of a replication of uniformity. For their purposes, all Muslims are alike, all Americans are alike. And as we get to the limits of that uniformity, the bad news would be that you arrive at bloody borders, or interplanetary misunderstandings. We may think of other ways of organizing diversity.

A question of the packaging of meaning can also be sensed here. When culturespeak suggests that culture somehow is pervasive and fuzzy, a main question to ask is what goes with what, for whom. The culture concept tends to suggest that some things go together, that certain ideas—knowledge, beliefs, attitudes, experiences, symbols—somehow cluster, become interconnected, and may thereby come to support each other. This is also something to actually look into. Again, much culturespeak, including cultural fundamentalism, leans strongly toward assuming that such entire complexes are the shared property of bounded groups—even the largest entities such as nations as civilizations—and that this is the normal and inevitable situation. Yet it is also possible that connections are on the one hand more partial, and on the other hand reach out in more open networks.

FRAMES OF CULTURAL PROCESS

To repeat, "change the social process and culture changes." That, of course, as you observe human life closely, may suggest almost infinite variety in the management of meaning. Taking more of a bird's-eye view, however, I would argue that it is practical, and takes you a rather long way in grasping the shape of contemporary culture, to identify a limited set of major organizational frames within which people now handle meaning together.[11]

Imagine yourself set down, individually as well as collectively with other people, somewhere in the contemporary world as a habitat of meaning. You keep going by taking in information from out there, some of it in forms shaped by others so as to be meaningful to you, some of it in forms perhaps more mute or so ambiguous that to a great extent you have to attach meaning to it more or less on your own, or together with others sharing much the same experience.

My suggestion is that for most people in the world now, in this over-all habitat of meaning one major organizational frame is the state, a second is the market, a third is movements. This is a fairly common-sense accounting scheme, yet some explanations are immediately called for.

"States" should be understood with upward and downward derivations, from the Security Council of the United Nations (and various other entities within "the United Nations family"—a dysfunctional family in some ways, but hardly entirely useless) to entities like the municipal council of Spoon River. State organization typically involves a territory with a population. It has taken the world a long time to get there, but in a general sense it is a form which is now everywhere. There have been important events along the way, such as that Westphalian Peace which once got the imagination of Olof Rudbeck the Elder going. There have also been individuals which, for better or for worse, have had a special part in turning people and territories into states: Prince Metternich in nineteenth-century Europe, the Belgian King Leopold who as an entrepreneur of colonialism managed to grab much of Central Africa for a Congo of his own, President Wilson with his post-World War I advocacy of self-determination, and the British and French diplomats Sykes and Picot who, drawing convenient boundaries in the Middle East after the Ottoman Empire collapsed, could create rather unlikely entities such as Iraq. Yet the fact is that since around 1960, with decolonization largely accomplished, at least the outward appearance of what a state is and does has become quite standardized.[12]

That certainly does not mean that all states actually accomplish quite the same things. For one thing some do more and some less, and some may indeed now be classified as "failed states." We saw some of the variations in this respect in Chap. 3, for example as in Thomas Barnett's contrast between the Core and the Gap, and in Robert Kaplan's account of the coming anarchy. What states can be expected to do has also changed over time. Here, as we consider the state specifically in its operation as an organizational frame for cultural process, we are interested above all in the involvement of the state apparatus in the production and circulation of meaning—the ideas, values, knowledge or whatever that are passed from that apparatus to the citizens, or subjects, or inhabitants of state territory, and sometimes to others outside. This can be handled for example through schools, universities, radio, television, museums, or national celebrations, all frequently although not always under state control. We are not so directly concerned, on the other hand, with what may be its supposed monopoly on the legitimate use of force, or with its provision of material infrastructure, although these may become significant a bit more indirectly as people make their own interpretations of them.

As far as the market frame is concerned, we should also for our purposes limit our field of attention somewhat. Lots of phenomena may be seen at least metaphorically as market matters, as long as choices are made between competing alternatives. What interests us here is where meanings are attached to items in a money economy—that is, when culture takes a commodity form. Here culture is transacted between buyers and sellers, perhaps with different kinds of middlemen in between. Moreover, we take notice also when commodities are somehow loaded with a lot of meaning: when much of their significance involves not just some material use, but a load of experience, an appeal to the imagination. The growth of the advertising industry particularly from the twentieth century and on is very relevant here. An example close at hand is Coca Cola, not least since "cocacolonization" has been an alternative term to "McWorld" in summarizing the spread of American consumer culture. Much of the promotion of the sweet brown liquid has had little to do with its taste or color, but typically involves inserting the brand into attractive social contexts and life styles. This kind of cultural activity does much to enrich, complicate and sometimes corrupt the habitat of meaning in its own way.[13]

Again, there is that tendency to think of culture as consensual, in a particular sense of "shared." But you can share something without agreeing. The ongoing traffic in meaning within and between human groups and networks is not all consensual—it is often enough a matter of their coming together in debates, shifting or quite continuous, with parties being more or less familiar with each other's viewpoints.[14] Some debates may be momentary, others enduring. Movements appear as a prominent form in cultural debates. The frame may be constant, but what is in it has an on-and-off character. Movements try to mobilize people for some common goal, either because something valued in the present faces a threat, or because something better can be envisaged for the future. The cultural process involves "consciousness-raising," conversion. Movements may stop being movements because they succeed or because they fade away. Some of them are very local, but if one looks again at the late twentieth century, it will be clear that some have been more or less of global scope: the peace movement, the women's movement, the green movement. While these may be in a way single-issue affairs, that issue may be so multifaceted that it can take up a great deal of space in the habitat of meaning. Not all movements, of course, are equally expansive in their cultural implications, but they contribute in their ways to keeping that habitat lively. In the twenty-first century, "jihad" has certainly been a keyword for what can go on in the movement frame.

States, markets, movements, then…but something is missing. Before the members of *Homo sapiens* got around to having any of these three, they were simply around each other: listening and looking, learning from each other that way, and using that learning in their contacts. And that fundamental fact is still there. It is a wide and central organizational frame of its own, not a residual category after what goes into state, market and movement frames has been identified, but basic to human existence.

The curious thing is that I have not really come across any widely used term that unmistakably refers with some precision to this frame—perhaps the concept is absent because, as the saying goes, it is not the fish that discovers water. [15] "Everyday life" may have the advantage of sensitizing to its centrality, but then probably we would mostly think that at least the state and the market nowadays also intrude into the everyday. "Conviviality" indeed refers literally to the key fact of simply living together, but it has been appropriated for somewhat more particular purposes. [16] So with some reluctance—since the paths through the academic-industrial terrain are littered with failed neologisms—I go for a term which has hitherto been used rarely if at all. The social philosopher Alfred Schutz, born in Vienna but in New York for most of his academic career, identified some general types of ways in which people can be seen to relate to one another; and for people who are simply in each other's presence, whether recurrently in situations of personal intimacy or quite briefly in situations of anonymity, he used the term "consociates." [17] Thus I derive from Schutz the term "consociality" as a label for that fourth, but actually first and most fundamental and ubiquitous, frame for cultural process.

Consociality includes everything from everyday interactions between family members to the sidewalk traffic of strangers in big-city streets, and in between these, contacts between friends and acquaintances, work mates, neighbors. It is within this frame we begin our lives as learners. Much of what goes on here is likely to be quite routine and repetitive, and there may be a tendency toward pragmatic conservatism in this: if it works, no need to change it. But looking more closely at the routines, one may sense that there is also a fair amount of versatile improvisation, and when circumstances change, people can change their lines of action. (A good thing when you live in a less than orderly environment.) Interactions within the frame of consociality are not always so deliberately communicative or instructional, but learning goes on even when nobody is intentionally teaching. Much of it is what has been termed "situated learning," observational and non-verbal; apprenticeship is a sort of more organized form of this.[18] (The key approach to field study in anthropology, "participant observation," is also a more systematic mode of learning which is in large part a simulation of what takes place within the frame of consociality.) If there is a dividing line between the public and the private, it runs through consociality, but whatever is defined as private is largely within this frame.

One may be tempted to assume that consociality is rather idyllic, but that would be a mistake. There can be power relationships and tyranny within this frame as well—even in quite intimate relationships. And there may be uncertainty and fear, if those present include strangers or known enemies. Being "street wise" in a complicated urban setting draws on building up one's own observational skills, and listening to the flow of local knowledge between consociates.

Cultural process within the frame of consociality may also draw more indirectly on what state and market machineries do to construct and maintain the environments within which consociate activities and interactions occur. Anthropologists have classically documented the ways in which hunters and gatherers, or small-scale cultivators, take their natural environment into account and build up more or less intricate knowledge of it, and beliefs about it. People who now live in cities and other more or less artificial environments may also pay some attention to facts of nature, such as the weather, but in large part it is human-made infrastructure that provides the practical circumstances of life. This infrastructure, however, is also often mostly mute. Much of the time it is within consociality it is interpreted and commented on, in the quotidian flow of experience and conversation.

Very few human beings are likely to live their lives mostly outside the frame of consociality. While there, on the other hand, they might at times pay only rather distracted attention when actors in the other three frames try to reach them as citizens, customers, or potential converts.

THE GLOBAL VILLAGE 2.0

After elaborating on what goes into the frame of consociality, it may be wise to take it a bit beyond Alfred Schutz.[19] "Co-presence" is the key idea, but need it be physical co-presence, as Schutz had it? By now it seems necessary to consider the implications of the ongoing evolution of the media as cultural technology.

The title of his best-known book, *Understanding Media* (1964), may be on the bland side, but otherwise Marshall McLuhan's way with words would seem comparable to those of the more recent scenarists. Of his most memorable formulations, "the global village" has the paradox, "the medium is the message" has the alliteration. And then there was already *The Gutenberg Galaxy* (1962), on the culture-historical significance of print. Probably these terms have stuck in the public mind rather more than some of McLuhan's various far-reaching claims about the ways new media were transforming the world and human consciousness.[20]

As things stood a half-century ago, however, one could have one's doubts about the precision of the concept of a global village. Over time, certainly, media had allowed culture to expand out of the face-to-face encounters of the real village, step by step: writing and literacy, print, telegraph, telephone, radio, film first silent, then with sound… One could reach out more and more widely, and one could record and therefore store more and more kinds of meaningful forms over time. Yet with the breakthrough of television, which was really the focus of McLuhan's concern, there was little that one could not show; one could do it in real time, from one corner of the world to another; and one could bring it into people's homes.

But it was still not really like in a village. Television was still largely one-way communication. What you had in audiences were shoulder-to-shoulder relationships, among people facing in the same direction toward the screen. A common term was "mass communication." Viewers could not do much to talk back, except turning the set off. In the real village, the dominant frame of cultural process is consociality, with everybody more or less involved in giving and taking, back and forth, in relationships more symmetrical in character.

It is from the late twentieth century, with the development of "social media," that we have had something more like a real global village. We may feel that "social media" is an unfortunate term; by definition, it would seem, all media are social. Mostly these newer tools may be more precisely described as interpersonal media. But the point is that with so much of the world's population online, in varied and flexible formats, the strictly physical co-presence, the literally face-to-face, does not carry the weight that it had in Alfred Schutz' time, or even in Marshall McLuhan's. It is definitely still important: in intimacy, for one thing, and in those uncertain situations of anonymity, for another. Nonetheless, much of the unregulated, more or less continuous flow of meaning between kinspeople, friends, colleagues and past or present neighbors is now less constrained by spatial distances. A large part of our lives is now taken up by screenwork.[21] Often enough, this is a matter of maintaining relationships already formed face-to-face. Yet it happens that relationships expand in the other direction as well, from screen to physical co-presence. So by now, the frame of consociality is defined by co-presence both—or either—physical and virtual.

Virtual co-presence is turning out to have all kinds of consequences. In some ways there may be more room for anonymity, less for privacy. At the interface between the virtual and the physical, there may be new facts and norms involving violence and sexuality. Mostly this shift toward the virtual matters on the small scale in people's daily lives, but it may even reach into world news. What became known in 2011 as "the Arab Spring" seems to have been stimulated by the fact that through the spread of social media, especially young people could get a stronger sense of just how widespread were those dissatisfactions that were generated by practical circumstances for which the state was held responsible.

So what had until then been the uncertain sentiments of "the Arab Street," as occasionally hinted at by foreign observers, could be transformed through laptops and cell phones at least for a while from consociality into a massive movement—"Come to Tahrir Square!" Some years later, the end result may seem uncertain. A reinvented state apparatus is apparently no less concerned with censorship than its predecessor, but the question is whether the meanings circulating in consociality can ever be returned to their old form. Thomas Friedman (2014e, 2014f), perhaps most technology-conscious of our scenarists, has devoted columns in the *New York Times* to forecasting the emergence of "The Square People," joining together in virtual as well as real public squares, as an emergent global force. More about that in the next chapter.

BETWEEN FRAMES

Fundamentally four frames, then: state, market, movement, consociality. It matters where in this scheme some complex of meanings is in motion. Consider for example Christian religion: it works out rather differently whether its ideas and expressions are handled by a state church, as it used to be in Sweden, or as it is in Roman Catholicism where the church has its own state, the Vatican; more or less in the market frame, as in American televangelism; by revivalist movements seeking converts and changing their consciousness; or in large part through the everyday and calendrical habits of consociality. While internally not wholly uniform, the frames show different tendencies in outreach, and they relate to time differently.

But then the frames do not exist insulated from one another. Many of the most interesting cultural phenomena in recent history have involved entanglements and hybrids between them, and instances when cultural complexes move between frames. For some seventy years until the end of the Cold War, World Communism was a movement doing the foreign work of a state, the Soviet Union. Later, the involvement of Saudi Arabia in the global expansion of Wahhabi Islam may be thought of similarly—even if no Eurabia has come out of it. Because the consociality frame is so basic to overall cultural process, a great many things are somehow anchored there. States can best claim to be nation-states if they are legitimate guardians of heritages and ways of life originating and voluntarily maintained in consociality; that is where "authenticity" is most likely looked for. Expressive arts tend first to be developed to some point by the "folk," among skilled amateurs, before they are transformed into commodities, so here there are continuous crossovers here from consociality to the market. When in the late twentieth century "world music" became a general label for popular music forms of Africa, Asia and the Caribbean taken up by radio stations and discotheques in Europe and North America, it was mostly a matter of mixed forms already resulting from passages between consociality and market in the former regions. Indeed, it has been noted as a widespread current tendency for cultural identities, such as those of ethnicity, certainly grounded in consociality, to take on corporate and commodity forms: *Ethnicity Inc.* (Comaroff and Comaroff 2009) More complicatedly yet, one may discern a borderless neoliberal jihad penetrating state apparatuses, somewhat paradoxically in order to make them more like market enterprises; what has been labeled "audit culture" is its rather protean academic form.[22]

It is striking that entanglements between frames often involve agents within other frames trying to monitor or steer whatever may be the flow of meaning within consociality. Much market research and opinion polling would belong here. The early twenty-first century state, in its concern with national security, has had the technological capability of eavesdropping on more or less whatever we say to each other by way of media technologies—surveillance at a level George Orwell's Big Brother of an imagined thirty years earlier could hardly have dreamt of.[23] When with inspiration from Michel Foucault "governmentality" for a time became an academic buzzword, it often referred to the state's shaping the conditions of everyday life in such ways that consociality would come up with the desirable kind of citizens. Again and again, it appears, there is scholarly or public concern over how the integrity of the relationships of consociality is threatened by invasions.

WHERE THE SCENARISTS ARE

So from where in this cultural landscape of today, and probably tomorrow, have our most prominent scenarists been reporting? They may not be too precise about this, but one can try to locate their postings. Samuel Huntington, again: as a political scientist, with a clash of civilizations scenario, he was clearly primarily concerned with the state frame, and with state machineries making friendships and alliances in large part on the basis of a sharing of one world religion or other. Historically, they might have had their origin in the movement frame; but as time passed, it might be that if these religions are to serve as bases of "cultural identities," people should engage with them continuously within their consociality. That would seem most likely to offer a sort of popular legitimacy to state action. Of course Huntington does not really trace and scrutinize these steps.

To Joseph Nye and "soft power," again, we will turn at greater length in Chap. 8. Another political scientist, he is primarily concerned with what the state does with culture. With one twist, however, he is concerned with how its management of meaning reaches people who are not citizens: people abroad. And it is another twist that in some considerable part, it is supposed to work by way of the market.

In Benjamin Barber's terminology, although it may at times seem a little fuzzy, "McWorld" mostly stands for the market, "Jihad" for certain varieties of movements. As he offers a satirical travesty of Karl Marx, it portrays the penetration of the market into all corners of social life: instead of "Workers of the world unite! You have nothing to lose but your chains!" there is now "Consumers of the world unite! We have everything you need in our chains!"[24] And the market does get a much larger part of *Jihad vs. McWorld* than the movements (which in this case are largely ethnic, regional or national; reactions to globalization). Here, most vividly, is that future in shimmering pastels, a busy portrait of onrushing economic, technological, and ecological forces that demand integration and uniformity and that mesmerize peoples everywhere with fast music, fast computers, and fast food—MTV, MacIntosh, and McDonald's—pressing nations into one homogeneous global theme park... (Barber 1996: 4)

Yet toward the end Barber (1996: 281) reaches another space:

It is not where we vote and it is not where we buy and sell; it is where we talk with neighbors about a crossing guard, plan a benefit for our community school, discuss how our church or synagogue can shelter the homeless, or organize a summer softball league for our children.

This sounds much like consociality, although for the political scientist Barber it is "civil society," and with good citizenship as a key vision, it is in large part consociality as it turns toward the state. Barber only gets there in the last of nineteen chapters, however, and does not spend much time on the ground.[25]

Thomas Friedman, "tourist with an attitude," is also mostly elsewhere. His olive tree metaphor, we have seen, is ambiguous: it can refer to culture and roots in a way that points toward consociality, but quickly shifts to conflicts and thus rather more toward movements and states. Yet toward the end of *The Lexus and the Olive Tree*, opening up Chap. 14 (out of 18), he is on a sidewalk in the heart of Hanoi. He goes there every morning to a tiny Vietnamese woman, who for a small fee allows him to weigh himself on her bathroom scale. Not that he really needs it, but it tells him how globalization (in the sense of the expansion of markets) emerges from the street level, and is driven by "the basic human desire for a better life—a life with more choices as to what to eat, what to wear, where to live, where to travel, how to work, what to read, what to write and what to learn." (1999: 285) Certainly Friedman is still in the market frame here, but perhaps one gets a sense that he is peeping into consociality and has his imagination stimulated by it.

One would perhaps expect that Robert Kaplan, with his boots and rucksack on around much of the world, would be most likely to immerse himself in life within the consocial frame—but no, not really. As one senses from his reporting on anarchy in Sierra Leone and surrounding lands, the bush taxi trips may not let him stay around quite long enough. Kaplan really get closest to everyday life and a certain level of personal familiarity on his "embedded" visits with soldiers on American bases.

Finally, back to Samuel Huntington again. As after the 9–11 events Kaplan (2001b) interviews him in *The Atlantic Monthly*, and suggests that Huntington has been right in his political forecasts most of the time, he also finds that his interviewee footnotes on-the-scene observers rather more than more than most academics do. That is because "there are no academic sources for recent events," Huntington responds; "there is only academic opinion."

That may or may not be so. In any case, we may remember from Chap. 4 that other Huntington book, *Who Are We?* (2004), on the cultural threat of immigration from Latin America, with one critical reviewer suggesting that Huntington did not seem to know any Hispanics well—no sign that he had visited with them, or listened to their views. That does not sound like an engagement with consociality either.

Perhaps it is fair to conclude that while the scenarists together give a rich, if hardly entirely complete or faultless, picture of what goes on, or can happen, in the organizational frames of state, market and movements, they are not so good in portraying culture in the frame of consociality. One may sense why this is so. Being in so many sites, yet not necessarily readily accessible from the outside, probably not so easily sorted into analytical categories, and seldom the stuff of hard news, this part of culture does not insist on so much attention. It is amorphous, uncentered, in large part private. Nonetheless, much of human life goes on here. (And perhaps if there had been more women among the scenarists, some might have been drawn to reporting on this frame?) If one may suspect that what happens in the future will often have its earliest forms in the sites of consociality, then either developing there or transforming and shifting into other frames, then it would seem to make good sense to pay close attention to these sites. I am reminded of one rather early contribution to the future scenario genre, not yet so globally oriented, and on the whole distant from the work considered here. The book *Megatrends* by John Naisbitt (1984) claimed that important new developments could first be spotted at a local level, even as they were rather inconspicuous to begin with. Therefore a method for identifying them was the scrutinize small, local newspapers—their reporters and editors were likely to have their ears close to the ground. We might sense that much of what they listened to was part of the flow of meaning within consociality. That, one has to add, was still at a time before many local newspapers died. New media, however, perhaps offer similar understandings.

Another of the writers in the scenario genre has a related proposal. In his *Facts Are Subversive* (2009: 184), considering the sort of situation referred to in Chap. 4, in the *banlieues* and tower blocks of urban Europe, Timothy Garton Ash comments that:

> In the nineteenth century, European imperialists studied the ethnography of their colonies. In the twenty-first century, we need a new ethnography of our own cities. Since European countries tend to have concentrations of immigrants from their former colonies, the new ethnography can even draw on the old.

Certainly a reasonable amount of such urban ethnography already exists. To what extent it can build on the heritage of colonial ethnography may be an open question. It is true, however, that it tends to offer a view of varieties of consociality.

What can we say, then, about that view of the culture concept, "a snowflake in June"?

For one thing, unlike that snowflake, this concept is unlikely to melt away. Perhaps one could just as well argue that in its entire shape-shifting complexity it is about as transparent as a Nordic snowstorm in midwinter. The view of culture I have suggested in this chapter is, one might say, maximalist; again, all the meanings and meaningful forms created and acquired by human beings as learning animals. When the term "culture" is actually employed, in what I have described as culturespeak, the tendency may be to use it in referring to ideas and expressions which are more durable, or more widespread, or of particular intricacy, or of notably high quality: in the latter case, examples of aesthetic or intellectual excellence, "highbrow." But as all breaking-off points along such dimensions seem more or less arbitrary, taking a comprehensive view seems not unreasonable.

Yet it also leads to a conclusion that "culture" cannot generally be taken to stand alone as an explanation of human conduct. The sense that human beings can attend to circumstances, can learn, unlearn and relearn, also takes us to a realization that culture is there in interaction with—although not as a mere reflection of—such realities as power and materiality.

The simple scheme suggested here of seeing culture as organized in large part into a handful of major frames may have allowed us to see in what parts of the contemporary habitat of meaning our scenario writers have been most active and present. One can, however, order one's understanding of culture, as an organization of diversity, in other ways as well. The next chapter will emphasize variations in scale.

Notes

1. The article cited by Acemoglu and Robinson is by Guiso et al. (2006). That article does not take a very inclusive view of thinking about culture either.
2. A "root metaphor," according to the anthropologist Sherry Ortner (1973: 1341), is "a symbol which operates to sort out experience, to place it in cultural categories, and to help us think about how it all hangs together."
3. In published form, the study in question is Ruth Benedict's *The Chrysanthemum and the Sword* (1946); Cooper adds that it "remains a classic to this day." Indeed, this was an interesting, inventive attempt at "studying culture at a distance," as Benedict could never go to Japan. It should be said, however, that many later Japan specialists in anthropology have not been so impressed.
4. Note Robert Kaplan's similar view of American history, as described toward the end of Chap. 3, but also Niall Ferguson's doubts, likewise mentioned there.
5. The subtitle of that book has changed from "A practical guide for improving communication and getting what you want in your relationships" in the original edition, to "The classic guide to understanding the opposite sex" in later paperbacks.
6. The work in question is *Culture: A Critical Review of Concepts and Definitions* (Kroeber and Kluckhohn [1952]1963)—the authors were assisted by a team of Harvard University graduate students, including Clifford Geertz, who would go on to have a very considerable influence of his own on how anthropologists would think about culture (see especially Geertz [1973]). The book includes an appendix on "the use of the term culture in the Soviet Union."
7. The pioneering discussion of the contrast between "the replication of uniformity" and "the organization of diversity" as understandings of culture was by the psychological anthropologist Anthony Wallace (1961). Although Wallace's prime example for making his point was extremely microsociological—involving new parents and their baby—the argument can very usefully be taken to larger-scale contexts.
8. A brief but comprehensive formulation complementary to that of Richards comes from Eric Wolf (2001: 313), one of the leading anthropologists of the second half of the twentieth century: "cultural sets, and sets of sets, are continuously in construction, deconstruction, and reconstruction, under the impact of multiple processes operative over wide fields of social and cultural connections."

9. One could note that just a few years after his "clash of civilizations" book, Huntington stood as co-editor of the volume *Culture Matters* (Harrison and Huntington 2000), in which most contributors (including Francis Fukuyama) agreed that due to their values, different cultures vary in their openness to development. But here culture is certainly changeable. His co-editor, the development specialist Lawrence Harrison, pushes that view very explicitly in a later book of his own, with its point of departure in a statement by Daniel Patrick Moynihan: "The central conservative truth is that it is culture, not politics, that determines the success of a society. The central liberal truth is that politics can change a culture and save it from itself." And so Harrison's book is titled *The Central Liberal Truth* (2006). Here, however, the argument is about values; again, the "clash" thesis is about identity. There does not seem to have been much cross-referencing between the debates (although there could have been).

10. I have commented on this and other forms of culturespeak in public use elsewhere (Hannerz 1999).

11. I have earlier discussed the four organizational frames as a conceptual tool primarily in two other publications (Hannerz 1992a, 1996)—see note 15.

12. Again, see the references to the work on the standardization of states by John W. Meyer and associates in Chap. 3, note 25.

13. Much critical scholarship has obviously been devoted to culture in commodity form, not least to popular culture, over the years; from the "Frankfurt School" (see Adorno 1991) at home and in exile from the 1930s on, to the up-to-date, globally oriented overview by Lash and Lury (2007). On advertising and American society, see Schudson (1984).

14. A perspective toward culture as involving conversations, and internal debates, was developed in anthropology by David Parkin (1978), in a study of the Luo people in Kenya; we may be reminded of the Luo-American background of a recent president of the United States.

15. Previously (Hannerz 1992a, 1996) I have used the term "form of life" for this frame, but I was never quite satisfied with it, as it seems more vague in its intended referents. What Appadurai (1996) has termed "ethnoscape," in his noted five-scape scheme accounting for the variety of cultural flows in the contemporary world, may bear a certain resemblance to what I have in mind, but is not so focused on particular kinds of interaction and experience. Some readers may also be reminded of Bourdieu's (e.g. 1977) concept of habitus, but that also seems less focused on particular interactional forms. "Sociality" is a notion which has drawn considerable attention in anthropology in recent times (e.g. Long and Moore 2013), but has been understood in rather varied ways, and does not seem sufficiently clearly bounded analytically vis-à-vis the other frames discussed here to serve our purposes here.

16. "Conviviality" was prominently placed in circulation some forty years ago for entirely different purposes by the anti-industrial futurist visionary Ivan Illich (1973), and the memory of his vision for the world could just possibly linger in some minds. Another prominent user of the term has been Paul Gilroy (2005), who employs it to describe an emergent open, tolerant co-existence in the context of cultural, ethnic and racial diversity.

17. Alfred Schutz (1967: 16) sees the term "consociates" as "equally applicable to an intimate talk between friends and the co-presence of strangers in a railroad car." Clifford Geertz, one anthropologist who has drawn on Schutz, has this to say about this category in social life:

"Consociates" are individuals who actually meet, persons who encounter one another somewhere in the course of daily life. They thus share, however briefly or superficially, not only a community of time but also of space. They are "involved in one another's biography" at least minimally; they "grow older together" at least momentarily, interacting directly and personally as egos, subjects, selves. Lovers, so long as love lasts, are consociates, as are spouses until they separate or friends until they fall out. So also are members of orchestras, players at games, strangers chatting on a train, hagglers in a market, or inhabitants of a village: any set of persons who have an immediate, face-to-face relationship. It is, however, persons having such relations more or less continuously and to some enduring purpose, rather than merely sporadically or incidentally, who form the heart of the category. (Geertz 1973: 365)

Alfred Schutz was surely Schütz in his Austrian early life, but in the phase when he wrote and published in the United States, the umlaut was gone.

18. On "situated learning" and apprenticeship see Lave and Wenger (1991) and Lave (2011).

19. That journal article where Schutz first discussed "consociates" was published in 1953, at a time when there was as yet not a whole lot of sophisticated media research, and when social theorists mostly did not take media into account.

20. For an updated, original-form account of McLuhan's significance, see Coupland (2010).

21. I take the term "screenwork" from the anthropologist Dominic Boyer's *The Life Informatic* (2013) which, with an ethnographic study of contemporary German news journalism as a point of departure, reflects on the overall impact of digital media in contemporary life. Boyer discusses the difference between McLuhan-age one-way media and more recent social media in terms of "radial" and "lateral" messaging; and he touches (2013: xv-xvi) on growing parallels between journalism and academic work (especially anthropology), as discussed briefly here at the end of Chap. 5.

22. On audit culture see Strathern (2000), and on its particular forms in anthropology, Brenneis (2009).

23. But much bureaucratic record-keeping in the world certainly still takes more old-fashioned forms; see for example Gupta's (2012) study of *Red Tape* in India. Timothy Garton Ash has contributed to the literature on state surveillance as well, through the memoir *The File* (1997), describing how the East German Stasi agency kept informed on him in the late Communist period.

24. In 2014 a Beirut-based correspondent for the *Financial Times* could report that when the troops of the Islamic State movement made camp, on their murderous advance through Iraq and Syria, there was a rising demand for Red Bull, the energy drink, for Bounty and Snickers candy bars, and for Pringles potato crisps (Solomon 2014). So perhaps with another variation, retrieving Mitchell's (2002) term: "McJihadis of the world unite, we have everything you crave in our chains!"

25. We could note that in *Jihad vs. McWorld*, Barber (1996) touches on a contest between market and consociality in a passage like this: "Long-lunch traditions obstruct the development of fast-food franchises and successful fast-food franchises inevitably undermine Mediterranean home-at-noon-for-dinner rituals—whether intentionally or not hardly matters."

In a later book, *If Mayors Ruled the World* (2013) too, the focus is on one level of organization within the state frame—but then we know that the relationship between big cities and the more comprehensive state level is often an ambiguous one.

CHAPTER 7

Culture: Between XL and S

In the midst of the "Arab Spring" of 2011, *New York Times* columnist David Brooks made one more revisit to the debate over Samuel Huntington's "clash of civilizations" thesis. Huntington, "one of America's greatest political scientists," Brooks suggested, had been "wrong in the way he defined culture." The aspirations of the people assembling at Tahrir Square, Cairo, were those of people everywhere, for human rights and liberty.

"In some ways, each of us is like every person on earth," argued Brooks (2011), "in some ways, each of us is like the members of our culture and group; in some ways, each of us is unique." That happens to be a formulation entirely parallel to a classic sentence by a prominent American mid-century anthropologist (Clyde Kluckhohn, mentioned briefly in Chap. 6).[1] Perhaps the point is actually so obvious that it has been made by any number of people at different times? But then Brooks, like Huntington, and no doubt a great many other people, links "culture" primarily to the middle category, where you are like some people, and different from others. Yet culture is not necessarily packaged that way anymore (if it ever was). If we proceed with the understanding of culture proposed in the preceding chapter, as the property of *Homo sapiens* as a learning animal, it is not by definition limited to such group-wise distribution within the species. It is conceivable that there is culture in some way or other acquired by all human beings. It is also possible that one human being can pick up meanings and meaningful forms which, at least in that individual's combination and handling of them, is quite unique. Culture can come in all sizes, between XL and S. This chapter, zigzagging between scenario writers, the sort of recent events they comment on, and certain classic ideas out of anthropology and sociology, may offer some sense of what a view of the present-day world in cultural terms may be like.

At the time when Kluckhohn wrote, what all human beings shared may have been expected to derive more or less directly from the givens of their biology. For Brooks, the claim came naturally that they all want liberty and human rights. By now, too, one view of globalization would tell us that cultural sharing is in large part a consequence of world interconnectedness generally, and the power of market forces especially. In an early column, Thomas Friedman (1998) reports on an interview with an elderly ex-prime minister of India, who talks about his four-year old granddaughter. She prefers Coke over Pepsi, and wants her pizza not home-made but from Pizza Hut. So in the era of cultural homogeneity, everywhere will be the same: "you won't be able to leave home again," says Friedman.

This, of course, is a McWorld story. I should say that I doubt brands like these are the best examples of what people everywhere have come to share through cultural diffusion. I would think it is more a matter of mundane things which by now they take for granted. In the late twentieth century, the examples I once used were matches, pencils and soap. At this point, with technological development rushing ahead, I might already be less sure of two of these. Perhaps t-shirts and cellphones now, or soon?

The Global Ecumene: A Cultural History of Openness and Flows

Anyway, there is much to be said about culture in relation to global interconnectedness, as it is in the twenty-first century, and also as it has been in the past. The geocultural map is not entirely unrelated to the geopolitical, but it is not the same. States today may operate significant cultural machineries, and hold on to power and material assets, but in the sense of nations, countries, they are not the kind of prime natural units, effective cultural containers, that they have sometimes been taken to be—even when language diversity in many regions, as in Europe, remains an obstacle to real transparency between them. This map has its own shifting flows as well as changing, and sometimes vanishing, borders. And clusters of meanings and meaningful forms of different sizes between XL and S continuously co-exist and combine in various ways.

For a moment, let us take note of an earlier commentator on world culture. In Chap. 3, starting out from Garreau's *Nine Nations of North America*, I compared the vision of that book with the effort of early twentieth-century anthropologists in the United States to map, in large part retrospectively, the culture areas of Native Americans. One of the major architects of that endeavor was Alfred Kroeber, long-term professor at the University of California, Berkeley.[2] But Kroeber had a wider range of research interests than that. Indeed, he was also concerned with The Big Picture. In *The Clash of Civilizations and the Remaking of World Order*, Samuel Huntington (1996: 40) lists him among the prominent scholars contributing to the comparative analysis of civilizations—although he then occurs only cursorily in two endnotes, and nowhere in the text of the book.

Early in 1946, Kroeber and his wife Theodora (who would become his biographer) crossed the Atlantic, on board the *Queen Mary*, back in service as a passenger ship, recently released from war duty. In London, Kroeber would give the slightly delayed 1945 Huxley Lecture at the Royal Anthropological Institute, under the title "The Ancient Oikoumene as a Historic Culture Aggregate." The Oikoumene was the name the Greeks of antiquity had given to what was to them the inhabited world. Kroeber now returned to it, to offer a selective cultural portrait of that world—much of Europe and Asia—as it had been, and to go beyond it with certain quick excursions to parts that the ancient Greeks knew nothing about (but which had connections to the Empire he was just visiting). A certain preoccupation with the minutiae of cultural history made him dwell on an assortment of topics which might by now seem rather surprising, and a bit weird: the wide distribution of cavalry, money, chess, eunuchism, astrology, printing, and more. Yet his principal point was that he identified the ultimate natural unit for his discipline as "the culture of all humanity at all periods and in all places." If we stick to that now, we see that the twenty-first century ecumene (as the term would become in an updated spelling) is larger than the ancient Greek one—it is a global ecumene, definitely culture of size XL.[3]

It seems to have been the right time for Alfred Kroeber to take an expansive view of things. His journey on the *Queen Mary* signified the postwar return of transatlantic academic travel. The immediate period after World War II could in fact remind us of that post-Cold War period when our global scenarios started appearing: a time when great-power Fascism was destroyed for the foreseeable future, when one could start thinking about another, improved world—without at least That Ideology. It was a time that would supposedly see the end of empires, and the recognition of human rights, and it had a new and inclusive organization labeled the United Nations. But then, soon enough, another major cleavage seemed to emerge as a threat to any new consensus. It has been claimed that when Samuel Huntington launched his "clash of civilizations" thesis, in 1993, he intended it as a dominant prophetic statement, a candidate to succeed the political scientist-historian-diplomat George Kennan's "Long Telegram" from Moscow in 1946, heralding the coming of the Cold War.

Yet for Kroeber at mid-century, it was time to think about the ecumene, and while his inclination to attend to the facts was probably always stronger than any urge to be in step with the times, one might sense that as he turned to the topic of civilizations, there was again an acknowledgment of openness and change. In his severe critique of Oswald Spengler, early twentieth-century civilization scenarist, Kroeber (1952: 154) pointed for one thing to a neglect of "the interflow of cultural material between civilizations." Elsewhere (1952: 404), he cautioned that one should examine civilizations "not as static objects but as limited processes of flow in time."

In terms of our Chap. 3 contrast between border thinking with flow thinking, these brief quotes clearly identify Alfred Kroeber as a flow man (although one who uses "flow" in two senses, in time as well as space). The point with regard to time is that culture is always in process, whether the process is one of repetition and continuity or one of change. But continuity cannot be taken for granted; processes can be interrupted, or grind to a halt.

By the most recent turn of century, "flow" had indeed made a new appearance in social and cultural thought as a kind of proto-theoretical metaphor, now referring primarily to spatial changes going with globalization. And there has been some debate about it.[4] Some have objected that it may make cultural process seem too easy, too smooth. I would rather think that it works well as a root metaphor, in the way it sensitizes to more diversity, leading on to further elaborations. Not all flow is of the same kind: there can be mighty rivers and tiny rivulets, separate currents as well as confluences, even leaks and viscosity in the flow of meaning.

Anyhow, with Alfred Kroeber and his dimensions of flow, we seem to be a long way from a view of civilizations as bounded units in the *longue durée*. Kroeber's listing of civilizations is also very different from Samuel Huntington's. For one thing, as a cultural historian working with a wide time frame, he identifies many more of them; civilizations, more-or-less-civilizations, aborted civilizations; temporary successes or eventual failures. I cannot resist citing his view of early Scandinavian ("Norse," or Viking) civilization: its "notable achievement of a highly wrought form in the single cultural field of poetry—in addition to war, pillage, and government—is strangely reminiscent of the pre-Islamic Arabs" (Kroeber 1962: 42). So that may seem like another civilization with "bloody borders."[5] And if the view of Olof Rudbeck the Elder, as described in the Prologue, tended to suggest a great deal of soft power on the part of ancient Scandinavians, Kroeber´s emphasis is rather the opposite. As for Islam, it is true that his view of it was also notably harsh, at least for the period nearest after the appearance of the Prophet, at the outskirts of that old Oikoumene.

Bringing thinking about civilizations closer to the present: when the well-known world historian William McNeill (also on Huntington's list of sources for thinking about civilizations) reviews *The Clash of Civilizations and the Remaking of World Order*, one may again be reminded of Kroeber.[6] McNeill argues that Huntington exaggerates homogeneity and boundedness, and finds yet more flows:

> civilizations are themselves diverse, with innumerable internal fissures and resulting frictions. Moreover, all human groups have to deal with strangers and outsiders, and across the millennia such dealings have become more and more pervasive and important. The flows between civilizations of information, goods, and services have increased precipitously in recent decades; and the innumerable human encounters that result, whether they are personal or only electronic, leave their mark on literally everyone today. (McNeill 1997: 20–21)

That view may be close enough to Amartya Sen's complaint, referred to in Chap. 3, about the bias of "civilizational confinement."

Alfred Kroeber died in a Paris hotel in the summer of 1960, eighty-four years old, on his way back from attending a scholarly conference he had organized, on the "horizons of anthropology." (When one of the participants had been curious enough to ask him about the unusual combination of invitees, Kroeber responded that they were all mavericks.) On the Berkeley campus, the present home of the university's anthropology department is named after him: Kroeber Hall. He left behind over 700 scholarly publications, and had probably spent some thirty years on his studies of civilizations. Another manuscript on the theme was published posthumously (Kroeber 1962), with an introductory note by Charles Le

Guin...Le Guin? A history professor, and also Kroeber's son-in-law—Ursula Le Guin, well-known pioneer science fiction author, is Kroeber's daughter. In the introduction to that book, Kroeber continued his critique of those earlier commentators on civilizations and empires—Gibbon, Toynbee, and again Spengler—whose views of the fate of such entities were dramatically declinist:

> That we shall shortly return to barbarism and anarchy is exciting news if true; but too much such preoccupation with the future, or how it can be saved, is calculated to disturb our understanding of the past and the present. (Kroeber 1962: 16)

We may remember that Gibbon's *History of the Decline and Fall of the Roman Empire* was among Robert Kaplan's favored readings as he contemplated the coming anarchy, and that Niall Ferguson referred to it as he reflected on the coming of Eurabia. Spengler and Toynbee, again, were also among Huntington's varied sources for his clash of civilizations argument, drawn upon occasionally but in any case cited more often than Kroeber. And Kroeber evidently felt that their work had an Orwellian, *1984*-ish twist: to control the future they corrupted the past.

What might be the reason to remember Alfred Kroeber now? One could perhaps be tempted to see Kroeber as an anti-Huntington, in his views of civilizations (and the time he spent studying them), future scenarios, and the public role of scholarship. Had there been a *Prospect/Foreign Policy* list of global public intellectuals in his time, Kroeber would hardly have been on it. An anthropologist of a later generation concluded that there was throughout Kroeber's writings "a strong sense of distaste for anything that had to do with politics, with involvement in nonscience, and I think also with sociology—all those enterprises that had to do, he thought, with trying to improve the world." (Wolf 1981: 49)

Most strikingly, however, there is his insight into the continuous openness and flux within the global ecumene; and his critical view of the facile formulations of some of those writers who had come up with Big Pictures before him. These contributions of his we may still find instructive. The global ecumene is not a "cultural mosaic" of clearly bounded pieces. Within it, culture may in principle get from anywhere to anywhere, depending on the movements of people and things, and on media flows through space.

Yet in some other ways his concerns are not now quite ours. Kroeber was not particularly interested in culture as meaning, as we are here, but rather in the externality of cultural forms which could be described, classified, and perhaps counted. This could have had a source in an early boyhood interest in natural history, where something like this had been the way to approach animals and plants.[7] It could be, too, that scholarly habits established in those extensive mappings of the traits of vanishing American Indian cultures continued to point in such directions.

Notably, there is also that distancing from sociology. Here, it seems, was one border that Kroeber guarded, rather more than he should have done. The reasons seem complex, probably having to do with personal background as well as features of the American academic scene in his days. But the terms of the divorce were unfortunate. If culture involves an "organization of diversity," as we see things here, you should not just leave organization out. A stronger, continuous sense of the social ordering of cultural openness and interconnectedness in the ecumene might have been helpful. Kroeber's Big Picture of world cultural history remains rather pointillist.

And then it seems he left the writing of imagined futures to his daughter, to be pursued in fiction in a more radical way. (As it happens, in certain of Ursula Le Guin's novels, a galactic civilization is served by an organization named the Ekumen.)

DAVOS CULTURE

We will leave Alfred Kroeber there, for the time being, and return to Samuel Huntington's view of the contemporary world. In *The Clash of Civilizations and the Remaking of World Order* and in the later *Who Are We?*, he warns his readers of the influence of Muslims and Hispanic-Americans—but there are also the intellectual adversaries which he finds in a way more close at hand. They are the people who somehow identify more with something global than with their nation, or their particular civilization. Among them are prominent intellectuals who proclaim that there is now such a thing as a "world civilization." For Huntington this is only Western cultural dominance in disguise, an updated version of "the white man's burden." When we find that this sort of view is held even by people domiciled in North America or Western Europe, but with roots elsewhere—like the author V.S. Naipaul, or the political scientist Fouad

Ajami—Huntington (1996: 66) rather unkindly cites, with approval, one Arab intellectual's epithet for such people: "White man's nigger."

Then Huntington also identifies as an eighteenth-century version of "universal civilization" those things civilized societies have in common, such as cities and literacy, which distinguish them from primitive societies and barbarians—"in this sense a universal civilization is emerging, much to the horror of various anthropologists and others who view with dismay the disappearance of primitive peoples." (Huntington 1996: 57) One senses here that his acquaintance with one discipline present on the Harvard campus, although across an intellectual fence, is about as close and up-to-date as a later reviewer found his contacts with the Hispanic-Americans—see Chap. 4.[8]

Most concretely, however, he finds his adversaries among the people assembling each January at a certain resort in the Alps:

> Each year about a thousand businessmen, bankers, government officials, intellectuals, and journalists from scores of countries meet in the World Economic Forum in Davos, Switzerland. All these people hold university degrees in the physical sciences, social sciences, business, or law, work with words and/or numbers, are reasonably fluent in English, are employed by governments, corporations, and academic institutions with extensive international involvements, and travel frequently outside their own country. (Huntington 1996: 57)

This is "Davos Culture," personified as "Davos Man." In *Who Are We?*, a decade or so later, they reappear also under such labels as "gold-collar workers" and "cosmocrats" (Huntington 2004: 268), still supposedly not reliable patriots of any country.

There is a vivid, gently satirical, closeup portrayal of Davos Culture as it was about the time when Huntington first identified it, in a short book by the prominent American publicist Lewis Lapham (1998), one-time *Harper's Magazine* editor.[9] Lapham describes the journey up the mountain, the gathering spots, the pecking order (different-color name tags for real participants and mere observers), speeches, conversations sometimes serious and sometimes inane, and an interview with Klaus Schwab (the Geneva economics professor who invented it all). Moreover, as an appendix, Lapham provides an incomplete list of participants at the 1998 Forum—a few hundred of them, including Bill Gates, George Soros, Archbishop Desmond Tutu, Speaker Newt Gingrich (advocating a "Pax Humana"), Prime Minister Viktor Chernomyrdin, Nobel Peace

Prize winner Elie Wiesel (commenting that "Nowhere else will you find a conference at which so many captains of industry are speaking about the soul"), Moroccan sociologist Fatima Mernissi, and...Robert Kaplan. Plus some twenty "scientists, mystics, and technoprophets."

Lapham's report suggests that there is a sort of intriguing culture-organizational hybrid here: new interconnectedness and debate, and with Klaus Schwab as cultural broker. Statesmen are in Davos enacting what states normally do in international relations, but very likely they are also in the market frame, selling and advertising their countries (see more about nation-branding in the next chapter). Businesspeople are no doubt also there engaged in marketing, with very select customers. So are various kinds of gurus, with their own enterprises and merchandise. And then in the end, if there is anything to Huntington's point of view, it all crosses into the movement frame, in a manner subversive of national boundaries and loyalties.

By now perhaps Davos Culture, at least as a local phenomenon, may be a success story, and also the victim of its own success. That temporary assemblage coming together in the Alpine town has continued to grow and grow, and has recently been estimated to draw some 2,500 participants. CNN is there with a cast or five or six star reporters and analysts; other media as well. But growing security concerns have turned the town, it is said, into "a virtual military protectorate." And one may guess that an increasing proportion are Davos wannabes, their lowly status again signaled by the colors of their name tags. Some of the publicity is dubious: the World Economic Forum is depicted as a site of conspicuous consumption. It has also gone multi-site, holding more conferences in other places than Davos. In between gatherings, too, the World Economic Forum also goes on with its work in a think tank mode.

Moreover, there are now a growing number of rival meeting places, scattered over the world. No Very Important Person would have time to go to them all. In the early years of the twenty-first century, too, a World Social Forum, with the motto "Another World is Possible," gained prominence as an annual meeting place for a variety of NGOs, social movements, and other grassroots activists. It was clearly intended as a left alternative to mostly neoliberal Davos; yet with time the boundary between them seemed to become just a bit blurred, and the alternative showed some internal contradictions.

In any case, of course, the point is that Davos Culture is not just a local phenomenon. If identifiable at all, it involves a loose, shifting network of people of some kind of elite status, open to a vaguely demarcated set of meanings and meaningful forms, marked by global center-periphery relationships, but with an intense annual event of cultural repackaging.

In *Who Are We?*, meanwhile, Huntington (2004: 362–366) ends up finding another set of labels to distinguish three alternative American views of how to relate to the world. The cosmopolitan point of view promotes open borders, multiculturalism, diasporas—the world reshapes America. In the imperial alternative, America remakes the world. American power is used to spread American values. As civilizational thinker, Huntington sees this as a matter of underestimating other people's attachment to their own ways. The third alternative, which is his own, is nationalist, and we have already seen in Chap. 4 where that takes him.

Of these three, it would seem to be the advocates of the cosmopolitan viewpoint who most nearly belong in "Davos Culture"—also known as "cosmocrats." "Cosmopolitanism," however, if we take it away from Samuel Huntington, is a complicated notion, relating to that interconnected whole world in more than one single way.

Three Faces of Cosmopolitanism

I have had my own experience in dealing with that notion. It began when I was giving a seminar talk at the University of California, Berkeley—in Kroeber Hall, but a quarter-century after Kroeber—on globalization, and a local colleague asked if I had thought about cosmopolitanism. I had to answer that mostly I had not. At the time, in the mid-1980s, this was not a concept with great academic visibility. But I sensed immediately it was something I ought to attend to.

Then soon afterwards, I had a deadline for organizing my ideas about it. I received an invitation to "The First International Conference on the Olympics and East/West and South/North Cultural Exchanges in the World System"—the title might seem unusual, but it was to take place in 1987 in Seoul, Korea, and it was one of a variety of events foreshadowing the Olympic Games to be held there the following year.

The paper I wrote was again armchair anthropology. It drew freely on readings of fiction and non-fiction, newspaper clippings, and some semi-classic and recent social theory.[10] My main point was that cosmopolitanism was an expansive mode of managing culture, searching for new experience, appreciating cultural diversity. Increasing global interconnections offered new opportunities for this, not least through travel. But then I also went to some effort to show that not all geographical mobility in the world was intended to seek new opportunities for cultural experience. Scandinavian tourists escaping winter at home for a week or two may just want sun and beaches, not so much fresh cultural experience. Migrant laborers are probably just looking for a livelihood. Refugees and exiles fleeing from oppression may only want to survive.

If members of such groups value the encounter with a new cultural habitat, fine—but one cannot take that for granted. The classic understanding of travel in the search of cosmopolitan experiences has been that it is a privilege which tends to go with other privileges. I pointed to the growth of a transnational occupational life where the pursuit of cosmopolitanism could be more a matter of choice, and where there might be a basic intellectual/esthetic expansive stance which could go with cosmopolitanism. Yet it is certainly also possible to use privilege to shut new experiences out.

This paper of mine was thus about cosmopolitanism as a matter of cultural outreach, of appreciating diversity to a degree for its own sake. In part this was simply because it was done for a conference about cultural exchange. Yet looking back, I could see that it also had to do with time and place—that conference was held in South Korea, at a certain time in history.

Among the participants were a few from Eastern Europe, and a sports sociologist from the Soviet Union. This was very remarkable, as the contacts between that country and South Korea were minimal at the time. Consequently our Soviet colleague, and actually our entire group, were closely watched. When we toured the country by bus after the conference was over we had a police car ahead of us, a blue light whirling on its roof. And when our Soviet colleague went for a walk by himself on a tiny road, he was surrounded at a discreet distance by plainclothes detectives with walkie-talkies.

This was still the epoch of the Cold War.

So under the circumstances, I had talked to the conference about one kind of cosmopolitanism, one of the faces of cosmopolitanism. This was the happy face of cosmopolitanism, of the pleasure of new cultural experiences from what is thought of as other cultures, other parts of the world— perhaps often in literature, art, music, food, drink, sometimes in travel (Fig. 7.1).

But then a couple of years later, when that Cold War came to an end (the fact which also led to the first wave of our global scenarios), another sense of "cosmopolitanism" could draw attention, in thought and debate, in a way it had not done for some time. Again, in that world without the

Wall and the Iron Curtain, it seemed more likely that borders could be crossed; here was "the world as a single place."[11]And so cosmopolitans could be people with particular moral and political principles, concerned with the needs and desires of humanity as a whole. They were world citizens. Perhaps one could still show a happy face if there were now better prospects for dealing with those needs and desires in a spirit of togetherness. Yet it was also becoming more obvious than before that there were a number of more or less urgent problems which also crossed borders, and which could not be handled on a national basis: global warming, world poverty and hunger, the spread of nuclear arms, trafficking, terrorism. So confronting these, a somber face was in order (Fig. 7.2).

If the term "globalization" had to a remarkable extent been appropriated to refer to the deregulation and expansion of markets, a more civic version of cosmopolitanism could suggest that human beings could relate to the world not only as consumers, or members of a labor force. In this sense cosmopolitanism could become a critique of at least certain qualities of global capitalism, as well as a search for ways of constraining it.

Yet somber-face cosmopolitanism had more varieties, and turned up in more sites. In Academia, the focus on ethics and politics became the more conspicuous understanding of cosmopolitanism in a number of

Fig. 7.1.   Happy-face cosmopolitanism

Fig. 7.2.   Somber-face cosmopolitanism

disciplines, such as in political philosophy and sociology. A concept of a "public sphere," for discussion of society's affairs, had thus far been debated mostly within national contexts. Now questions turned to how it could be transnationalized.[12] Here one could also return to early thinking: back to the Stoics of Greek antiquity, and to Immanuel Kant's *Perpetual Peace*. But there was a revived debate, too, over a split between cosmopolitanism and patriotism.[13] Huntington, of course, emphasized such a split, particularly in *Who Are We?* Yet it is an idea which has shown up in various contexts in history. Cosmopolitans, supposedly, cannot be trusted to be loyal with their own country—they are "rootless." In Russia, in the days of Empire as well as those of the Soviet phase, a "rootless cosmopolitan" was frequently the epithet for a Jew; we get back to that in Chap. 9.

Still in Academia, this conflict could be resolved by recognizing a middle road, that of the "rooted cosmopolitan." It was entirely possible, argued the philosopher Kwame Anthony Appiah (1996), to find satisfaction in one's own country and its way of life, and yet appreciate the diversity assembled as others made their own choices. Appiah could speak with some personal authority here: he was an American academic, but he had been born and had grown up in what is now Ghana, with a West African father and a British mother (and a grandfather who had been a prominent minister in the British cabinet after World War II). It was especially his father, politically prominent at the time of the Ghanaian struggle for independence in the 1950s, who had impressed on his children the fact that one could be a patriot and a citizen of the world, too. And for members of the Appiah family, it became a fact of life that you could develop roots in more than one country.

Quite probably it is actually easier to be a cosmopolitan, with both a happy and a somber face, if you are rooted than if you are rootless—if you know that there is one milieu, or even more, where you can always feel at ease, competent, accepted, secure. Those who are forced into exile, or whose home countries are in chaos, might find it more difficult to embrace the entire membership of the species *Homo sapiens*, and the diversity of the world.

Cosmopolitanism in the political and moral sense, in any case, did not only find a place in scholarly arguments. In the post-Cold War period, it also developed more noticeable forms in politics itself. There were what we may see as bottom-up varieties, in more or less grassroots commitments, often concerned with more specific issues and areas—such as gender rights issues, environmentalism, freedom of speech—although these preoccupations could be seen to converge into a more general sense of interconnectedness in a "global civil society."[14] The activists at the World Social Forum, with their vision that "Another World is Possible," belonged here. But there were also top-down cosmopolitanisms, cultivated by at least some statesmen and politicians, perhaps under a rubric of "global governance" (less provocative than "global government"). Such ideas could find a place in Davos Culture, although not always in the same corner of it, as they also could be located at different points on a left-right scale.[15]

The organizational and intellectual engagements of moral, civic, political cosmopolitanism are still with us, but it seems not with the same intensity as in the 1990s. With the early twenty-first century influence of Osama bin Laden, George W. Bush and Vladimir Putin, the vision of a borderless world could only suffer.

What might be the affinity, if any, between cosmopolitanisms of happy and somber faces? Are these merely different kinds of sentiments which, through a certain weakness of western languages, have come to share the same label? It may well be possible to be a cosmopolitan in one way but not the other. Yet one might hope that the enjoyment of the riches of world culture, the sense that people from everywhere contribute to it, can also be a resource when one has to show the worried face; that it gives people some of the strength needed to confront the challenges of the troubles of the world, and some sympathy for fellow human beings even when they are far away.

No doubt the media, in that early sense of Marshall McLuhan's "global village," have contributed importantly—if not altogether unambiguously—to the growth of both these kinds of cosmopolitanism from the late twentieth century onwards. It is in no small part through the media that people can now gain access to much of the cultural diversity of the world, experiencing it and enjoying it: literature, art, music, dance or whatever. By way of the television screen, in large part through feature programs, they can enter other peoples' temples, gardens, and kitchens. But it is also through the media that they can follow what happens far away, be moved by what happens to their fellow human beings, reflect on their own commitments as citizens of the world. World watching through the media, and now mostly through news programs, they can respond to famines, earthquakes, tsunamis, planes flying into skyscrapers, civil wars, and what may or may not technically qualify as genocides.

I have once termed one variety of such responses "electronic empathy"; the kind occasionally mobilized by the stars of the entertainment world, and perhaps of politics, in giant relief efforts: "We Are the World." But it also appears that people can react differently, or simply not react, to the experience of such remote disasters. Another recently circulating term has been "compassion fatigue" (Moeller 1999). Too much bad news from the world out there may become more than one is ready to handle. When I studied the work of newsmedia foreign correspondents, and talked to a great many people in the international news business, I became aware that at least some journalists and editors were concerned that reporting on conflicts and disasters abroad could even make their readers, listeners, and viewers more defensive, more insecure, more hostile to what was outside the borders. It could offer materials for neo-nationalism and xenophobia.

Recognizing two faces, we may already sense that we are dealing with a concept which should more often be used in the plural form: cosmopolitan-isms. Yet even if the happy face and the somber face are those who tend to draw most attention and comment, we should be aware that there is also a third face: I would call it "cosmopolitan with a straight face." (Fig. 7.3)

This is a matter of simply managing cultural diversity as a fact of life, coping with it without seeking it out, mostly without attaching particular value to it. Straight-face cosmopolitanism is now quite widespread in the world. I touched on it in Chap. 4, as a characteristic of my one-time home city Malmö and of much of contemporary Europe; certainly it is widespread in North America and various other regions as well. Migrants may tend to become straight-face cosmopolitans, but in the present-day world we do not have to travel to experience diversity, because it tends to come to us, in our work places and neighborhoods—and "you gotta deal with it." It is, of course, a variety of cosmopolitanism particularly likely to appear in big cities, drawing people of many different backgrounds, from many places.[16] In large part it involves mere tolerance, combined with a certain confidence in one's skill in handling diversity as a feature of continuous social traffic. At times

Fig. 7.3.   Straight-face cosmopolitanism

one may discern a certain instrumental value in for example such features of social life as a functioning ethnic division of labor, or multilingual skills, without attaching value to differences for their own sake.

Not all contemporary urban environments, it should be understood, work equally well in breeding this kind of cosmopolitanism. Some become habitats of fear and distrust, ethnic conflict, and defended, bounded turfs. Others work better as learning environments, offering not least what Elijah Anderson (2011), urban sociologist, has identified as "cosmopolitan canopies," local settings where people can mingle and relaxedly observe each other, building up capabilities and a measure of trust—where it might even become easier to take the step from straight-face to happy-face cosmopolitanism.

Summing up, we find that cosmopolitanisms come in different sizes. However much of the global cultural inventory it may relate to, the happy-face, cultural-experiential variety operates often in an individualized version of cultural connoisseurship; or it may bring a small group together to cultivate and celebrate it. The political-civic version may be XL at least in the sense of its ambition to reach out, and may involve organizational forms of varying scope. Straight-faced cosmopolitanism often operates at a more or less local level, not intentionally extending very far in space. But there may be other variations here as well.

Moreover, the three faces of cosmopolitanism tend to have special affinities with different organizational frames, as we encountered them in Chap. 6. The happy face involves preferences in cultural consumption, going in large part with the market. And when diversity is valued, it suggests that a homogenizing "McWorld" is not so entirely dominant in this frame. When tourism and other travel also goes with a happy face, it may involve glimpses of other people's consociality—but also perhaps a commoditization of the latter. The somber face of cosmopolitanism, gazing at the world's problems, is a meeting place of state and movements: top-down cosmopolitanism or bottom-up cosmopolitanism. And straight-face cosmopolitanism, handling nearby diversity practically as one of the facts of life, is in large part a matter of consociality.

THE GLOBAL VILLAGE 2.0: THE SQUARE PEOPLE

Back to Tahrir Square, Cairo. David Brooks took the 2011 scene, symbolic key site of the Arab Spring, as an expression of universal human aspirations. Three years later, we already noted, his *New York Times* columnist colleague Thomas Friedman (2014e, 2014f) contextualized that and a series of similar events rather more specifically in a two-part commentary: "We have seen them now in the squares of Tunis, Cairo, Istanbul, New Delhi, Damascus, Tripoli, Beirut, Sana, Tehran, Moscow, Rio, Tel Aviv and Kiev..." They were "the Square People." Perhaps Friedman's intent would be lost in some translations. In any case, these are not what we would usually mean by "street people": they are newly connected middle classes, "mostly young, aspiring to a higher standard of living, seeking either reform or revolution (depending on their existing government), connected to one another by massing in squares or through virtual squares or both, and united less by a common program and more by a shared direction they want their societies to go."[17]

If the world were really flat, Friedman might possibly have seen as far as the 1999 protests at the meeting of the World Trade Organization in Seattle as well, and he only gets to the 2011 Occupy Wall Street movement on Manhattan as he considers the difficulties such emergent groupings confront. One might see parallels with these, too, although their adversaries were not of the same kind. Later yet, a few months after Friedman had his columns on the Square People, there was again a similar development in Hong Kong, with Occupy Central, "the umbrella movement" (using umbrellas as a protection against the pepper spray of the police).

Certainly the world has seen protest gatherings in public places before— that at the Bastille in Paris in 1789 may remain at the top of any ranking list. In Beijing, exactly two hundred years later, the Tiananmen Square People did not have Internet, but the fax was the new technology that made some difference, and apart from that another, more localized means of written communication, part of a Chinese heritage: wall posters.[18] Yet recently the Square People have seemed to show up with increasing frequency, and in many places—those Friedman listed were in four continents. So, he suggests, "a new global force is aborning."

Perhaps in a way, and in a way not. One could still see these diverse groupings as more or less local, emerging out of consociality in protest against repressive and mostly corrupt state machineries which are near at hand. They may not be so directly globally connected in stricter organizational terms, but often enough they are globally or at least transnationally inspired, by examples set in other places, across a border or far away. There is a clear linkage between the Square People at Tahrir Square and that desperate hawker who not long before had set himself afire in a small town in Tunisia.

In part these linkages are created through older-style media: television, radio, even print. Yet what is new is to a degree that growth of an aspiring but dissatisfied youngish middle class, and definitely the technologically updated mode of consociality. These, as Thomas Friedman points out, are people of Internet, cellphones, Facebook and Twitter. That is how they can so readily get together at real public squares or virtual squares.

So, says Friedman, with a reference to Samuel Huntington's writing a decade earlier, "Move over Davos Man, the Square People are coming."

Possibly another forecast one might sympathize with, but which needs some more consideration. Coming straight out of loosely organized consociality to the Square, these phenomena may be materials for—following Fernand Braudel, as we drew on him in Chap. 5—"event history." Perhaps a kind of instant culture, size M. But at this point, they risk being the sort of meaningful events which academics have tended to classify as "collective behavior": short-lived, perhaps getting their fifteen minutes of fame in world history. Concealing too much internal diversity, they could go nowhere or into chaos, failing to make it from agitated consociality to a movement. The interface between cyberspace and the "real" world of bodies and of physical and material power remains critical. Here Friedman indeed notes that the crucial question is whether they can go "from *disruption* to *construction*," referring at this stage to New York's Occupy Wall Street as one which could not. Another alternative, of course, is that what the Square People began is hijacked—by some preexisting organization, doing its own construction work.

Anyway, whatever is the future of the Square People, we could now note that their arrival was not foreseen in the early batch of global scenarios. They were not seen between the stampede of the Electronic Herd and the ambiguous traditionalism of the Olive Tree, and certainly not between the clashing civilizations; they were not part of the coming anarchy; and there would have been no need for them after the end of history. The scenarist who may have come closest was perhaps Benjamin Barber, with his plea for civil society. But then the entire coming role of the interpersonal media, the "Global Village 2.0," was not really expected in these scenarios either.

Culture in Corners

One of my favorite formulations about cultural process is from a well-known mid-twentieth century sociologist, Everett Hughes: "whenever some group of people have a bit of common life with a modicum of isolation from other people, a common corner in society, common problems and perhaps a couple of common enemies, there culture grows." (Hughes 1961: 28)

That says a great deal about the self-organization of diversity in social life—and yet it needs some scrutiny. Typically that corner in society is some site within the frame of consociality, where people get together over some kind of shared concerns. To describe these as "problems" may narrow the possibilities too quickly: they may just have shared interests, or goals, or some other kinds of ideas or experiences. Indeed, common enemies may or may not be there.

But what is "a common corner," "a modicum of isolation"? Very often this kind of viewpoint toward cultural organization has been applied to what the social sciences have described as "subcultures," a slightly treacherous term insofar as people not so involved in the relevant academic fields risk misunderstanding that prefix "sub." It could be taken to mean that the cultural entities in question are substandard...or subordinate... or subversive?

No, this is not what the term means—with an analogy from natural history, "subculture" is to "culture" as "subspecies" is to "species." It is a section within a larger unit, a part within some whole. And so in sociology and anthropology the label has been classically applied to such entities as youth cultures, or occupational cultures (Everett Hughes' formulation comes from a study of medical students), or ethnic minority cultures, or life styles.

What, however, would then that larger unit be, the "whole"? In an era before ours, it would most likely be assumed to involve a "society," which in its turn would be understood to be a nation, a country—a territory and a population with supposedly clear borders. And then quite possibly, the subculture with its peculiarities could be contrasted with what would be described as "mainstream culture," a construct loosely referring to what was shared by a majority, not needing much attention in itself but somehow taken for granted as a standard.

One could sense that there is some conception of such a mainstream in notions referred to in Chap. 4: Samuel Huntington's Anglo-Protestant tradition in the United States, or the German *Leitkultur*. The problem, however, tends to be that on closer inspection, that mainstream itself fragments along various lines, to display gender differences, generational differences, urban-rural differences, class differences... So perhaps it serves best as a useful contrastive fiction.

What is perhaps more important for our purposes here, in any case, may be that the corners in question are often not so local any longer. They are not necessarily sites in physical space, but corners in that Global Village 2.0, with updated forms of consociality—somehow coming together in interaction over shared meanings. So Davos culture, for one, becomes a subculture within the global ecumene.

And there are others. They may not be entirely contained within the frame of consociality, but can involve entanglements with other frames as well. Often enough, under current conditions of diversified large-scale and small-scale media channels, and easy travel, they come together as groups of consumers, of cultural forms from the market frame. In such instances especially, subcultures are also often described as "scenes."

Return to that Arab Spring again: the closest to a forecast of that multi-site complex of events I came across was in a lecture I heard, about a half-year earlier at a conference in Vienna, by Mark LeVine, an American specialist in the contemporary history of the Arab World (what he continuously refers to as MENA, the Middle East & North Africa)—but also a rock guitarist. In the fall of 2010, LeVine could describe his contacts with other musicians, whom he would seek out and play with wherever he traveled in the region, and his experience at live concerts drawing audiences from far and wide; audiences in veils, blue jeans, and sneakers. These people shared a taste for the tunes and texts of hard rock, in forms which blended global inspirations with local musical traditions. Moreover, the political sentiments in these mostly youthful audiences, LeVine found, were oppositional to the regimes in power. He compared the situation to that in Central Europe in the late 1980s, before the crumbling of the Iron Curtain. So these were young men and women who would, the following year and beyond, make up one portion of the Square People. Tahrir Square and such places became their new scene. A proto-movement drew its cultural strength in considerable part by followers standing shoulder to shoulder as popular culture consumers—and again, the culture consumed was not entirely of a McWorld variety, but more hybrid.[19]

Before the conference lecture I heard in 2010, LeVine had already approached his vision of what might happen next in the book *Heavy Metal Islam* (2008). It has seemed to me that there is a parallel between his personal immersion in the MENA musical scene and that of another contemporary historian, Timothy Garton Ash, in the oppositional intellectual circles of Central Europe twenty years or so earlier. LeVine has not reached an equally wide public, however, and his own stance has been more a part of the adversary culture at home as well. A few years earlier yet, his book *Why They Don't Hate Us* (2005) began with a brief critique of the scenarios of Francis Fukuyama, Samuel Huntington and Thomas Friedman, argued against prevalent views of anti-Americanism in the world as understood in the United States in the period (referred to in Chap. 4), and suggested that the mildly conservative stances of many of the good people in the Muslim Middle East had their contemporary American parallels among the evangelical Christians in Kansas.[20]

MICROCULTURES

We are approaching the lower end of the cultural scale, with entities definitely size S—in this case almost literally in corners, sometimes indeed cornered. They have been called microcultures, or small-group cultures, engaging some handful of individuals: perhaps a dozen, or twenty or so, or simply the members of a household.

One early study of more or less microcultural phenomena, although using other terminology, was published in *Public Opinion Quarterly* in 1948. The authors, Edward Shils and Morris Janowitz, would go on to become leading sociologists, but at the time they had fairly recently served in the Intelligence Section of the Psychological Warfare Division of the Supreme Headquarters Allied Expeditionary Force, and their article was on "Cohesion and Disintegration in the Wehrmacht in World War II."[21] Shils and Janowitz had found that what had mattered most to the stubborn resistance of German soldiers toward the end of the war was the quality of interpersonal relationships, rather than ideology or political commitments. In his squad or platoon the soldier gave and received affection, and could identify with the leadership, and in such groups there was also an accumulation of shared experience. It was only when such sentiments of *Gemeinschaft* fell apart, with disintegration or the threat of physical destruction, that soldiers were likely to surrender or desert; although it also happened that under hopeless conditions, they came to a joint decision.

I am reminded of Shils and Janowitz as I read what, a half-century or so later, in *Hog Pilots, Blue Water Grunts*, Robert Kaplan (2007: 6–7) writes about the part of the non-commissioned officers, the "noncoms," the NCOs, in shaping the ground-level collective spirit in the American military. The wider context may have been very different, but similarly in day-to-day endeavors, it was "a world of platoons, squads, and teams: a world of NCOs, who worked at the lowest tactical level, where operational success or failure is determined."

But we should not think that a concept of microculture can only serve us in understanding people in uniform. Some number of TV sitcoms, at least from the 1970s on, have portrayed microcultures, in households, offices or groups of friends. These show, too, that microcultures are not always modest, lowly entities—the *West Wing* series, revolving around a fictional U.S. president, was a case in point. It is in the nature of things that microcultures are usually not very durable: perhaps often a decade or less. (Yet entities such as genealogies, heirlooms and anniversaries may help extend their existence even in the face of surrounding changes.) Much of the cultural process within the consociality frame, however, is likely to go on within them. The most complete and concrete forms of cultural sharing may occur here—"I know, and I know that you know, and I know that you know that I know." More general opinions and assumptions can be shaped in such contexts, but they are packaged together with experiences of and ideas about particular personalities, settings and events. Trust often grows under such conditions.

One relevant notion here may be "groupthink"—not a term in much academic use, with any general and abstract definition, but in fairly wide popular use. The notion suggests that the people involved in a microculture shield themselves off from ideas from the outside, and maintain a mostly undesirable intellectual uniformity. ("Bunker mentality" is another relevant expression.) Yet one could discern an alternative where the group involved is somehow more of a microcosm of the diversity outside, and thus perhaps engaged in continuous debate.

For one more example from recent history, return once more to the Mediterranean region, not so far from Tahrir Square. In his book *Talking to the Enemy* (2010), the American but Paris-based anthropologist Scott Atran engages in a wide-ranging, yet at the same time closeup study of violent Islamists. So he takes us, for one thing, to the rather grim Mezuak neighborhood in Tetuán, Morocco—just next to the Spanish enclave of Ceuta, mentioned in Chap. 3, where African migrants from just about everywhere try to get into what pretends to be a part of Europe. In Mezuak, boys would grow up together, going to the same primary school, playing soccer in the field below the mosque, watching TV (mostly Al Jazeera) at Café Chicago, getting their stylish haircuts at the same barbershop. And in these settings "they earnestly debated the meaning of world events through the filter of their common experiences." (Atran 2010: 49)

But then some of the boys left Mezuak. After the young men got across to mainland Spain, they did menial jobs, played bit parts in the criminal underworld, as in drug dealing, and largely found themselves in the Spanish version of the kind of European urban milieux sketched in Chap. 4: *banlieues* and others. Then from there on, five of them together, they took the step toward the suicide bombings which ended their lives, and those of nearly 200 others, mostly morning traffic commuters, in three Madrid railway stations on March 11, 2004. Together with the London bombings in July, 2005, and the Paris massacres of 2015, this is so far the major acts of recent jihadist terrorism in Europe. Meanwhile, some other men, from the same boyhood circles in Mezuak, became jihad martyrs in Iraq instead.

Those who planned the Madrid massacre, Atran (2010: 206) concludes, were "a hodgepodge of childhood friends, teenage buddies, neighborhood pals, prison cellmates, siblings, cousins and lovers"—"almost laughably incompetent, though tragically only a bit less so than Spanish law enforcement and intelligence."

Then Scott Atran (2010: 50–51) went to Ceuta as well, and sat down in a café with a group of young men much like those across the border in Tetuán. He asked them who were the men they admired most. A Brazilian soccer player, in a Barcelona team, came first. In third place was Osama bin Laden. In between, second in their ranking list, was the Terminator—Arnold Schwarzenegger, understood by them as the Hollywood figure (but probably not as puzzled as in Niall Ferguson's view—see Chap. 3), rather than as a governor of California.

GREAT AND SMALL MEN IN HISTORY

Finally, back in that state, with Alfred Kroeber. For a period, as Kroeber worked away in his documentation of Native American peoples and their cultures, he had as one of his collaborators a man named Ishi.

In 1911, after apparently spending several years alone in the wilderness of northern California, a "wild man" had walked into one of its small towns. The local sheriff had seized him, and put him in a cell. But the news of the event spread, and Kroeber and his colleagues read about it in a San Francisco paper. Could this be a member of one of the peoples they had believed were extinct? They cabled the sheriff, and one of them took the train up north to collect the man. Soon they could place him on their cultural map—he was, it seemed, the last Yana Indian. And so Ishi came to spend some five years, until he died in tuberculosis, with the ethnographic collections of the University of California, slowly picking up some English, doing odd jobs, and serving as an informant for ethnographers and linguists.

Several decades later, Alfred Kroeber, who had long been reticent in talking about him, suggested to his wife Theodora (apparently less of an ivory tower writer than he) that she might write a book about Ishi. It was in 1961, the year after Kroeber died, that the book appeared: *Ishi in Two Worlds*. It became a bestseller, and so "the last Yana Indian" probably became, after they were both gone, better known around much of the world than Kroeber himself. Then again, toward the very end of the century, he was once more at the center of some interest, and controversy.[22] It became known that before Ishi's body had been cremated at his death, as he had wished, his brain had been removed, in some presumed scientific interest, and sent off to the collections of the Smithsonian Institution in Washington. In an era of changed sensibilities, this was viewed as utterly inhuman. In the end, the brain was repatriated to California, to be properly buried, in 2000, by Native Americans, of a group that was still around.

With Ishi we reach, in one form, the end of the scale of cultural organization, where some cultural configuration is carried and handled only by a single individual—absolutely size S.[23] At his death, it would seem, something identified as "Yana culture" seized to exist as living practice, although still there in written documents and museum artifacts. But the story is presumably only unique in being so well told. Through human history a great many cultures, with their own ethnic identifications to signal boundaries, have disappeared, as some last remaining representative has died; from natural or other causes.

We may tend, however, to be less interested in endings than in beginnings. There is an old concept of mythical "culture heroes," outstanding individuals who shaped things more or less forever after, and there was an era when one could be more unqualifiedly inclined to celebrate "the great man in history"—it was in the nature of things at the time that the gender bias tended to disregard people like Jeanne d'Arc and Catherine the Great. Individual-centered periods and places may also have allowed a larger intellectual niche for notions of "charisma." Then perhaps as some of the most notorious villains left the world scene such notions became unfashionable; perhaps by now the pendulum has swung somewhere midway, where there is a sense that given certain social-structural conditions, there may be some opening for politico-cultural entrepreneurs to begin to refashion other people's environments, and not least their habitats of meaning.

So perhaps Klaus Schwab, of the World Economic Forum, could be a modern-day culture hero for Davos Man? In *The Lexus and the Olive Tree* (1999: 12), we remember, it is part of Thomas Friedman's early future scenario, too, to recognize the occurrence of "super-empowered individuals"—here he points to Osama bin Laden as one example, at a time when the Al Qaeda leader was perhaps usually known as a target of US missiles, and not yet as the individual most responsible for the 9-11 to come. In such instances, obviously, the unique individuals do not remain alone—in one trajectory, something may perhaps begin with their influence in a microculture, and then move on into a movement frame and grow there. And possibly it ends with the creation or takeover of a state.

Yet between Ishi and the culture heroes, the diversity of size S culture is virtually infinite. We began this chapter by noting, for one thing, that within the vast habitat of meanings which surrounds them, individuals can make their very own selections, so that their particular combination and handling of them becomes quite unique. And the way culture moves in the world now, this may allow some room for The Little Man in History as well. As media offer people a very wide choice of sources of information and opinion, there is the strong possibility that some will choose to attend mostly to those which support views and tastes they already hold. Thus yet another member of the *New York Times* stable of columnists, the veteran foreign correspondent Nicholas Kristof (2009)—he already appeared briefly in Chap. 6—has suggested critically that what the media consumer selectively assembles may be a very special "The Daily Me," narcissistic rather than cosmopolitan.

In Chap. 4, discussing the landscape of Eurabia, we encountered the young Norwegian Anders Behring Breivik—perhaps a case in point here?[24] Breivik's parents went their separate ways early, his contact with his father lapsed in his youth, while he had a complicated relationship with his mother. He tried varieties of 1990s Oslo youth culture (hiphop, graffiti), but his efforts seem not to have been highly thought of among those he wanted as peers. For a period, he then engaged intensely with Internet war games, alone in his room, while mostly avoiding direct interpersonal contacts. Later he set up an Internet business selling fake academic credentials, but that was not successful. His early attempts to make contact with the Freemasons failed, as did his later efforts to establish himself with the major Norwegian neo-nationalist party. If Ishi left the wilderness to establish himself in his final years at the margins of the wider American society, Breivik went the other way. Withdrawing from most ordinary face-to-face consociality, he rented a small outlier farmstead where he could be alone, building bombs and putting the final touches to his Manifesto, a 1,500-plus-page document. Not entirely a "Daily Me" selection, as it drew eclectically on some more mainstream sources as well, but (to repeat) a larger part was from generally xenophobic or specifically anti-Muslim web sites and print sources, prominently of the Eurabia genre. Here Breivik went on ranting about the "political correctness" of Norwegian public opinion, the evils of multiculturalism, and the threat of Islam.

Interestingly, the title of the document was *2083: A European Declaration of Independence*—an Orwellian allusion to 1984? In any case, while in large part a compilation, the result was a scenario all his own. He posted it on the Internet, signing it Andrew Berwick and trying to make it seem as if it originated in London, just before he drove to downtown Oslo to place the bomb that would leave a government building in ruins, and then continued to the island summer camp of young leftists where, in a fake police uniform and with a revolver and an automatic rifle, he carried out his massacre.

THE S-XL LEAP IN THE GLOBAL VILLAGE

We have come a long way from the XL of the global ecumene to the S of Ishi and Breivik – finding that while civilizations were never so bounded, and always changing in time, the world is now a quite open organization of diversity.

But it is time to realize that the distance between S and XL, moving in the other direction, can now also be quite short. More or less in the same family of conspicuous twenty-first century events, groupings, sites and individuals as Tahrir Square, the Davos Club, different-faced cosmopolitans, the boys from Mezuak, and Anders Behring Breivik is, after all, 9-11.

It can take very little in the way of assets for a handful of people, or even only one, to reach large-scale results. That morning in 2001, the nineteen Al Qaeda terrorists had at their disposal some box-cutters and rudimentary skills in steering an aircraft: hardly in themselves Weapons of Mass Destruction. Yet they hijacked two planes to crash into the World Trade Center, one into the Pentagon, and one, less successfully, in the middle of nowhere in Pennsylvania. And if you have one plane hit into that first tower in lower Manhattan on a weekday morning, the media will be there for live reporting even as the second plane crashes into the other tower, less than an hour later—not too many places in the world where you can achieve such immediate global reach.

Thus terrorism aims at, and may achieve, dramatic change in the habitat of meaning. Even though locally thousands of lives were lost, 9-11 was above all a communicative event.[25] It inserted itself into global memory, and also changed the way facts and suspicions would be handled in the future, leading to the extreme social and material costs of surveillance of the security state. In *Talking to the Enemy*, Scott Atran (2010: 278) says much the same: "to terrorize and destabilize, terrorists need publicity and our complicity. With publicity, even failed terrorist acts succeed in terrorizing; without publicity, terrorism would fade away."

Downtown Manhattan is obviously a special case. During the period, also around the millennium turn, when I was most engaged in studying international news reporting, it struck me how extremely unevenly it was distributed over the globe. I referred to this in Chap. 3, in relation to "Afro-pessimism": the limited number of professional reporters just could not be everywhere. Thus conditions of relative everyday normality would very likely not be on the global newsbeat.

Moreover, even events of great significance to people in some locality or region of the world could draw very limited attention in the media elsewhere, or be disregarded altogether. In January 2015 (we saw in Chap. 4), the world watched as a few terrorists in Paris killed a dozen people at the office of *Charlie Hebdo*, occupied a kosher food store, took hostages, and were then killed themselves. At much the same time, it could still take several days for word of mouth to reach even the nearest northeastern Nigerian regional capital that Boko Haram, another grouping of violent Islamists (already globally known for kidnapping hundreds of schoolgirls, taking them away to a threatening future), had struck again in some remote towns and villages, killing—how many? Hundreds? Or was it thousands? It never seemed to become quite clear.

It is true, too, that not all world-wide distributions of powerful pictures are intentional. When some low-level American military staff at the Abu Ghraib prison in Iraq (perhaps with a microculture of their own) seemed to think that humiliation of inmates was fun, and wanted to share their images with friends, they hardly had in mind millions of viewers either in their home country or in the Muslim world. But they did get them.

Anyhow, as digital technology has continued to develop, with cellphones just about everywhere, and when you can take and send pictures with many of them, leaps from S to XL may become more common in the global village.

NOTES

1. "Every man is in certain respects like all other men; like some other men; like no other man" was Clyde Kluckhohn's formulation (in Kluckhohn and Murray 1948: 15)—if in our more gender-conscious age that seems to exclude half of humanity, that is surely not the way it was intended at the time. Kluckhohn, a Harvard professor, was still active when Samuel Huntington arrived at the same university, and since he was interdisciplinarily involved and was the first director of the Russian Research Center at the university, it seems probable that the two met. Again, together with Alfred Kroeber, Kluckhohn also edited that famous compendium of definitions of culture to which I referred in Chap. 6, note 5.

2. The New Jersey-born son of a German immigrant family, Kroeber was a pupil of Franz Boas, founding father of academic anthropology in the United States, at Columbia University, and was first to earn a doctorate in anthropology there. But then he soon established himself at the University of California. See also the biography by Theodora Kroeber (1970), and Wolf's (1981) illuminating account of Kroeber's role in American anthropology.

   Boas, a German immigrant, had been influenced by Friedrich Ratzel's (see Chap. 3) writings while a geography student in Germany; and so Kroeber may once have been pointed toward Ratzel, and his early use of the ecumene concept, by his mentor.

3. "Ecumene" is a concept that can be used at different levels. The earliest use of a notion of "global ecumene," including Eurasia as well as the New World, that I have come across is by William McNeill, one of the pioneers of world history, in his classic book *The Rise of the West* (1963)—see also note 6. I have used it frequently, perhaps beginning in Hannerz (1989). By now it has been used by some handful of writers, from several disciplines, to indicate interconnectedness and shared history, by way of interactions, exchanges, and the awareness that grows out of them. There is possibly some risk that "ecumene" is taken to refer primarily to religious organization, as "ecumenicism" has been prominent particularly in twentieth-century strivings toward positive contacts between major faiths, but that is obviously not the intended understanding here.

4. Again, see Chap. 3, note 5, on notions of "flow" in anthropology and adjacent fields.

5. Arnold Toynbee (1947: 156–160), too, took a similar view of "the abortive Scandinavian civilization."

6. Perhaps somewhat surprisingly, William McNeill makes no mention of Kroeber in *The Rise of the West*, although the lively mid-twentieth century intellectual milieu at the University of Chicago of which he was a part

included strong anthropological influences. One gets a sense of connections and differences between Kroeber and his Chicagoan contemporaries, however, in the anthropologist-philosopher Milton Singer's introduction to a posthumously published set of Kroeber's essays, *An Anthropologist Looks at History* (1963), which includes a number of Kroeber's texts on civilizations.

In a retrospective introduction to a new edition of *The Rise of the West*, a quarter-century or so after the first publication, McNeill ([1963]1991: xv) also finds his book "an expression of the postwar imperial mood in the United States"—for all his admirable overview of South and East Asia, the main theme is there in the title. This is also the somewhat critical conclusion of another prominent world historian (but Islam specialist) in the same Chicago milieu, Marshall Hodgson (1993: 93, originally written in a 1966 letter), likewise engaging with civilizations and the Oikoumene; one could note that there is no mention of Hodgson in Huntington's "clash of civilizations" book. The veteran anthropologist Jack Goody (e.g. 2006, 2010) was among those who have made an effort to write a less Eurocentric world history.

William McNeill has continued to make important and original contributions to world history: see for example McNeill (1995, 2000). His most recent take on the subject is in *The Human Web*, a book co-written with his historian-son (McNeill and McNeill 2003). After discussing the classic writings of Herodotus and Thucydides in Greek antiquity, McNeill (1991: 269) notes that their successor did not quite keep their standard: "As a man of letters, more interested in a good turn of phrase and an effective moral than in the stubborn complexity of human affairs, Xenophon presaged the subsequent degeneration of historical writing into a branch of rhetoric." Here McNeill seems to share some of Kroeber's concern with the uses of large-scale history; relevant also to matters discussed in Chap. 5.

7. Elsewhere (Hannerz 2010: 92) I have noted that Kroeber in one early (1936, but later anthologized) paper argued that small-scale, "primitive" cultures had helped make anthropology scientific: "they came to be accurately and dispassionately analyzed much as a biologist dissects a worm or a crayfish." (Kroeber 1952: 76). Hardly the kind of parallel anthropologists would be comfortable with any longer, but perhaps not so strange to someone remembering a childhood spent with microscopes, beetle and butterfly collections, and cages for living creatures.

8. Herzfeld (1997) is one Harvard anthropologist who has commented on Huntington's work.

9. Returning to Lapham's book after some years, I find it reminiscent of Leibovich's later report on the Washington, D.C., elite, *Our Town* (2013)—very possibly there is some overlap between the populations. For additional

reporting on the World Economic Forum as a meeting place for power elites, see e.g. Rothkopf (2008) and Freeland (2012).

10. The paper was published a few years later (Hannerz 1990); appearing in an edited volume that received a lot of attention, it has been widely cited, and occasionally misrepresented. After that I have had occasions to return to the topic of cosmopolitanism with a wider perspective, for example in Hannerz (2004b). For that wider view, see also for example Vertovec and Cohen (2002).

11. I connect the notion of "the world as a single place" with Roland Robertson (1992), one of the pioneer sociologists of globalization.

12. Jürgen Habermas, German social philosopher, had a major role in getting the "public sphere" debate going, but largely in a nation-state framework; Nancy Fraser (2007) most effectively took it on to a transnational setting. For a further update, see Nash (2014).

13. The work of Ulrich Beck (e.g. 1999, 2006), referred to in Chap. 2, note 1, on cosmopolitanism and "risk society" focuses on such cosmopolitan matters. Martha Nussbaum's (1996) discussion of the contrast between cosmopolitanism and patriotism drew considerable comment. In this context, Benjamin Barber (1996: 33) makes an appearance as one of those who find cosmopolitanism too culturally thin—it "offers little or nothing for the human psyche to fasten on." His preferred civil society evidently has its strongest locus in a state, and is linked to a "civic patriotism." A range of viewpoints toward a civic cosmopolitanism are exemplified by Yates (2009), and in other contributions to that issue of *The Hedgehog Review* where Yates' article appeared.

14. For a discussion of the idea of "global civil society," and the growing presence of non-governmental organizations (NGOs), see Kaldor (2003).

15. For an overview of the theory and practice of "global governance," see Stade (2014). One could sense some thinking of this kind in Robert Cooper's (2002) suggestion that the "premodern" world might have some use for a new imperialism inspired by cosmopolitan values—see Chap. 3.

16. A considerable part of the recent anthropology of cosmopolitanism has dealt with this straight-face cosmopolitanism—sometimes under labels such as "vernacular cosmopolitanism." For a range of views, see Werbner (2008) and Glick Schiller and Irving (2015). While not drawing centrally on a such a vocabulary, the New York anthropologist Roger Sanjek's *The Future of Us All* (1998) offers a comprehensive view of straight-face cosmopolitan urban neighborhood politics.

17. For accounts by the actual participants in the Arab Spring, at Tahrir Square and elsewhere, see al-Saleh (2015).

18. On the role of the fax in the Beijing events of 1989, see Calhoun (1994: 204). I am grateful to Göran Leijonhufvud, veteran China correspondent

for the leading Stockholm newspaper Dagens Nyheter, for drawing my attention to the part of wall posters as a medium of public opinion and protest during the volatile twentieth century history of the People's Republic.

19. For a broad view of varieties of hip-hop as political protest music, with a point of departure in the Arab Spring, see Morgan and Bennett (2011).

20. Moreover, Mark LeVine also appeared on a list, emanating on the right wing of American politics, of the hundred most dangerous academics in the United States. *Why They Don't Hate Us* featured an endorsement by Thomas Frank, author of *What's the Matter with Kansas?*

21. Morris Janowitz, incidentally, was Samuel Huntington's early colleague and competitor in the sociology of the military. On military microcultures see also Chap. 8, note 2.

22. The main publications relating to the controversy over Ishi's brain are by Kroeber and Kroeber (2003)—the editors are Alfred Kroeber's sons, both academics—and Starn (2004).

23. Anthropological commentators have had different, rather esoteric labels for such cultural entities: subjectivities (Biehl et al. 2007), mazeways (Wallace 1961), idioverses (Schwartz 1978), propriospects (Goodenough 1971).

24. My main sources on Breivik, his life history and sociopolitical context are Bangstad (2014) and Seierstad (2015). As it turned out, Breivik had a near counterpart in the United States in 2015, as the young Dylann Roof likewise posted a manifesto on the Internet, against the takeover of the country by African-Americans, before going on a shooting spree in a classic Black church in Charleston, SC.

25. Another obvious instance is from mid-2014, when the Islamic State, a media-sophisticated organization with Caliphate ambitions in the Middle East, effectively seized the world's attention with its video beheadings of European and American captives (later, two Japanese as well).

CHAPTER 8

Soft Power

Of all the catch phrases coined within the global scenario genre, Joseph Nye's "soft power" may in the long run have been the most successful. True, Nye (2004a: ix) could reminisce about speaking about soft power at a conference in Washington, supported by the U.S. Army, and high officers had listened sympathetically—but when someone asked one of the other speakers, Secretary of Defense Donald Rumsfeld, about his opinion of soft power, Rumsfeld had replied, "I don't know what it means." Nevertheless, the concept has become very widely used, also among writers and speakers who have no idea of its origins.

Certainly Nye's concern with soft power was primarily intended to make a point in an internal debate within the United States. He first developed the concept in the book *Bound to Lead* (1990), in a period when a prevalent view was that America was in decline. After that, he served for a while as Assistant Secretary of Defense in the Clinton Administration. By the time of *The Paradox of American Power* (2002), he had to caution instead against triumphalism. A couple of years later, with the Iraq conflict going on, in the book *Soft Power* (2004a), that still had to be a main theme. Evidently Nye had become increasingly disaffected with early twenty-first century American foreign policy, and saw a decline in soft power as the government increasingly used hard power in ways which increased anti-Americanism and subverted the credibility of soft cultural assets. In an article in *Foreign Affairs*, he argued that it was too often "outgunned in the propaganda war by fundamentalists hiding in caves."

Above all, "Americans will have to become more aware of cultural differences; an effective approach requires less parochialism and more sensitivity to perceptions abroad." To wield soft power, he concluded, Americans must first learn to listen (Nye 2004b).

But then it turned out that the world listened, and his key concept crossed borders easily. Early in the 2000s, when I spent a few months as an academic visitor in Tokyo, I used the opportunity to learn a little about Japanese responses to some of the current scenarios for the world.[1] In particular circles, there had evidently been a measure of sympathy with Huntington's "clash of civilizations" argument because of his stance against multiculturalism at home; this resonated with their preferences for a homogeneous society in the Japanese context. (Huntington's *Who Are We?* was not yet around.) But other views were more critical. In this country which had been involved in what Huntington might have seen as two major civilizational clashes, in the Russo-Japanese War a hundred years earlier, and then in World War II, there were still those commentators who preferred to see civilizational encounters as culturally productive.

By the time I was in Tokyo, however, the Huntington scenario was no longer so much in the news among Japanese academics or other commentators. Instead, the notion of soft power had become one with a certain appeal. It was also true, however, that just as Huntington's critique of multiculturalism had to a degree been domesticated, one could discern that soft power could become "made in Japan." For a nation which had been demilitarized after World War II and which had suffered much from the uses of hard power, the possibility of making friends and exercising influence by peaceful means was clearly attractive. And Nye's emphasis on the part that popular culture could play in soft power was central. My Tokyo informants would note that Japanese popular culture had recently diffused widely in the world, and hoped that could be a goodwill resource to Japan in international politics as well, especially in its Asian neighborhood. Not least in countries like Korea, China and Taiwan the memory of Japanese warfare and occupation from the first half of the twentieth century was still there. But the recent success of Japanese popular music and television series, and the enthusiasm of younger generations for hit tunes and idols from Tokyo and Osaka, could turn out to be soft power assets.

Having encountered the Japanese conception of soft power, I was more prepared to look for it elsewhere. So I Googled. In *The Hindu*, the quality (and despite the name, basically secular) daily newspaper out of Chennai,

I found one prominent columnist, sometime diplomat and politician, Shashi Tharoor (2003), noting that India had Bollywood which made Syrian and Senegalese movie goers look at the country with stars in their eyes. And India had fashion designers, and Misses World and Universe, and software developers; and above all it had free media, energetic human rights groups, and the recurrent spectacle of remarkable general elections which make it an example of the successful management of diversity—so "let us not allow the spectre of religious intolerance and political opportunism to undermine the soft power which is India's greatest asset in the world of the 21st century."[2]

Then a little later I found an op-ed piece in what was still the *International Herald Tribune* by the Swedish foreign minister at the time, Carl Bildt (2006), pointing to the risk of a "true Huntingtonian clash of civilizations" and arguing for a "profound strengthening of the soft power of Europe." And so the concept of soft power continued to spread. Now it seems to be just about everywhere; it would not be difficult to offer many more examples. By 2012, I could learn about South Korean soft power as resulting from the new world-wide popularity of the Gangnam style in popular music. What that would imply for Japanese soft power in Seoul I could only wonder.

Meanwhile, back in the United States, soft power ideas had a career of ups and downs.

Joseph Nye certainly aimed at reaching a wide public with his argument. As he took it on one more round with the book *Soft Power* (2004a), it had back cover blurbs from foreign policy and academic notables, while the back flap, apart from a presentation of the author, carried another comment, by the musician and defense analyst (or so it says) Jeffrey "Skunk" Baxter: "*Soft Power* belongs right next to Sun Tzu, Samuel Huntington, and the latest copy of *Rolling Stone*...Joe, you rock!"[3] But then some years later, Nye's (e.g. 2008) emphasis shifted to a notion of "smart power," the strategic combination of hard power and soft power, adapted to the needs of the situation. Presumably, it would be difficult to be against "smart power" as a matter of principle—even if it sounds rather like Theodore Roosevelt's "speak softly and carry a big stick." Some would also note that the soft power concept was used in a way that was not very analytically precise: there was a tendency to make it include whatever was not hard power. In an article in *Foreign Affairs*, another policy commentator, Walter Russell Mead (2004), suggested that we also need a concept of "sticky power," for economic power, to highlight the way partners in economic transactions tend to remain involved with each other. That term, however, does not itself seem to have stuck. Yet more recently, with a U.S. Congress turning more conservative, Nye (2011a) found that in its funding decisions, it was waging a "war on soft power." Another U.S. Secretary of Defense, Robert Gates, evidently understood soft power better than his predecessor Rumsfeld, and had even used the term in making a case for a greater national capacity to use it, but that did not help much. Nye could cite even what he considered a friendly member of Congress who told him that "you are right about the importance of combining soft power with hard power, but I cannot talk about soft power and hope to get re-elected."

But let us turn to more of a scrutiny of the concept itself and its possible referents. Considering the alternatives, it is easy enough to feel a certain sympathy for soft power. Yet one should perhaps beware of taking too rosy a view. Again, the idea is to co-opt rather than coerce people; "if I can get you to *want* to do what I want, then I do not have to force you to do what you do *not* want to do" (Nye 2002: 9). This may sound much like a certain older concept, and Nye is clearly aware of this. He makes a nod of recognition toward the fact that "thinkers such as Antonio Gramsci have long understood the power that comes from setting the agenda and determining the framework of debate," and one of his papers (Nye 2003) carries the title "The velvet hegemon." In other words, what is soft power to one may be undesirable cultural hegemony to someone else, and yet another observer may remind us of that not-quite-so-old idea of "cultural imperialism" (which, it is true, could be seen as one of the more benign forms of imperialism).

Once we make that connection, Benjamin Barber's McWorld may not seem so far away, although Barber's emphases are different. We may sense, too, that Samuel Huntington's argument about civilizational alliances forming on the basis of shared cultural identities is in its own way a soft power claim. And there is the diplomat Robert Cooper's (2003: 127) discussion of his maxim, "Foreign policy is not only about interests," where Cooper begins with a brief story of how Harold Macmillan met President Kennedy in 1957 to talk about nuclear politics. (Perhaps Tony Blair, the later prime minister for whom we have learned that Cooper originally wrote this text, did not notice, but Cooper got the year wrong—there was of course no President Kennedy in 1957.) In a sensitive situation involving major current strategic and technical issues, the British prime minister chose to emphasize his country's history. The question was really not about a calculus of national interest, but about Britain's perception of the kind of country it was and wanted to be. Those foreign policy analysts who draw on realist understandings of interests may try to remove what they see as the "emotional element" from the conduct of politics—but the trouble with their view, in Cooper's opinion, is that nations are communities, and it is in the nature of human communities to return to their roots and myths when their identities and destinies are affected. The nation is likely to "respond as the heart urges rather than as the head advises." (2003: 136)

ORIGINS KNOWN OR UNKNOWN

Again, then, varieties of arguments about the power of culture are recurrent in the scenario writings. A somewhat parenthetical aside may be in place here: an underlying assumption of much soft power thinking is that people have an idea about where attractive cultural imports come from. Quite a long time ago, however, a leading American anthropologist of the period, Ralph Linton (1936: 326–327), offered an example (a sometime classic in the discipline, although by now certainly mostly forgotten) of the workings of global cultural flows.[4] It goes on for a full page, but just quoting it selectively demonstrates Linton's point:

> Our solid American citizen awakens in a bed built on a pattern which originated in the Near East but which was modified in Northern Europe…He takes off his pajamas, a garment invented in India, and washes with soap invented by the ancient Gauls…ties around his neck a strip of bright-colored cloth which is a vestigial survival of the shoulder shawls worn by seventeenth century Croatians…On his way to breakfast he stops to buy a paper, paying for it with coins, an ancient Lydian invention…When our friend has finished eating, he settles back to smoke, an American Indian habit…While smoking he reads the news of the day, imprinted in characters invented by the Semites upon a material invented in China by a process invented in Germany. As he absorbs the account of foreign troubles he will, if he is a good conservative citizen, thank a Hebrew deity in an Indo-European language that he is 100 percent American.

It does not seem that this citizen, or most of his compatriots, were much affected by the enduring soft power of the Gauls, the Croatians, the Lydians, or the Chinese. The point is that the origins of cultural things are sometimes known to their users, and sometimes not. Yet at times these origins become an important part of the understandings people have of the phenomena in question, and this is where some potential for soft power may be present. So for such purposes, countries should try to get their own cultural products to move out into the world, but the origin of these products should also be clearly marked so that people elsewhere know where they come from, and do not forget.

The history of Japanese exports over half a century or so is instructive here. We may still remember that immediately after World War II, as the country tried to get its industries going again, its products tended to be regarded as low quality; "Made in Japan" pretty much signified trash. Then as Japan developed high-quality cars and electronic goods, with brands like Toyota, Sony, Canon and Toshiba, they met world-wide success, but consumers elsewhere may not have paid much attention to their origins. Only more lately have things like sushi och karaoke, and popular art forms like manga och anime, carried a more clearly Japanese identity. One Japanese cultural sociologist, Koichi Iwabuchi (2002), has written about this as a contrast between phenomena with and without "cultural odor." "Odor" may not be the term I would have chosen, but in such terms, obviously, those Japanese observers who thought recent popular culture would have some soft power effect elsewhere in Asia hoped to reach at least young noses.

With regard to the identifiability of American popular culture exports, it is frequently not in doubt. The people and the scenery in movies and TV series are unmistakably American (except when foreigners are brought in for contrast and Othering). Speech and song are in English (unless the former is dubbed, in some larger language areas), which is not the first language everywhere else. But the role of English as *the* dominant world language is of course another soft power factor, as it reaches where no single other language does—and at the same time, the global strength of American popular culture has surely itself contributed to the position of the language.

Yet at one remove, it may be that some U.S. exports have lost that "cultural odor." In the first step, soap operas, sitcoms, talent contests and the like are imported into other markets in their American original; in the next stage, the formats have been naturalized, so that the contents are Japanese, Swedish, Nigerian or whatever. One might see that there is a kind of standardization of global cultural diversity in this, but the openings for soft power may no longer be so clear.[5]

SOFT POWER CONTEXTS

But then soft power ideas also fit into the overall equations of power rather differently in different contexts. To begin with, we could note that soft power has sometimes followed in the footsteps of hard power. The arrival of American popular culture with the occupying forces after World War II still leaves certain marks even in Tokyo's urban landscape; the strong exposure to it may more generally have had a part in developing those cultural forms which would later supposedly be an asset for Japan's own soft power.[6] Probably the impact of American music, movies, fast food and soft drinks in Western Europe after that war and during the Cold War which followed could also draw on a U.S. military presence. (Possibly the importance of military bases as cultural bases was no longer quite so strong by the time Robert Kaplan did his field studies in such locations, if by then soldiers remained rather more inside the gates during off-hours.)

Furthermore, in the internal American debate in which Joseph Nye has been primarily engaged, there has been a choice involved, between soft power and hard. Elsewhere, it is likely that soft power is an appealing notion to those who, comparatively speaking, do not have much hard power anyway, which in the end may be everybody except the Americans. This creates the paradox of the soft power idea that it may in some ways have become more popular at the periphery than at the center, more relatively useful to those who received it (the rest of the world) than to those who originated the idea (the Americans). Soft power becomes a consolation prize.

Generally the idea is that soft power is something nations (and possibly regions, such as Europe) can have, and something they should be aware of and cultivate carefully. Moreover, they should avoid exhibiting undesirable characteristics that would detract from the buildup of such power. The concept thus comes to work as a new tool of self-reflexivity—what are we in our country good at, how do we want to be perceived by others? Getting soft power is a matter of building a brand.[7] Indeed, something called "nation-branding" has also become a considerable image-making industry in the early twenty-first century.[8]

Usually, even in the recent past, when historians, anthropologists and others have looked at states becoming involved in cultural management, this has tended to be a matter of building and maintaining a nation, creating an imagined community, emphasizing a shared identity and safeguarding a shared heritage; turning "peasants into Frenchmen," as the title of one important historical study had it. This kind of cultural management operates mostly inward. In contrast, soft power is externally oriented. It aims the promotion of a national brand at outside audiences.

Great powers, and not least past empires such as those of Britain and France, may long have engaged in varieties of soft power politics, viewing it in large part as a matter of spreading their varieties of civilization. But in the past, generally speaking, the conduct of international politics may have been more the turf of a restricted elite, quite possibly inclined toward some version of *Realpolitik*. While some of that is still there, now the game seems to have become at least a little different. Large states and small states operate here in something like a global market, competing to a degree with the soft powers of other national brands. In part the public presentation of the national self to the world may be a matter of attracting business investments, in part one of drawing tourists, but there is also a more diffuse claim to general recognition. A growing interest in something termed "cultural diplomacy" is part of this; hosting international conferences and sports events are among the concrete manifestations. And anyone who has been watching CNN International on TV in recent years has certainly seen much of this in a vivid (although somewhat standardized) form of imagery, blending culture with nature— "Incredible India" perhaps to begin with, but also a wide range of other countries, not least from the Balkans, Central Asia and Africa, hoping to catch your attention.

BETWEEN STATE AND MARKET

So states are reaching out beyond their borders. Yet things get more complicated, for one thing, by the fact that the state machinery itself does not always have much power over the national production of culture. The Chinese government, increasingly soft power conscious, has tried, rather controversially, to insert "Confucius Institutes" into universities in various parts of the world, and its leaders have warned against excessive foreign cultural influence (which can surely be understood to be in very large part American).[9] In the early 2000s, Nye could argue for more support for U.S. broadcasting outlets aimed at audiences abroad, particularly in the Middle East, such as Radio Sawa and the TV station Al Hurra. But then again, in the following decade, he saw Congress waging its "war on soft power" (2011c).

Instead, much of that cultural production that reaches out abroad, and which should be convertible into soft power, is in the hands of other actors—outsourced, as it were, especially to the market. The popular culture to which Nye has assigned great weight is the obvious instance. Here the state and its cultural policy may turn into a sort of hostage, with little control over the messages going out from the commercial cultural industries. Some commentators have certainly pointed out that of the entertainment products for which "Hollywood" has come to stand as a summarizing symbol, many do not exactly offer a very favorable view of American life, with their depiction of violence, racism, messy personal relationships, and very conspicuous opulence. In this, it has moreover been suggested, one can see the roots to an anti-American reaction among young men in Muslim countries: their lives and future prospects are complicated enough anyway, and stories of family problems and more or less independent young women are hardly to their taste.

On the one hand, then, in such instances, instead of soft power one may get something more like its opposite. On the other hand, it could be argued that a rosier picture, more like straight propaganda, might be so lacking in credibility that it would not do much for soft power either. Audiences may just appreciate a realistic portrayal of problems and weak spots (although presumably that can be handled in different ways). Perhaps the most successful American soft power is really a distracted, unintentional soft power—power with the back turned, not missionizing, facing toward home, yet picked up by an attentive world. It may be that to determine what may or may not be the soft power of popular culture, whether American or otherwise transnational, we would be well served by some more close-up ethnography of media use and audience responses.[10]

THE POWER OF DIVERSITY

Not all Joseph Nye's own explorations of soft power resources seem entirely convincing. While his interests have primarily focused on American uses, he too sees it as a more general concept with a wider, although uneven, potential elsewhere in the world. Yet some of his discussion of this in the book *Soft Power* appears superficial, not going much beyond a search for foreign stars that may be familiar to his audience. A claim, for example, that the Nobel Prizes in literature of Gao Xingjian and V.S. Naipaul would do much for the soft power of China and India seems dubious—one is actually in exile in Europe, the other a critical member of the diaspora.

Nor does it seem certain that the fact that the Houston Rockets have a Chinese basketball star will do all that much for the soft power of the People's Republic (Nye 2004a: 88).

Certain of Joseph Nye's colleagues or competitors in the global scenario industry have not been so enthusiastic about the idea of soft power either. Niall Ferguson (2004a: 20–21) concludes that Nye may have overestimated the reach of American media products, and that current American soft power is hardly any more awesome than that of the British Empire in the old days. And in his book *The Age of the Unthinkable* (2009: 76–77), Joshua Cooper Ramo, managing director of the consultant firm Kissinger Associates, argues that "soft power was one of those beautiful academic ideas that failed a lot of tests of practical foreign policy." It is not difficult to find people and places where one enjoyed American popular culture, and still saw the United States as an adversary. Ramo notes that Kim Jong-Il, North Korea's ruler at the time, grew up watching Clint Eastwood movies. And we saw in the preceding chapter that the young men in Ceuta, North Africa, who had the Terminator, Arnold Schwarzenegger, second highest on their popularity list had Osama bin Laden in third place.

One argument here might be that soft power could not rely very much on what is in large part youth culture enthusiasms—young people, after all, are mostly not so strong a force in national political decision-making. Against that it might be replied that perhaps early influence will turn out to be enduring. There is a striking report by Maureen Dowd (2006) on the visit of Junichiro Koizumi, one of the more flamboyant Japanese prime ministers of recent times, to Elvis Presley's Graceland, in the company of Laura and George W. Bush. The prime minister had grown up near an American base and probably had a considerable early exposure to American popular culture. Now, at Graceland, after arriving at Memphis on Air Force One, Koizumi did his own karaoke performance of "Love me tender" and other Elvis numbers.[11] Indeed, in the early 2000s, he was one of the United States' best foreign friends. So perhaps here soft power might have been at work?

In any case, it is not fair to connect the idea of soft power so narrowly to popular culture. It has hardly been so unusual that what sticks in the public mind from those striking catch words summarizing global scenarios has been something a little different, and less complex, than the author originally intended. Yet Joseph Nye certainly has pointed to a wider range of outlets of American culture with a certain outreach in the world. Academia offers some of them: in an earlier chapter, we have already encountered Benazir Bhutto's reminiscences about her experiences on the Harvard campus. When American universities move out to establish overseas campuses, they may do so for their own reasons, but perhaps they are also creating outposts for soft power.[12] What initiatives in offering MOOCs on the Internet will lead to, globally as well as for campuses on the ground at home, remains to be seen.

Continuing with that view of culture as an organization of diversity which I advocate in this book, however, let me conclude with a slightly different perspective toward soft power, and how contemporary American culture may connect to it. First, a few ethnographic vignettes. The first is from a summer day some years ago, when I was in a supermarket in the southern Swedish town close to my summer home. I was at the magazine shelf, distractedly leafing through various offerings, when I came across one magazine with page after page of color pictures of large old rusty cars; roadside, or heaped on top of each other in junk yards, or with mountain sceneries in the background, or among grazing cattle. A document of environmental decline? Or yet another critique of consumer capitalism? No, this was the report of a Swedish enthusiast of a very special journey across the United States, through the country of the magnificent antique cars, those which in mid-twentieth century Sweden were known as "dollar grins," as they were indeed American and their fronts seemed to resemble wide smiles. His route, from coast to coast, was a pilgrimage laid out through four-lane Interstate highways or dusty country roads to take him past as many of those aging steel beauties of 1950s Detroit as possible, even as many of them had now come to a final rest.[13]

My second vignette I draw from another contributor to the global scenario genre, Thomas Barnett. To repeat, in his book *The Pentagon's New Map* (2004) it seems that the "clash of civilizations" is really between Pentagon and Wall Street. Rather like early Fukuyama, with his "end of history," Barnett expects that democracy and the market are on their way to triumph in the world, and he sees the task of the American military mainly as making sure that less orderly parts of the world—his "The Gap," discussed in Chap. 3—will not mess up the process. But while he develops his argument he also offers concrete insights from his work connected to the US Navy. Early in 2001 he had been in Mumbai, India, as a member of the American delegation when the Indian navy celebrated its fiftieth anniversary. Barnett was to lecture to an audience of several hundreds, including some twenty admirals who were heads of naval forces in different parts of the world. Despite the fact that his colleagues at home had warned him that he must adapt his presentation to this audience, he somehow came to do much the same Powerpoint presentation which used to go down well in the United States.

That actually worked beautifully, and in the next few days he received a lot of compliments from all those visiting admirals. So how come his materials, with their origins from Washington, "inside the Beltway," succeeded so well in reaching this audience? Well, actually his listeners were wonderfully tuned-in culturally. Most of them had studied in the United States, and about half of them had graduated from the college of the US Navy. It dawned on Barnett that he was really at a sort of alumni reunion party.

My third and final vignette is from New York, and drawn on an anthropological study of young Swedes which Helena Wulff (1992) conducted there in the late 1980s. There were many of them, although nobody would know exactly how many. But it was a fact that anyone speaking or at least recognizing Swedish, and traveling in the subway or on city buses, could again and again hear Swedish spoken, between two or three of these young people.

Part of the charm of New York to them was clearly what it was not— that is, Sweden. Here they had a temporary free zone, a place where they could more easily disregard where they were from, and what they would probably sooner or later return to. Young Swedish bankers and stock brokers could mix with Swedish film makers or hair stylists of the same age, or au pair girls a year or so out of a small-town high school. They could party together and go for coffee at the Swedish church, without any expectation that this would be their enduring network once they took up their positions back home. The fact that they interacted at all had something to do with the fact that their Swedish identity did mean something to them, but only within a repertoire of possibilities realized in different contexts. (And there would be some who basically left their Swedishness behind altogether.) Here, for a period of their lives, was a measure of liminality, a relative lack of structure, with new openings as an important ingredient.[14]

Some of them would in fact remain in New York. But others returned to Sweden, and when Wulff interviewed some of them again back in Stockholm it was clear that "at home" was no longer quite what it had been, and the period in New York had not become a parenthesis without significance. For some it had become an important stage in their careers, a valuable item in a professional résumé, and again and again the opinion came up that in their particular line of work, whichever it was, it had become impossible to advance unless one had some American experience.

(Perhaps those admirals in Mumbai would agree.) But for many, too, it had become a wider matter of life style, with a whiff of nostalgia. They sought out an urban life that would remind them of New York, they went to the movies where they recognized street scenes, and they reacted with some disdain when they saw or heard America or at least New York described in a way they thought was erroneous or superficial.

These three cases show some of variations in contemporary American culture, and the responses of some people from elsewhere as they encounter them. Through this diversity, its sheer size and what has at least for a long time been its great prosperity, America has had something special to attract very many even across borders, and hardly any country has had much of a chance to compete with it. That, however, has been the strength not of some general, homogenized mainstream, or its bestselling cultural commodities, but the appeal of its subcultures: whether of professions or life styles, of esthetic persuasions or generational preoccupations (or even of regional character, as in those "nine nations"). You may be an admiral commanding a fleet somewhere in the world or a lover of vintage cars, and either way you may have your particular Mecca somewhere in the United States, where your subculture is more developed than anywhere else. The globalizing changes in transport and the media now make it easier than before to make one's own way to this Mecca, or to keep in touch from a distance with what goes on there. Those highly varied cultural commitments have also been drawn into the center-periphery relationships of transnational culture. For historical or present-day reasons, some of these subcultures may have their particular charismatic local centers somewhere in the American geography: New Orleans for jazz enthusiasts, Silicon Valley for digital entrepreneurs, Harvard Square, Cambridge, Massachusetts for varied academic subcultures (or for alumni or alumnae like Benazir Bhutto). But then some places may accumulate centrality in very diverse subcultures; New York tends to be many Meccas in one.

It may be that those admirals from around the world, or vintage car enthusiasts, or young Swedes in New York, could encapsulate themselves in their particular little worlds somewhere in a corner of the wider American cultural diversity. For many of them, however, that kind of little world becomes an entry point into a rather more general American experience, a wider set of cultural skills. From this may just follow an openness to American soft power which is just as broad as that which popular culture may stimulate. But perhaps it has a greater depth, and is less volatile. It may be in a way both soft power and sticky power, in the sense that it is open to ideas and symbols, and at the same time involves rather durable entanglements. I would suggest that grounding an understanding of soft power in an understanding of the organization of diversity may well point to one considerable American advantage: other countries may be on the rise as global powerhouses, but probably it will be a long time before any one of them could offer such a wide range of transnationally attractive cultural strengths.

Then, however, such soft power may not be so uncomplicatedly manageable. If political strategists would prefer a soft power which is always at hand as a resource for the state, this might not be it. The diversity of cultural linkages may lead to a variety of commitments which mirrors that of the American domestic political map. It may be seen on that map as red, blue, green, purple, pink or whatever. Or in other words, the soft power of diversity will be matched by a not so easily managed diversity of soft power.

Notes

1. For one thing, I had long conversations with the political science professor Takashi Inoguchi, who shared my interest in future scenarios. Inoguchi's (e.g. 1999) quite complex mapping of geopolitical, geoeconomic and geo-cultural scenarios of American origin includes Fukuyama, Huntington, Barber, Kaplan as well as several other writers. We met at Inoguchi's office at the main campus of the University of Tokyo, in the Institute of Oriental Culture, an intriguing survival from that World War II period when Japan had been most actively playing with maps, focusing on its "Greater Asia Co-prosperity Sphere." That time was long gone when we met, but the institute in its later rather liminal situation offered some autonomy from the more conventional discipline structure of the university.
2. Tharoor's argument about Indian soft power is also in a book of his essays (Tharoor 2007).
3. As one of those endorsements was from then-Senator Chuck Hagel, one could note that with time Nye could line up two Pentagon chiefs against one—if Donald Rumsfeld did not know what soft power meant, his successors Gates (see below in the text) and Hagel did.
4. Ralph Linton was a contemporary of Alfred Kroeber, a key figure in the preceding chapter; theoretically influential, but hardly as organizationally powerful. Toward the end of World War I, Linton served in the American Expeditionary Force in Europe, and it is notable that in a brief 1924 piece on "Totemism and the A.E.F.," (reprinted in Linton and Wagley 1971), he

adumbrated some of what was said about the nature of microcultures in Chap. 7: "By the end of the war, the A.E.F. had become organized into a series of well defined, and often mutually jealous, groups, each of which had its individual complex of ideas and observances... The individual complexes bound the members of each group together and enabled them to present a united front against other groups."

5. I have discussed this more extensively elsewhere (Hannerz 1992a: 238ff.).

6. See on this a study by Shunya Yoshimi (2003), cultural sociologist at the University of Tokyo. The Roppongi neighborhood, Tokyo's most famous entertainment district, got its start as such during the Occupation when U.S. soldiers with their base there created a new nightlife. And Harajuku, where Tokyo youth have recently met to display new fashion styles was where American officers lived in an affluent area named Washington Heights. When they left, Japanese media and fashion professionals moved in.

7. Such building a brand is also the opposite, it seems, of what Michael Herzfeld (1997b) has referred to as "cultural intimacy," those national characteristics which may be recognized at home, but which become a bit embarrassing when noticed by the outside world.

8. On nation-branding see the theoretically informed overview by Aronczyk (2013).

9. On the Confucius Institutes, see the critique by the anthropologist Marshall Sahlins (2014). For more general overviews of early twenty-first century Chinese approaches to soft power, see Kurlantzick (2007) and Shambaugh (2015).

10. I am reminded here of early transnational studies of the reception of *Dallas*, certainly a series showing not only rosy sides of American life, among television viewers in different parts of the world (Ang 1985, Liebes and Katz 1993).

11. The version I read in the *International Herald Tribune* at the time may have been slightly different; as I remember it, peanut-butter-and-sliced-banana sandwiches (an Elvis favorite) were served aboard Air Force One.

12. For an overall discussion of the globalization of Academia through overseas campuses, see Wildavsky (2010); for a reflective case study of teaching at the Georgetown University campus in Qatar, see Mitchell (2013).

13. For a more recent account of Swedish car enthusiasts and old Detroit products, see Tenold (2014).

CHAPTER 9

Scenarios from Everywhere

A conspicuous brawl broke out in the pages of the *London Review of Books* in late 2011, as Pankaj Mishra reviewed Niall Ferguson's book *Civilisation* (2011) under the title "Watch this man." Mishra, a prominent Indian commentator on culture, politics and history, and a forceful writer, had made a rapid career from modest North Indian provincial beginnings to engagements with literary and intellectual circles on both the Anglophone sides of the Atlantic, and now spent most of his time in London; his best-known book so far was *Temptations of the West* (2006), shaped as a journey between some major historical and contemporary sites of South Asia's encounter with imperialism, modernity and globalization. Ferguson, again, was now mostly in the United States. What irritated Mishra about Ferguson's work was that it still exemplified, in his view, and in a formulation by a Chinese commentator a century or so earlier, "white people's histories."

One may be reminded here of the prognosis, in 1903, by the Black American scholar W.E.B. DuBois in his *The Souls of Black Folk*: "The problem of the twentieth century is the problem of the color line—the relation of the darker to the lighter races of men in Asia and Africa, in America and the islands of the sea." Considering what would follow – in the United States, and with the decolonization of what would for some time become the Third World—one might conclude that this could have been the summary of one remarkably successful global future scenario. (And DuBois himself, moving on to become a founding father of Pan-Africanism, was

209

indeed an early global public intellectual: born in Massachusetts, with some years of study at the University of Berlin, then a Harvard doctorate, he died in 1963 in exile in Accra.)

Against such a background, Pankaj Mishra's sensitivity to any unicolor dominance in a twenty-first century celebration of European imperial history may not seem so surprising. In particular, he saw it as disregarding Asian achievements in precolonial times, and ignoring a century of development of Asian anticolonial critique.

In the issues of the *London Review of Books* that followed, Ferguson first responded that Mishra's review had been a "crude attempt at character assassination" and had implied that Ferguson was a racist. So he demanded a public apology. From there on, the exchange tended to swing between epithets and matters of detail, and drew more media attention. Mishra's view of the world certainly had its sympathizers in London as well as New York. *The Guardian* (November 14), commenting on one side of the Atlantic, asked in a subtitle whether it was "time for them to step outside and settle it once and for all?" *Wall Street Journal* (December 5), on the other side, noted that the battle "hasn't made it to court, yet," and went on to compare British and American litigation practices.[1]

Soon afterwards, Pankaj Mishra's book *From the Ruins of Empire* (2012) appeared, bringing into view some of the figures who formulated and propagated early critiques of Western colonialism, and offered alternative visions: the Persian-born but remarkably itinerant, mostly nineteenth-century figure Jamal al-Din al-Afghani; the Chinese scholar-publicist Liang Qichao, in exile much of his early twentieth-century career in Japan, the rising Asian power; Rabindranath Tagore, with roots in an established Bengali upper class and the first Asian winner of a Nobel Prize in literature; many others more in passing. But those times had not only their heroes, but also their villains and fools. Mishra's mini-portrayal of the maharaja of Bikaner, present as somehow representing British India at the peace conference in Paris at the end of World War I, also offers a glimpse of Mishra's vivid style.[2] At the previous turn of the century, the maharaja had already been to China to support the British as they quelled the Boxer Rising. In the war just passed, he had been briefly present for a skirmish at the Suez Canal. At Versailles, site of the peace conference,

he became a striking figure at the discussions with his ferociously curled moustache and jewel-studded red turban, insisting on showing the leaders present the tiger tattooed on his arm (Clemenceau [the French leader] was impressed enough to undertake a shooting trip to Bikaner in 1920, from which he emerged with possibly the only positive short-term result of the Paris Peace Conference: two dead tigers.) (Mishra 2012: 200–201)

A couple of decades later, Mishra went on to point out, the early Japanese triumphs in Southeast Asia in World War II were favorably received by significant parts of local political intelligentsias, and did much to undermine European hegemony as the earlier empires returned at the end of the war.

USA: Up? Down?

Civilization (with a *z*, of course, in printings destined for the American market) hardly offered any major surprise for readers already familiar with Niall Ferguson's general viewpoint. But it was linked to a television series—and moreover, in tune with the twenty-first century times, it offered some new vocabulary for the superiority of the West: competition, science, property rights, medicine, the consumer society, and the work ethic were now "killer apps."

Yet could the entire global future scenario genre by this time keep going, renewing itself? Of the early contributors, Samuel Huntington was no longer around (although still occasionally harangued by other commentators). Some of the others might find that they were repeating themselves. Perhaps they moved on to other projects. (Niall Ferguson became Henry Kissinger's authorized biographer.) Others again could possibly feel that proclaiming new futures again and again was difficult, and in any case not entirely credible. So what might keep the genre going? Who could provide the Big Picture now?

Once more it seemed that the Ferguson-Mishra confrontation to an extent did not only involve different understandings of history: "who controls the past controls the future." But the question also came back about who writes for whom, from where to where about where, in the global scenario genre.[3] Again, with its centers on the Atlantic coastline of the Northeast, much of the scenario production has taken place in one or two of Joel Garreau's "nine nations of North America"—with a supplementary site in his West Coast nation of Ecotopia, at Stanford University. Much of the lands in between, as far as this line of enterprise is concerned, is fly-over country. Perhaps more importantly, the diversity of the political map of the United States is not equally represented either, insofar as the scenarists are mostly of the right or center-right, not so much of the center-left, and hardly at all, with regard to public off-campus visibility, of the left (unless Noam Chomsky and Naomi Klein were to be included). It is likewise true that to the extent that they are academics, disciplines are not so evenly distributed. The scenarists are mostly historians and political scientists—not for example geographers, economists, sociologists or anthropologists. Yet we are primarily concerned here with global distribution—where in the world do scenarios grow?

The base of the scenario genre in the United States has shaped some particular emphases. A recurrent set of questions is "Up?" "Down?" American influence in the world is celebrated, or there is a concern with its decline. In this, scenarists may be involved as participants or as observers. Niall Ferguson began his writing career as a celebrationist, in his retrospective view of the British Empire and in his desire that the United States should play a similar part. Then with time a declinist tendency has grown more pronounced—conspicuously in *The Great Degeneration* (2012), subtitled "How Institutions Decay and Economies Die."

But again, even before that, he identified an economic deficit, a manpower deficit, and an attention deficit, all undermining potential American power. His engagement with the dystopic vision of Eurabia leaned, from some distance, in the declinist direction as well.

In the prospect of an end to history Fukuyama may have suggested a likely triumph of capitalist democracy, rather more than of the United States as a nation, although that could have seemed like a distinction without a difference (and to repeat, it is true that that his enthusiasm was already somewhat mixed). Paul Kennedy issued an early warning with his historical view of the decline of overextended empires. Thomas Friedman may have been mostly on the celebrationist side, although his co-authored *That Used to Be Us* (2011) points in another direction. Joseph Nye has argued for soft power both when his surroundings have leaned toward declinism and when there has been more celebrationism. Most recently he has expressed his doubts about declinism in *Is the American Century Over?* (2015), pointing to the enduring American combination of varieties of power: hard, soft, economic. Robert Kaplan appears to have been consistently a warrior and a worrier.

As the Ferguson-Mishra confrontation was going on, the American journalist Ethan Casey (2011), hostile to the former and with some past personal acquaintance with the latter, writing for the Indian public affairs magazine *Open*, also raised the question what American audience Mishra was actually writing for: "Has Pankaj Mishra Ever Been to South Dakota?" The United States, all of it, Casey argued, was crying out for a new Alexis de Tocqueville. If Pankaj Mishra would only get away from the Eastern Seaboard,

> I wish he would consider addressing his incisive intelligence, reporting skills and narrative talents to an attempt to understand my country as the deeply troubled, various, and extremely interesting society that I know it to be.

Certainly other countries may have had their moments in history when they have shouted "Up!" (Olof Rudbeck the Elder, we saw in the Prologue, was a seventeenth-century Swedish supercelebrationist in his *Atlantica*.) But it is a familiar tenet from the sociology of knowledge that people tend to develop their perspectives from where they are in the social order of the world: American preoccupations with "Up?" or "Down?" may not come so naturally to observers everywhere. Does some of the renewal of the genre of global future scenarios come from writers with other vantage points? And what can this do for a world's thinking about itself? Finally, the time has come to sample some of the scenarios, or scenario-related points of view, with origins different from those of that pioneering "One Big Thing" Quintet, and those others introduced in Chap. 1.

AMERICAN HALFIES

We do not have to go outside the United States to find some of them. Again, for all of his Harvard connections, the African-American W.E.B. DuBois, with his early forecast of the "color line" as the major twentieth-century problem, already exemplified how different backgrounds can bring different perspectives. A few of the critical comments on the later set of scenarios also came from well-placed and established thinkers with other cultural connections in the world out there. We have already heard Amartya Sen, from his corner of Harvard University, rejecting Samuel Huntington's civilizational scenario. A little after 9–11, from slightly further south on the Atlantic coastline, Eduard Said, at the time still alive and well at Columbia University (and already, with his *Orientalism*, a strong intellectual adversary of Bernard Lewis), summarized his view of the Huntington thesis in a chapter in *The End of the Peace Process* (2000), under the title "The Uses of Culture"—his argument was not so unlike Sen's.

Then we also find authors of more fully developed contributions (or approximations) to the genre, with names not so much like, say, Huntington, Kennedy, or Kaplan—instead, Chua, Khanna, Zakaria. Those who have followed the recent history of anthropological scholarship may sense a parallel with the rising presence there, from the late twentieth century onwards, of what one representative of the category has, perhaps at least semi-seriously, described as the "halfies": "people whose national or cultural identity is mixed by virtue of migration, overseas education, or parentage" (Abu-Lughod 1991: 137).[4]

So these are writers moving into the global scenario genre mostly a decade after the pioneering cohort, in the new century. Amy Chua begins her book *World on Fire* (2003: 1) with a striking reminiscence:

> One beautiful blue morning in September 1994, I received a call from my mother in California. In a hushed voice, she told me that my aunt Leona, my father's twin sister, had been murdered in her home in the Philippines, her throat slit by her chauffeur.

Chua herself, now a law professor at Yale University, is American-born, the daughter of a young Philippine-Chinese couple who had recently arrived in the United States in pursuit of higher education. And in their ethnic background, with the implications it had in their country of origin, she finds the social context of that murder. The Filipino Chinese are "a tiny but entrepreneurial, economically powerful" minority. Her aunt had clearly been well-off, a candidate for in-house robbery. From that family experience, then, Chua proceeds to an overview of "market-dominant minorities" in a wide-range of countries around the world—the Chinese here and there in Southeast Asia, other groups in South Africa, Nigeria, Russia, Bolivia and elsewhere, groups that could profit conspicuously in a changing political economy. Early enough, in the introduction, Chua points out that *World on Fire* stands in contrast to Thomas Friedman's market-celebrating *The Lexus and the Olive Tree*. In her view, "the global spread of markets and democracy is a principal, aggravating cause of group hatred and ethnic violence throughout the non-Western world."

Following on that, Chua's *Day of Empire* (2007) is very much a post-9-11 book. Again, it begins with a family story: the way her parents (not least her ambitious, demanding father), and then she and their other children, became part of an open and welcoming American society. Now, however, she finds the United States as the hyperpower on the world scene, with "empire" as an increasingly attractive prospect in public debate at home, and meeting with widespread dislike abroad. And then there is Samuel Huntington's *Who Are We?*: "he almost goes out of his way to be inflammatory and insulting—suggesting for example that Mexican Americans are multiplying like rabbits and that they may try to take back California, Utah, and Texas." (Chua 2007: xxix) Even so, she senses that Huntington is right that the country needs more of what she calls "glue," to hold it together. But his basic error is to find the source of it only in a single group.

So "glue" becomes Chua's key metaphor, and tolerance is also a central notion. She takes the reader on a quick tour of empires from ancient history onwards, arguing that those who did well were those who were open to newcomers and handled diversity well; and they declined when they no longer did so. Arriving at the present, her portrayals of other possible world powers may seem more persuasive in some cases than others. Perhaps predictably, China gets a rather favorable review, and she finds Klaus Schwab at the World Economic Forum, Davos, putting on an Indian turban as he discusses investment opportunities in—guess where. Europe perhaps seems more troubled. Coming back to the United States and its place in the world, she underlines, first, the value of a relatively open immigration policy, not least to attract the best of human capital from elsewhere. Second, as American business goes abroad, outsourcing is not necessarily an evil, as it provides advancement opportunities for local talent, and thus makes friends and allies. And third, multilateral international cooperation is the best way of dealing with problems that cross borders. That may remind us of that cosmopolitan with a worried face, from Chap. 7—the world citizen, perhaps even engaged in "global governance." And the "glue" metaphor shows a certain affinity with that of "sticky power," encountered in Chap. 8.

Remarkably, the paperback edition of *World on Fire* carries endorsements by Barbara Ehrenreich, author of *Nickle and Dimed*; the conservative economist Thomas Sowell; and by *Mother Jones* magazine; and *Day of Empire* has blurbs by Robert Kaplan, Niall Ferguson and Paul Kennedy. (Robert Kaplan in turn gets a blurb from Amy Chua on the back of *Monsoon*.) After these two books, however, Amy Chua's public visibility has not depended so much on endeavors in the scenario genre. What contributed even more to her fame was her next book, *Battle Hymn of the Tiger Mother* (2011), a memoir rather sardonically describing her tough-minded childrearing practices—an international bestseller, placing her on

Time magazine's list of 100 most influential people in the world, but also supposedly starting something called the Mommy Wars. Then, with her husband and fellow law professor Jed Rubenfeld, she wrote *The Triple Package* (2014), a fairly controversial book about how three personal characteristics—a superiority complex, insecurity, and impulse control—have made members of some ethnic groups more successful than others in American society. This possibly comes a little closer to the scenario genre, although it is still the Tiger Mother marching on, broadening the field of vision, but perhaps with much the same vantage point.

Parag Khanna's book *The Second World* (2008) had a conspicuous sort of trailer in the *New York Times* Sunday Magazine before publication. About that time, he was based at a Washington think tank, reputedly offered opinion and advice to Barack Obama's first presidential campaign, and was somewhat surprisingly at the same time a Ph.D. candidate at the London School of Economics. Born in Kanpur, North India, Khanna had had a mobile childhood, growing up in the United Arab Emirates, Germany and the United States.

The book title could raise some eyebrows. The "Second World" used to be the state socialist bloc, until the Soviet Union fell apart. For Khanna, barely two decades later, it is basically what is not quite Europe or North America—starting with Ukraine and going East, also including Latin America, but leaving Africa south of Sahara to the lingering Third World. So in this Second World, Khanna sees other powers rising, competing successfully with the United States, although not least in Asia doing their politics quite differently. Khanna travels widely but quickly, offering rather thumbnailish observations on geopolitics and globalization: seven pages on Russia, seven on Afghanistan and Pakistan together, five on Mexico, seven on Brazil. Extensive reading goes into the globetrotting as well. He begins by finding Arnold Toynbee's account of a journey around the world the best guide for his own project—although Toynbee made his journey only after writing his twelve volumes on civilizations, whereas Khanna travelled first and wrote later. He sees, too, the tension between Toynbee's and Spengler's views of civilizations as a predecessor of that between Francis Fukuyama's and Samuel Huntington's. All this earns *The Second World* an endorsement from Robert Kaplan.

Having received his doctoral degree, and still based at the Washington think tank, Khanna is next ready to instruct his readers in *How to Run the World* (2011). What readers? Khanna suggests that this is "Generation Y geopolitics;" that is, for a generation conventionally understood to include people born in the two decades or so after 1980. So here is a geopolitics different from that of Rudolf Kjellén a century earlier, and from that of Samuel Huntington, a half-century older than Khanna himself. Even so, presumably Khanna does not mind if those from generations earlier in the alphabetical order try to catch a glimpse over the shoulders of tribe Y.

The realities to be confronted now, Khanna argues, are those of a neo-medieval world order: most fundamentally one where states are no longer the only important actors, but where business and NGOs also play major parts. As in the middle ages (at least in certain regions), cities are more important than countries. The way to handle it all is through diplomacy—although not just old-style diplomacy, but mega-diplomacy. In the neo-medieval landscape we encounter a diversity of identities, actors and organizations, many of a hybrid nature; philanthropreneurs, eco-raiders, celebrity diplomats ("Madonna has helped put Malawi on the map"). Yet diplomacy is now really for everybody, not least the members of the Generation Y, "cause-mopolitans" equipped with mobile phones and skilled users of Internet. (One might find it easier to imagine Khanna's Generation Y at home in the regions around the North Atlantic, rather than in some other parts of the world.)

What, then, will come after neo-medievalism? Having accompanied Khanna somewhat breathlessly through this era, one might be comforted but a bit surprised that the next Renaissance, presumably after mega-diplomacy has done its work, is much like contemporary Europe, solving its problems through transparency and negotiation—that Europe which we have seen (in Chap. 3) the very real diplomat Robert Cooper describing as "postmodern." (Cooper, however, is one author Khanna does not cite.) As for other continents, for one thing, he takes a lightheartedly irredentist stance toward existing but problematic political borders in Africa and the Middle East—"Inertia is not a legitimate reason to prolong cartographically imposed suffering." (2011: 79)

Khanna is clearly well-read, and sometimes strikingly eclectic in his references. On leadership, of a kind conceivably useful in mega-diplomacy as well, he draws on the how-to book *The Seven Habits of Highly Effective People*—quite likely available next to bestselling scenario texts in airport bookstalls, although in the management section. It would seem that he is also an effective networker: over 200 people are listed in his acknowledgments. What is mostly absent from the pages of *How to Run the World*, on the other hand, in contrast not least with Amy Chua's books, are accounts of personal experience, and insights drawing directly on that. Khanna's

composition of the neo-medieval world is vivid, often entertaining, sometimes irritating. The back cover of *How to Run the World* had "advance
praise" by Klaus Schwab, Davos (who may well have found Khanna's combination of stakeholders appealing), and Nassim Nicholas Taleb, author of
The Black Swan (see Chap. 5). Later reviewers, on the other hand, many of
them veterans in world-watching, were often rather unenthusiastic, asking
for more coherence, and greater depth.[5]

Among the halfie cohort of scenarists, the more enduring public presence is that of Fareed Zakaria. Growing up in a prominent Bombay
Muslim family, Zakaria made his hemispheric move to the United States
in 1982, in his late teens, to go to college.[6]As a Yale undergraduate he
studied history with Paul Kennedy; from there he went on to political
science at Harvard, with Samuel Huntington and Joseph Nye. So early
on, it would seem, he was socialized into the intellectual milieu of what
would become the global scenario genre. His first two books, it should be
said, did not fit so directly into it. *From Wealth to Power* (1998) originated
as his doctoral work, with Huntington as thesis adviser. It grew out of
some impatience with the academic drifting apart of political science and
history, and centered on the explanatory importance of changing state
power, with an American focus. The next book, *The Future of Freedom*
(2004), warned that democracy, introduced all by itself, did not necessarily lead to a good society. Voters could indeed place bad people in almost
unlimited power. Here Zakaria's view of the need to combine state power,
the rule of law, and political democracy, and getting to them in the right
sequence, would seem to belong broadly in the range of views offered for
example by an early (pre-clash) Huntington, and a late Fukuyama (on the
path to Denmark). But it was *The Post-American World* (2008) that took
him fully into the community of scenarists.

Despite what one might expect on the basis of the title, this is not a
declinist tract. As an immigrant, Zakaria remains qualifiedly upbeat about
his adopted country.[7] The point is that recent change in the world has
entailed "the Rise of the Rest." Some countries have a larger part than
others in this, but Zakaria agrees with Parag Khanna (and many others)
that states are no longer so dominant in the landscape of actors.

It may be his semi-detached view as a halfie that allows Zakaria occasionally to take a somewhat ironic view toward his more recent compatriots:

> Americans may admire beauty, but they are truly dazzled by bigness. Think
> of the Grand Canyon, the California redwoods, Grand Central Terminal,

Disney World, SUVs, The American armed forces, General Electric, the Double Quarter Pounder (With Cheese), and the Venti Latte. Europeans prefer complexity, the Japanese revere minimalism. But Americans like size, preferably supersize. (2008: 87)

In *The Post-American World*, Zakaria devotes special attention to China ("The Challenger") and India ("The Ally"). As for China, he emphasizes its inclination to *Realpolitik*, but also a certain historically continuous mindset: "Few Chinese have really internalized the notion that abstract rules, laws and contracts are more important than a situational analysis of a case at hand." (2008: 113) Yet "Like every non-Western country, China will make up its own cultural cocktail—some parts Eastern, some parts Western—to thrive in the twenty-first century." (2008: 114)

The reader will certainly find, however, that Zakaria remains closer to India—and that he takes a more up-to-date view of it than his old teacher Huntington did in his "clash of civilizations" interpretation:

Indians understand America. It is a noisy, open society with a chaotic democratic system, like theirs. Its capitalism looks distinctly like America's free-for-all. Many urban Indians are familiar with America, speak its language, and actually know someone who lives there, possibly even a relative. (2008: 150)

As a halfie, again, Fareed Zakaria can also draw on personal experience in contrasting varieties of learning, and learning how to learn, in a very good school in Mumbai and in an American college. In school, the emphasis had been on rote learning (but that was not really so essentially Asian—it was a surviving import from Europe). In college, it was on developing the critical faculties of the mind. With regard to civilizations, he notes, they are of different kinds, have different sorts of bases. Confucianism is not a religion at all, but a philosophy. Hindus (like Confucians) do not believe in God—but they believe in hundreds of thousands of them. "Every family forges its own distinct version of Hinduism." (2008: 153) So Hinduism, it seems, has its internally diverse base in millions of microcultures.

What, then, should the United States do in the post-American world? Most importantly, get out of the "fear and loathing" stance which had grown strong after 9–11.[8] Apart from that, develop a sense of priorities; stick to broad rules, based on values rather than narrow interests; engage with everybody, whether friends or challengers; find varied, often bottom-up organizational solutions to problems that often now involve more kinds of actors (that sounds a bit like Khanna's mega-diplomacy); think asymmetrically—problems with small enemies are not always best handled through large attempts at solutions; seek legitimacy. Concretely, at the time of writing, Zakaria saw little of this in the conduct of the country's foreign affairs.

More lately, President Obama has been observed taking *The Post-American World* (as well as Thomas Friedman's *Hot, Flat and Crowded*) as summer reading to the beach. Fareed Zakaria's public presence, however, has not depended on his books alone (even as these have been translated into numerous languages). Only some ten years after his arrival in the United States he was named editor of *Foreign Affairs*, the flagship journal of American foreign policy debate; while editor, he published Huntington's first "Clash" article—and then also the ensuing debate. From there, he moved to become editor of *Newsweek International*, and later a columnist at *Time* and the *Washington Post*; he contributed to a couple of TV news shows before getting his own weekly one-hour program, "Global Public Square," on CNN as well as CNN International. As a Harvard Ph.D., television personality and print columnist, he is clearly the kind of public intellectual with a comfort zone including academic as well as media worlds—also a Davos veteran, and in recent times more continuously and frequently visible than anybody except perhaps, again, Thomas Friedman.

On his "Global Public Square" program, Zakaria displays his diplomatic skills in interviews and the conduct of panel discussions, usually smoothly deliberative, a style unlike the shouting matches otherwise common in political talk shows on American TV. By 2011, he could interview Benjamin Barber on the latter's controversial earlier contacts with Colonel Khaddafi, recently deposed Libyan dictator; both Joseph Nye and Niall Ferguson appear as occasional panelists. One could perhaps suspect that the "Global Public Square" tends to offer The World According To Harvard (however much internal diversity that could involve), yet the range of invitees is fairly broad, and they often agree to disagree. Furthermore, in the program segment "Fareed's Take" as well as in his print columns, Zakaria takes a stronger view of his own: it becomes apparent, for example, that he has tended to favor more of an American opening toward Iran, and is doubtful toward the workings of the regime in Saudiarabia.[9] And as the topic became hot, his favorable view was clear toward an immigration policy reform which would be more generous toward those who had at one time or other made their entrance illegally across the U.S.-Mexican border. In a *Washington Post* column (Zakaria 2014), he reminisced that he had been a college sophomore when he decided he wanted to become a U.S. citizen.[10] It had taken him through much paper work and a passage through several formal immigrant statuses, via a "green card" and a civics test, to reach there, after seventeen years, in 2001. Yet he did not view illegal immigrants with any hostility. So here it seems that his opinion has become quite distant from that expressed by his one-time mentor Samuel Huntington, in *Who Are We?*, a decade earlier. (And closer to that of Amy Chua.)

Then a little later, when President Obama made a brief but intensely celebrated visit to Delhi in January 2015, to attend the Republic Day parade but certainly also to engage in serious deliberations with the Indian leadership, Fareed Zakaria could still get an hour with him, sitting down in some secluded spot, for a wide-ranging interview for the "Global Public Square." Of course, Barack Obama likewise has a Harvard degree. Moreover, he is a sort of halfie, too.

London, Hamburg, Paris, Beirut/Paris

With some contributions to the scenario genre, however, there are indeed other countries heard from. Starting in an earlier phase, we have seen Great Britain contributing (also through transatlantic commuters), a number of writers to the scenario genre: Paul Kennedy, Robert Cooper, Timothy Garton Ash, Niall Ferguson. From there as well, there has been an occasional later voice speaking from that sort of South/North, East/West halfie background. In *After Empire* (2010), Dilip Hiro, born in what is now Pakistan but long in London, a prolific writer on many topics, forecasts an unstable multipolar world, with a key role for oil-rich countries in opposition to the United States. In *Ghosts of Empire* (2011), Kwasi Kwarteng, born in London by Ghanaian parents, sometime Conservative member of parliament, with a Ph.D. in economic history from Cambridge, has offered intriguing insight into the ways the backgrounds and personal quirks of individual colonial servants, working frequently quite independently in governing sizeable areas, affected the outcome on the ground in various territories once under British rule. Kwarteng does not engage in an open polemic with Niall Ferguson, but his portrayal of the Empire is certainly quite different.

Engaging more directly with the present and the future, there is a prominent voice from Germany: Josef Joffe, editor of *Die Zeit*, leading newsweekly broadsheet out of Hamburg. His book title *Überpower* (2006) in its hybridity already suggests an ambition to build a bridge across the Atlantic; and the book seems to be aimed as much at an American readership as at anybody else. Indeed it is a book about American power at its zenith—and then not so many years later there would be another book by Joffe named *The Myth of America's Decline* (2014).

Josef Joffe is again someone combining media and academic scenes—but with the twist that he seems to do so transatlantically, with his media engagement primarily in Europe (through *Die Zeit*), and his academic homelands largely in the USA. (Although his books evidently do well in the latter country, he writes op-ed pieces and reviews for American newspapers and magazines, and shows up as a guest at Fareed Zakaria's Global Public Square.) He has everything from an American high school diploma to a Harvard Ph.D. (with memorable undergraduate years at Swarthmore College in between); lately, there have been recurrent periods at Stanford University.[11] Harvard connections also show up quickly on the covers of *Überpower*, through endorsements by Fukuyama, Nye and Zakaria, while inside the book, there are references to Huntington, Nye and Ferguson. Not, on the other hand, to Benjamin Barber or Paul Kennedy, elsewhere on the American campus map; and not to the journalists Thomas Friedman and Robert Kaplan. (But Friedman gets a retrospective blurb on the back cover of *The World is Flat*, where Joffe's *New York Times* review of *The Lexus and the Olive Tree* is quoted.)

On second thought, one might wonder if even in the depth of Joe Joffe's mind, *Überpower* really originated in German. His memories of arriving in the United States as a student are in many ways not so different from Fareed Zakaria's. Yet the Hamburg vantage point comes through in some ways.

Like a number of scenarists, Joffe draws the world map in his own way. A key divide is between the Berlin-Berkeley Belt—"the West," with Australia, New Zealand as outliers, and Japan, Korea, Taiwan and Israel as honorary members—and the Baghdad-Beijing Belt. The latter may seem like a rather haphazard construct, not so convincingly supported through sparse footnote references. (If India is within that belt, as a conventional map would suggest, it does not get much space in the text; here Zakaria, Khanna and Mishra might all disagree.) [12]Yet Joffe in large part focuses on western Europe, and particularly on Germany and France. Here, as editor of a major newspaper in the region, he has a clear view of the flow of current debate. In that early twenty-first century period when much

European public opinion was against America's most conspicuous armed activities, Joffe could deal, critically and rather polemically, with some of the more prominent political and academic voices within that opinion. At the same time, he could note that in some circles, anti-Americanism in Europe had older and deeper roots.

What, then, would be the task of an Überpower? To avoid mistakes, for one thing: Joffe agrees that the 2003 Iraq War was one. Then perhaps not so surprisingly, Joffe sees a model in his old compatriot Bismarck's policy of placing his country at the active center of collaborative relationships with competitive neighbors. But one could note that Fareed Zakaria (2008) also had taken that nineteenth-century Iron Chancellor as a source for useful strategy. Soft power may be a good thing, too, although Joffe does not think it always works. In a way, his imagery of American cultural influence has a rather McWorld-like quality. (We may remember from Chap. 1 that Joseph Nye, introducing the soft power notion, quoted Joffe on how America through this asset "rules over an empire on which the sun never sets.")

Then in *The Myth of America's Decline* Joffe confronts "declinism"— he acknowledges that his original sense of it came from a late 1980s essay by Samuel Huntington, "a teacher who became a friend."[13] This is not solely an American preoccupation, he notes: in his time, Oswald Spengler was the "high priest of doom," and later on it was a theme in the work of the social philosophers of the "Frankfurt School."[14] As an observer of the political scene in the United States, however, Joffe discerns a striking recurrence over a half century or so: in the electoral cycle, challengers and newcomers dramatize the threat of decline, incumbents do not. So by 1960 Sputnik stood for the Soviet challenge, and John F. Kennedy as presidential candidate could offer the new, fresh alternative. Later there would be "Japan as Number One," most recently what he describes (with another neologism) as the modernitarianism of China. By 2008, there was Barack Obama with "Yes We Can." Incumbents tended to be more happy with things as they were. The notable exception was Jimmy Carter, with a rhetoric of "malaise" (drawing on poor academic advice) as he sought reelection in 1980— and that did not work out well.[15]

On the whole, based on the record, Joffe is not impressed by declinism, although he can see some point in it: "to foretell is to forestall," "to praise others is to prod America." By the twenty-first century, he concludes, the United States may not necessarily be best in everything. But it still wins the decathlon, and that again makes it indispensable. Yet beware: "Just because Declinists have always been wrong does not guarantee that they will never be right." (2014: 263)

Over now to Paris: Houellebecq's novel *Submission* focused on France, was declinist in its own way, and was undisputably fiction. But France also has a long tradition of America-watching; starting with Alexis de Tocqueville, and going on from there.[16] (And often, at least from World War II and Charles de Gaulle onwards, with some worry about American dominance.) Publicist-politician Jean-Jacques Servan-Schreiber's *The American Challenge* (1969), proclaiming that the United States was comprehensively superior in its economic war with Europe, became a bestseller. Jean-Francois Revel followed with *Without Marx or Jesus* (1971). In a way, one could perhaps see them as instances of vicarious celebrationism. The philosopher Bernard-Henri Lévy we referred to briefly in Chap. 4, in connection with his critical view of Huntington's *Who Are We?* His book *American Vertigo* (2006) is perhaps something like what Ethan Casey wanted from Pankaj Mishra: a perceptive foreigner's view, from on the road, of more of the United States. He has a brief encounter in Boston with the young Illinois politician with the odd name ("Barack Obama") who had just entered a wider public consciousness with a visionary convention speech. But Lévy also goes West—yes, to South Dakota, passing the Corn Palace, the tourist trap just off the Interstate highway with a multicolor façade entirely made up of corn cobs; talking to Russell Means, Amerindian activist, at the Pine Ridge reservation; inspecting the sculpted presidential faces at Mount Rushmore; walking through Castro District, San Francisco; deciding that if he had to choose one American city to live in, it would be Seattle. And much more. This is not so much in the global scenario genre. But it was an American sojourn in between times when some of the genre's frequent fliers were returning home to ponder what was happening to their country. One could perhaps compare the Lévy account with Robert Kaplan's *An Empire Wilderness* (1998) and Thomas Friedman's (with Michael Mandelbaum) *That Used to be Us* (2011). Kaplan, also traveling mostly in the western half of the country, with excursions to Mexico and to Canada, is concerned in large part with growing inequality, and with fragmentation. Friedman, dwelling more on institutions and not least on education, worries about failing competitiveness. Lévy, for his part, seems more subtly, complicatedly optimistic. The political heritage is alive enough for the country to pull through, and there really is no Empire.

But these America-watchers would not be French if they all agreed. Emmanuel Todd finds rather more of such world dominance, but also leans toward declinism, in *After the Empire* (2003), more of a full-scale scenario attempt. Todd presents himself as a historian and an anthropologist; the latter identity comes through not least in a consistent interest in the implications of kinship structures, a traditional focus of the discipline. (A strong patrilineal emphasis, he argues, is really more important in shaping Arab society than its religious allegiance. And family authority patterns tend to infiltrate state structures; an interesting example of what in our Chap. 6 terminology would be a case of entangled consociality and state frames of cultural process.) With this goes Todd's enduring concern with demography.[17] As his surname may suggest, too, he notes that there are American linkages on both his father's and his mother's sides of the family. His doctorate is from Cambridge (the one in England).

Literacy leads to a changing demography, Todd points out, and much of the world is now on its way to lower birth rates, with generations hardly more than replacing each other. This leads to political upheavals, such as in the Middle East, but they are temporary. Todd sees a great deal of value in Fukuyama's vision of the trend toward liberal capitalist democracy, but goes beyond it. Education can lead to a further cleavage between those with little more than literacy and those highly educated, and the latter may in the end be more inclined toward oligarchy than democracy.

He discerns that the United States is well on its way in that direction. Moreover, when the world generally tends toward peaceful trade, and when democracies generally do not fight each other, the United States finds itself under the threat of isolation out there, between the oceans, no longer needed by the world. So geopolitics strikes again: the country will try to make a place for itself as a global troublemaker. But there is hope on Todd's (2003: 58) horizon: "There is nothing to prevent one from imagining that a liberal and democratic Russia might one day protect the planet from America's aggressive attempts to regain its global imperial status."

Well, no. Imagination is basically free.

This is an intriguing, and intellectually complex, scenario. One should perhaps be reminded, however, that it originated in those early years of the new millennium when there was also said to be a deep divide in the Atlantic between the Martians and the Venusians, gazing at each other in mutual incomprehension. Of the first eight endnotes of *After the Empire*, four refer to Joseph Nye, Benjamin Barber, Paul Kennedy and Samuel Huntington respectively. (Three more refer to writings by Norman

Podhoretz, Noam Chomsky and Henry Kissinger.) Francis Fukuyama shows up in note 11. So Todd is obviously well acquainted with the scenario genre as it has emerged in the United States. American scenarists have not been equally inclined to cite Todd.[18]

Dominique Moïsi, with *The Geopolitics of Emotion* (2009), takes another view again. His global scenario went through a familiar kind of passage: it started as a syndicated newspaper column, turned into an article in *Foreign Affairs*, and then grew into a book. And the title of that first article had a Huntingtonian allusion: "The Clash of Emotions." Moïsi, too, has had his off-and-on Harvard connections (as a graduate student, and as a visiting professor), although his enduring base is at the French Institute of International Affairs (IFRI).

Moïsi sees three emotions—fear, humiliation and hope—as shaping the contemporary world. Such an emphasis on emotions may seem counterintuitive, insofar as we might usually take these to be individual, and shifting even fairly quickly in time. But it turns out to be a vehicle of imagination which takes Moïsi a long way. This is yet another kind of geopolitics. Emotions matter as "they impact the attitudes of peoples, the relationships between cultures, and the behavior of nations" (2009: 29)

At present, painting with a broad brush, he sees a culture of hope in much of Asia (China, India, Southeast Asia). A culture of humiliation is there, with significant exceptions, in much of the Arab-Islamic world. A culture of fear is widespread in Europe, and—here Moïsi evidently agrees with Fareed Zakaria—in North America. He also admits, however, that not all countries fit readily into the scheme. Among the more complex cases are Russia (humiliated after the crumbling of the Soviet Union, fear exacerbated by xenophobia, but then perhaps rising toward hope again), Iran (humiliated in the past by Western domination, rising with new energy but with regime eccentricities as a diversion), and Israel, with its combination of hope and fear. Africa is between despair and hope.

Again, as a frame for portraying the early twenty-first century world, the three-emotions combination has some persuasive strength. If one considers it together with the understandings of culture in Chaps. 6 and 7, one may have further questions. The scheme appears to lean toward an assumption of "replication of uniformity" rather than "organization of diversity." The state frame can alternatively cultivate all three emotions, and this may be what Moïsi like many scenarists is most concerned with. Movements, perhaps likewise. Does the market frame in a greater part deal in hope? And to what extent do these emotions really penetrate frames of everyday consociality?

Attributing emotions to countries and continents, moreover, Moïsi's preferred scale is surely XL. (And in the terms of the historian Braudel, as noted in Chap. 6, this seems to be conjunctural, medium-term history.) Taking his scheme around, we may see sentiments of humiliation strong in certain microcultures, such as that of the Tetuan gang responsible for the Madrid bombings. Thomas Friedman's Square People are strongly into hope, wherever they turn up. In the end, perhaps we feel that beside hope, fear and humiliation there should also be a recognition of Greed. It may be most conspicuous in certain size M cultures in corners of society: at its worst in kleptocracies or crypto-kleptocracies in Russia, China, Africa and the United States (perhaps just about all well served by technicians in Zürich). Is Davos Man mostly there, in milder forms, or does he engage with hope as well? (Hardly much humiliation.)

Making emotions carry such a heavy interpretive burden, too, one may wonder if there should not be some more explicit attention to the place of ambivalence in human life. Rhetorically and methodologically it may be inconvenient, yet being of two minds about things is hardly so unusual.[19]

Finally, however, Dominique Moïsi offers two vivid alternative scenarios for the world—using fully the freedom of fiction. These scenarios are both from November, 2025 (some fifteen years from the publication of his book). The beginning setting for both is Tel Aviv, Israel. The first of them is 1984ish Orwellian, but updated: fear prevails, the country's population has been declining, as both Jews and Arabs have been fleeing the atmosphere of violence and a life in an oppressive state of near-martial law. But things are hardly better elsewhere. Terrorist networks have used biological weapons successfully in major Asian and European metropoles in the "White Death" attacks of 2019–2020. Borders have been shut down, dissident groups have been banned, military checkpoints and physical searches are omnipresent in everyday life. The president of the United States who took office in 2013 had been a far-right conservative of isolationist inclinations who quickly announced a reduction of the armed forces. By 2025 they were largely deployed along the heavily fortified Mexican and Canadian borders. There was not much left of a European Union. Belgium had exploded in 2010, and then Catalonia, Scotland and Wales declared themselves independent. Turkey is on the verge of implosion, Russia has installed puppet governments in Kiev and Tbilisi. China's war of conquest with Taiwan became long and costly. Generally, the Asian culture of hope had been eroded by environmental degradation. Overall, the notion of a "clash of civilizations" had become a self-fulfilling prophecy.

There is also, however, Moïsi's alternative scenario. Hope prevails. Back to Rabin Square, Tel Aviv: today this is the site for celebration of the fifth anniversary of the Middle East peace treaty. Palestinians have their own country, but there are also the beginnings of a Middle Eastern Common Market, with Lebanon, Israel, Palestine, Syria and Jordan as members. The wise investments of the Gulf emirates had contributed to transforming the region. Chinese, Indian and Japanese technology are helping turn Africa into "the planet's greatest locus of economic growth and opportunity," while Brazil and Argentina are taking the lead in creating the Latin American counterpart of the European Union. Turkey is about to join the latter, while there is a new climate of confidence between Russia and its European neighbors. Ukraine, now an EU member, serves as a perfect bridge. "Encouraged by a president with multicultural roots and interests, Americans began studying the cultures and languages of other countries." There was a run on passport offices, too, when they turned with new enthusiasm to travel, and they were leading the struggle for environmental protection. At the United Nations a dynamic, charismatic new secretary-general has at her (yes) disposal a streamlined bureaucracy and a strong military force ("mercenaries of peace," mostly Gurkha regiments from Nepal). In the Security Council, France and Britain have given up their permanent seats in favor of a representative of the European Union as a whole.

Indeed, Dominic Moïsi has allowed room for his imagination. But the world needs hope, he concludes, and dedicates his book to his father, who was in Auschwitz but survived.

Amin Maalouf, also a Parisian, has another background. His family is from the mountains of the Levant, in what is now Lebanon, and of a local Christian denomination which was already there in the Arab world before Europe became Christian, and before the Prophet Muhammad and Islam appeared. His father was a newspaper editor in Beirut, and in his twenties he himself began a career as writer and editor there. But then when the civil war broke out, he left for Paris and established himself as a writer of both fiction and non-fiction.[20] (That was a few years before the young journalist Thomas Friedman arrived in Beirut to begin his career as a Middle East correspondent, resulting in due time in the book *From Beirut to Jerusalem*. Friedman [1989:23] offers a vivid view of the wartime city: "I came to think of Beirut as a huge abyss, the darkest corner of human behavior, an urban jungle where not even the law of the jungle applied.")

If "empire" has again become a keyword of debate, Maalouf's historical horizon indeed goes back to an earlier version, when Rome ruled on
all sides of the Mediterranean, and much of his writing engages with the
shifting times since then. His space of sensibility has clearly developed
between his Lebanese and French experiences, although it is not confined
to these. For the novel *The Rock of Tanios* (his books tend to get translated, also into English) he was awarded a Prix Goncourt, although he
may have drawn more international attention for his fictionalized account
of the life of *Leo Africanus* (1988). This famous early sixteenth-century
traveler, aka al-Hasan al-Wazzan, was born in Muslim Spain, went into
enduring exile in North Africa, and from there traveled, it seems, as far
south as to West African Timbuktu. To the east, he had been on a pilgrimage to Mecca when he was captured by Christian pirates and offered as a
present to the Pope, who soon found his knowledge strategically valuable.
And so out of the Vatican, after being baptized a Christian, Leo Africanus
achieved his reputation on the north side of the Mediterranean.[21]

On the non-fiction side of Maalouf's work there was soon *The Crusades
through Arab Eyes* (1984), portraying the period, mostly the twelfth and
thirteenth centuries, when Muslims as well as Jews became the victims of
those invading northerners who were mostly described not as "crusad-
ers," but as "Frankish," *Franj*—the term *faranji* is still in rather widespread, somewhat distancing use for western aliens in Muslim regions of
the world.[22] It was a period of schism between the West and the Arab East,
Maalouf concludes in the final lines of the book, which is "deeply felt by
the Arabs, even today, as an act of rape" ([1984]2006: 266).

In 2011, Amin Maalouf was elected to the *Academie Francaise*. As far
as the genre of future scenarios is concerned, two of his books more or less
belong in it: *In the Name of Identity* (2001) and *Disordered World* (2011).

One might think that with someone like Maalouf, France has its halfies,
too, with a capacity to draw on a double set of foundational experiences
for insights into complicated realities. That, however, is not, strictly speaking, the way Maalouf himself thinks about his own identity, or identities
in general:

> So am I half French and half Lebanese? Of course not. Identity can't be
> compartmentalised. You can't divide it up into halves or thirds or any other
> separate segments. I haven't got several identities: I've got just one, made
> up of many components in a mixture that is unique to me, just as other
> people's identity is unique to them as individuals. (2001: 2)

In a way, again, this is not so different from what we heard from Amartya Sen saying about identity, in Chap. 3, in his polemic against Huntington. The identity of a human being is a complicated, multifaceted entity. Yet Maalouf seems to be even fiercer in his emphasis on individuality: as that human being turns experiences and beliefs into a single coherent whole, the resulting identity is unique, shared with nobody else. This is reflected in his view of religions as well: faith is a personal, a spiritual achievement of the mind and soul which ought not to be collectivized into large-scale identities.

Turning such matters into totalizing allegiances, either-or forms of identity politics, is a path to mistrust and conflict. He could see this in Lebanon, first in odd ways of portioning out national political offices on the basis of "confession;" then long battle frontiers stretching through his old home town. But in large part the world is now one of migrants, and children of migrants. In France, and in Germany, he could see people born in these countries, but of Algerian parents in the one case and of Turkish parents in the other. Their natural inclination was to acknowledge and integrate past as well as present sources of identity, but this was not accepted in the societies which were now their homes. What should be there instead, in Maalouf's view, is mutual respect—acknowledgment of both difference and similarity, as well as a right to criticize. And the mass of people who now find themselves in these in-between positions have a special role to play in forging links, eliminating misunderstandings; acting as bridges and mediators between cultures.

What Maalouf sketches, then, is a moral philosophy of modernity and globalization, with dignity and reciprocity as key concepts. Over time, both Islam and Christianity have had their periods of openness to the world and to change, as well as dark periods of closure and intolerance. While both have influenced the regions where they have dominated, both have also been shaped by what was already at hand there.

Since the nineteenth century, however, the tendency has become forever stronger for the modern and the global to become the property of one culture. When modernity bears the mark of the Other, Maalouf argues, some of the people who confront it will assert their difference by brandishing symbols of atavism. Today it is the response of some Muslims. Taking the example of a country which at the time of his writing was more or less in a state of civil war, however, he finds it more important to consider its present and its recent past than what is more remote in time:

You could read a dozen large tomes on the history of Islam from its very beginnings and you still wouldn't understand what is going on in Algeria. But read 30 pages on colonialism and decolonisation and then you'll understand quite a lot. (2001: 66)

Even as he reminds us of the long-ago ravages of the *faranji*, one might reflect, Maalouf seems not to be an advocate of *longue durée* history *à la* Fernand Braudel. (Samuel Huntington and Robert Kaplan may be for it—see Chap. 5—but Lévy, Todd and Moïsi do not mention it either, so its original French base no longer seems so strong.) This is rather conjunctural history. For Maalouf, a key figure of recent Arab imagination is Gamal Abdel Nasser, the Egyptian president in a volatile period.

Recently, too, Maalouf has also noticed that some of his closest French friends speak of globalization as a catastrophe:

This is because they now see globalisation as synonymous with Americanisation, and they wonder what future there will be for France in an increasingly standardised world, and what will become of France's language, culture, prestige, influence and way of life. (2001: 74)

Looking back to the preceding chapter, it is not difficult to see changing fortunes of "soft power" here, with accompanying nostalgia, but for Maalouf some empathy with his present compatriots comes easily enough.[23] So what does he see as a better kind of global interconnectedness?

It would be one where we fight for the universality of human values, and at the same time against standardization, against hegemony, "against everything that stifles the full variety of linguistic, artistic and intellectual expression"; "against everything that makes for a monotonous and puerile world." (2001: 107) Reciprocity becomes the key principle. Whichever part of the world you are from, you should be able to see something from your own culture adopted all over the world…including North America.

Language has a special place on Maalouf's agenda for a desirable kind of globalization. Again, one can sense that it is not least a French sensitivity: the growing hyperlanguage status of English entails a declining role for what has been another world language of sorts. But in principle, for Maalouf language is important because it involves both identity and communication—and the more contexts where you can communicate while demonstrating your identity, or more of your identities, the better. So national languages, even if like Icelandic they are spoken by rather few people, should not be allowed to get impoverished as domains of use are taken over by a global language even at home. Moreover, in contexts where native speakers of two languages come together, they should preferably not turn to a third language. Maalouf inserts the question into the multilingual European Union:

> Will future relations between Germany and France be in the hands of Anglophones from both countries, or of French-speaking Germans and German-speaking Frenchmen? A little common sense, lucidity and will-power should be enough to ensure that commercial, cultural and other exchanges remain chiefly in the hands of those with a special interest in their opposite numbers; an interest they have demonstrated by a meaningful cultural investment, such as familiarising themselves with their interlocutors' language of identity. (2001: 140)

Maalouf ends *In the Name of Identity* on a note of modesty and quiet optimism. Authors, he reflects, may have high hopes for the response to their work, and its lasting impact. As he reaches his final manuscript page, he has a simpler wish for his book:

> May my grandson, growing up and finding it one day by chance on the family bookshelves, look through the pages, read a passage or two, then put it back in the dusty corner where he found it, shrugging his shoulders and marvelling that in his grandfather's day such things still needed to be said. (2001: 164)

That may still become true. In *Disordered World* (2011), however, Maalouf in large part comes back to his enduring concerns. This is in a volatile period: between editions, the Arab Spring takes off, people gather in Tahrir Square and elsewhere. But the preface of the original edition begins: "We have embarked on this century without a compass."

Maalouf continues to find his own way navigating between the Arab World, Europe (with France in it), and the world as a whole (with America in it). He comes back now to developing his view of the era of Gamal Abdel Nasser. Nominally independent, yet still under Western domination, and recently humiliated by defeat at the hands of that new little state of Israel, most Arab regimes by the mid-twentieth century suffered from a lack of popular legitimacy. Throwing out a corrupt monarchy in a military coup, Nasser captured the imagination of people across the region. Indeed, legitimacy is a key concept in *Disordered World*.

By restoring Arab dignity, Nasser earned specifically the variant Maalouf terms "patriotic legitimacy," at least for a while. He did not govern particularly well, but he was among the handful of leaders of the "non-aligned movement" which asserted a more real independence on the part of what was becoming known as the Third World. (He also drove a number of the more cosmopolitan minorities out of Egypt, including the family of the coming Bat Ye'or who gave us "Eurabia.") Most importantly in the region, there was his triumph, political if not really military, in the Suez Crisis. For a moment in history, in the late 1950s and the 1960s, it could seem as if the Arab World was pulling itself together. Then it fragmented again, along complex lines which Maalouf knowingly accounts for, and after the Six Days War in 1967, humiliation was back. Nasser died not long after.

I actually heard Nasser speak once, on May Day 1965, in Tahrir Square, in front of an enthusiastic, handkerchief-waving crowd—and I certainly recalled that moment when another kind of Square People came together there, on my television screen, in 2011. I can sense that Amin Maalouf, beginning to develop his own curiosity about the world around him, and growing up in a home with a newspaper editor father, absorbed very personally the ever-shifting story of these times. This may be an instance where generational as well as regional experience has mattered in scenario writing. Looking back at the period a half-century or so later, in any case, Maalouf can see this as a baseline for what has happened in Arab society later. When Arab nationalism did not succeed, there was some scattered leaning toward socialism, but with the crumbling of the Soviet Union, that was not a credible alternative either. Yet in this part of the world, the end of the Cold War was a bit more of a side show. What really mattered was the emergence of radical Islamism as a remaining oppositional alternative, a way of confronting the sense of domination.

For an optimistic moment at least, Maalouf could see another way— "the people's patience was not infinite." Yet at the time of his writing, the movement toward change was already slowing down. On balance, he identifies himself as a skeptic, yet an activist. The debate over global warming, as it was in the early years of the new century, offers him an example. Even if he was not yet entirely convinced by the arguments, he found that humanity could not afford to neglect them, and not act on them. To do nothing *could* lead to disaster. The burden of proof must be with the do-nothings. And this is his line of reasoning in dealing with the twenty-first century world generally.

In the Name of Identity had been a book without footnotes and references, and Maalouf's opponents mostly remain nameless. This is not so in *Disordered World*: at least there is a reasonably extensive bibliography where Thomas Friedman, Samuel Huntington, Bernard Lewis, Joseph Nye and Fareed Zakaria appear (along with many others), and "the end of history" and "soft power" show up passingly in the text. Evidently Maalouf is familiar with the world of the American scenarists. With regard to "the clash of civilizations," Maalouf starts out gently (or perhaps a little ironically?): "To see in today's conflicts a clash between six or seven civilizations…is enlightening and intellectually stimulating, as is evidenced by the number of debates it has given rise to." (2011: 213) But of course he does not agree with the thesis. The world is more complicated than that.

Nevertheless, culture is central to his concerns: "Today the role of culture is nothing less than to provide us with the intellectual and moral tools for survival." (2011: 158) That requires building a shared civilization, based on principles of the universality of human values as well as the diversity of cultural expression. The universality of values means that there can be no acceptance of things like tyranny, the caste system, forced marriage, nepotism and corruption—such cultural relativism would involve not respect but contempt. The valued diversity would rather find its forms in language, literature, arts, craftsmanship, cuisine… Instead of "global tribes" who detest each other, there are fellow human beings. In this twenty-first century, no longer strangers, only traveling companions.

Maalouf sees some promise in Europe. It is not flawless, but at best it could turn out to offer a model for how peoples can leave old animosities behind and find a mode of coexistence which draws on the diversity of both natives and immigrants.

And then again there is America. It remains problematic, once more in terms of legitimacy, when a country with five percent of the world's population can exercise such global influence. But then, strikingly, Maalouf finds new hope personified in the advent of someone named Barack Hussein Obama:

> More than ever, the world needs America, but an America which is reconciled with the world as well as with itself, an America which exercises its global role with respect for its own values as well as others'—with integrity, fairness and generosity. I would even add with elegance and grace. (2011: 248–249)

TWO-FACED RUSSIA

From Paris eastward, from Beirut northward: in Russia debates over directions in the past, present and future have been an enduring feature of the intellectual and political landscape. The triumph of world communism was, of course, for a long time its dominant global future scenario. Since that passed into oblivion, there may have been no major contributions to the genre as we view it here. On the other hand, Moscow allows us a glimpse of how scenarios from the outside can be received in another setting; and then we may also see how Parisian perspectives suggest understandings of how recent Russian experiences, and reactions to them, point toward a future.

As Russian debates are mostly conducted in Russian, they tend to be less accessible to most of the outside world, but fortunately there have been some of those migrant minds that Amin Maalouf points to, serving as bridges and mediators. Andrei Tsygankov (2003), international relations scholar with his early academic training from Moscow in the *perestroika* years, now based in the United States, has reported on the Russian reception of "the end of history" and "the clash of civilizations." It was not uniform, and it changed over time. Fukuyama's perspective was initially viewed more favorably among Russian liberals, in the final period of Soviet decline. With its emphasis on deep-lying differences and on conflict, the Huntington scenario, arriving on the scene a little later, could meet a certain understanding among those intellectuals and politicians still preoccupied with the centrality of the state, and not least among remaining national communists. Yet due to their ethnocentrism, neither scenario was in the end acceptable to Russians, Tsygankov argues; so he concludes that those theorists who wish to be influential across borders which are both political and cultural need to frame their ideas so as to make them more fit to travel.

The "end of history" and "clash of civilizations" scenarios arrived in Russia, obviously, in a period of dramatic changes, but reactions to them also had deeper roots. This country has certainly never needed to depend on imports from the outside world for large scenarios—again and again with implications for the present and future, even when they have dwelt on the past.

It is a past which has kept raising questions about what kind of country it would be, and where it would fit into the world. Early in the eighteenth century, Czar Peter the Great, impressed with what he had seen during a journey in western Europe, transformed his administration, ordered beards to be shaved off, and shifted his capital to an extreme western corner (actually on past Swedish territory), with a harbor on the Baltic. Later in the century, a reluctant immigrant German princess became the long-reigning empress Catherine the Great, and engaged in conquests through North Asia, reaching the Pacific Coast—while importing scientists from Europe, and keeping her correspondence with Voltaire going.

So should Russia turn outward or inward, toward the West or the East? In the nineteenth century, there would be varieties of Slavophiles, idealizing the peasantry and the Orthodox Church, rejecting individualism and rationalism. Later in the same century came the *narodniki*, radical populists and anti-czarists, turning occasionally to revolutionary terror. Some decades into the twentieth century, Eurasianists (whose Eurasia was of course not that of George Orwell in *1984*) looked with favor at the historical interactions between Slavs and Mongols in the steppe lands, asking if the cultural influences of Genghis Khan's Mongol Empire had not in the long run helped save Russia from too much Europeanization. In such politico-intellectual clusterings, one could still find some ambiguity and paradox. The Slavophiles drew some inspiration from the German cultural nationalism, with its academic wing, flourishing at the time.[24] One could borrow the form, without the content. The Eurasianists did not meet in Irkutsk or anywhere thereabouts, but in anti-Stalinist exile in large part in Central Europe (where, it is true, they could witness the same continental troubles that made Oswald Spengler's *The Decline of the West* a Euro-Pessimist bestseller, and take in the kinds of geopolitical thought offered by people like Ratzel, Kjellén, Haushofer and Mackinder, as sketched in Chap. 3). In some ways, there were differences among them. In more precise geocultural terms, a Slavophile would hardly be a Eurasianist. But what makes them similar is what they were against: moving any closer to the West.

During much of the Soviet era, there was hardly much open debate over this. At least as we try to understand it, looking back from afar, it might appear that in local scholarly worlds, some denizens to a degree hibernated, but gained some wiggle room by paying lip-service to a regnant but basically stagnant ideology, then proceeding with mostly empirical work. By the time the Soviet Union was a world power, its international engagements reflected in scholarly circles as well. (Moscow and Leningrad had their own Africanists.) Part of the story could be told as a rise and fall of academic microcultures, their inhabitants watching their borders. Toward the end of the period, world language absorbed one additional Russian concept: *samizdat*.

Then by the late twentieth century again, the questions were still there. What in much of the world was World War II, we may remember, was to Russians as often The Great Patriotic War. And what further west was, above all, the end of the Cold War was in Russia, with the *perestroika* and the end of the Soviet Union, a period of domestic upheaval and dramatic decline of international position. Some enjoyed the new opportunities for intellectual and cultural exchange across borders, and for travel.[25] Moscow had its Square People too, in August 1991, gathering spontaneously in structureless communitas. A smaller number of people were more or less discreetly transiting from *nomenklatura* to oligarchy. For a much larger number, however, things were not going well. Viktor Chernomyrdin, sometime prime minister (and at least one-time member of the Davos Club, we may remember from Chap. 7), earned some of his renown at home for malapropisms and other revealing off-the-cuff oneliners: "We wanted the best, but it turned out like always."

One Big Picture thinker, hardly known in the world outside Russia and its "near abroad," seems to call for attention here.[26] Lev Gumilev, born in 1912, was the son of two famous Russian poets. The father was executed by the Soviet regime in its early years, and the son, consequently forever suspect, spent long periods in the Gulag during the Stalin era. (In between, he served in the Red Army in the Battle of Berlin.) Evidently, this gave him time to think—but although he could get some books sent to him, the library facilities were presumably not great. Then when he was back in freedom, he first earned a doctorate in history, yet found it difficult to break into the academic establishment in the historical discipline. By then based in Leningrad, he went on to get another doctorate in geography, more tolerant of unorthodox thinking.

Gumilev concerned himself with issues of nationality and ethnicity. These had been forever important in the Russian empire and in the Soviet Union—Stalin himself had played a part in formulating an official view of them.[27] While ethnic Russians went on being just Russians, a sort of unmarked standard, other groups used whatever were the rules of the game in their own way to improve their standing. As the end of the twentieth century came closer, the game itself seemed to become another one. With demographic change and internal migration, tensions grew between ethnic Russians, people from the Caucasus (such as Georgians and Chechens), and newcomers from Central Asia. It seems the people, or peoples, of Russia had to face that "Who Are We?" question again.

In Gumilev's answer there was a connection back to older Eurasianism, and at the same time he offered a kind of natural history of the *etnos*, the basic cultural grouping. The *etnos* developed in its geographical habitat, a biosphere, and depending on the characteristics of that habitat, it would engage in battles, exchanges or modes of coexistence with other peoples, resulting in a wider pattern which we might translate as something like a civilization. One could speculate that the dearth of libraries in the Gulag left its durable mark on Gumilev's thinking here: it took his *etnos* narrative away from documented history, away from existing bodies of social theory, and into something more like a geopolitical mystique. The primordialist, inward-looking tendency seems clear. Moreover, commentators scrutinizing Gumilev's work more closely and comprehensively find a streak of that old Russian variety of anti-Semitism, with Jews as "rootless cosmopolitans"; for Jews are understood not to fit into the organic connection between man and land.

Seen from the outside (to the extent that it is possible), Gumilev's style of depicting the shifting career of the *etnos* have reminded some observers of Spengler and Toynbee. A more recent parallel has been suggested with Samuel Huntington: fundamental cultural units draw on sources of their own, over their borders battles are fought. But not everybody seems to find that similarity so striking.

If Andrei Tsygankov, looking over the not-so-successful entries of the Huntington and Fukuyama scenarios onto the Russian scene, found them insufficiently adaptive to global intellectual travel, one could surely take the same view of Lev Gumilev's Big Picture of things. Yet in Russia, at one point, indeed as Gumilev was nearing the end of his life (he died in 1992), after his work had long subsisted in scholarly obscurity, it rather suddenly made its strong appeal to the public imagination. As a new millennium began, critics could report that in his home country, "all bookshops are flooded with his works and his name is widely known across the entire post-Soviet space." (Shnirelman and Panarin 2001: 2) School curricula were redesigned under the inspiration of his writings. It seems his sense of the essentials of peoplehood resonated with the feelings of a great many who had found old official views unsatisfactory, and who perhaps could not find their way to more narrowly academic presentations at all.

Evidently finding Gumilev's Eurasian tendency to its liking, for the purpose of building a national identity, the new republic of Kazakhstan named a university after him, and issued a postage stamp with his portrait. This would seem to qualify him as a transnational, although not exactly a global, public intellectual; even though his public presence was in large part posthumous, and hardly anything that he has written has been translated into and published in English.

Again, the *perestroika* years and the early post-Soviet years were a trying period for many Russians. It is good to have, from this period, some insightful ethnography, not least by Americans who came to Russia for field work.[28] (They did not all go to Moscow either—Muscovites, some at least, are rather unlike other Russians.) One of the richest pictures, however, is offered by another migrant scholar fitting Amin Maalouf's conception of the cultural bridge builder: Serguei Oushakine, Russian-historian-turned-American-anthropologist, thus once more a halfie of sorts. For a monograph titled *The Patriotism of Despair* (2009), Oushakine draws (among other things) on extensive field research in south Siberia, in what had long been his own home town. He comments on Gumilev's late rise, and on local protest against "looting by greedy Moscow capitalists," and educational issues, but not least on activities and sentiments among war veterans (from the conflicts in Afghanistan and Chechnya), and among the mothers of fallen soldiers.[29]

There is a sense of pervasive loss and trauma, and of the withdrawal of what used to be a nearly omnipresent state apparatus from everyday life—from entanglements with what we would see as the frame of consociality—and from responsibility in situations of crisis. Back, quickly, to Dominique Moïsi here: we sensed before that as Moïsi offered the large picture of the geopolitics of emotion, his cultural scale was basically XL. Oushakine takes our understanding of Russia to size M or even S in his more close-up ethnography, and then back at least to L. Moïsi, we can also remember, saw Russia as a complex case within his scheme. It had been humiliated as the Soviet Union fell apart, a sense of fear had resonated with xenophobia, but then perhaps there had been a turn toward renewed hope. Oushakine agrees. "Various forms of the patriotism of despair," he writes, "provided a key base of support for the resurgence of Russia's national assertiveness." (2009: 7) Perhaps Amin Maalouf comes in here as well, with his emphasis on patriotic legitimacy: after a period of humiliation, there could be room on the early twenty-first century Russian scene for someone a bit like Gamal Abdel Nasser.

VOICES FROM SINGAPORE

Maps again: even without the lands which left to become "the near abroad," what remains Russia is a very large country, stretching over more time zones than any other. Singapore, on the other hand, its inhabitants say fondly and ironically, is a "red dot on the map."[30] (The color here does not seem significant.) Under the circumstances, it is not so easy to turn mostly inward. So Singaporean voices are often heard addressing the world, commenting on the world, and occasionally reporting to Singapore from elsewhere. One prominent voice was certainly for a long time the founding father of the city-state, long-time prime minister Lee Kuan Yew, who died in 2015, aged 91. Returning home from studies in Cambridge (England), with a law degree, young Harry Lee rebranded himself for public purposes with his Chinese name (the majority of Singaporeans are ethnic Chinese), helped drive out British colonialism from what was taking form as a Malaysian federation, and then found his city pushed out of that entity by the leadership of the Malay majority. And so as leader of what unexpectedly had become an independent republic, and more or less a one-party state, he rather ruthlessly pushed a rapid modernization policy. Approaching the year 2000, in a *Wall Street Journal* interview series about the most important inventions of the millennium, Lee responded, "air conditioning"—this had improved mental concentration and the quality of work.[31] After over thirty years he retired as prime minister; but after some time his son was the prime minister, while he himself was in a historically and globally unique official position as the Minister Mentor (abbreviated MM in the local media).

Briefly in the 1990s, Lee Kuan Yew had been among those who gave some support to a rhetoric of "Asian Values"—another XL-size culture notion, with limited intellectual credibility in its own right, claiming a base partly in a Confucian heritage but serving mostly as an alibi for a politics of soft authoritarianism, and largely gone with the wind of the late 1990s crashes of several Asian economies.[32] Interviewed by Fareed Zakaria (1994: 111), during the latter's term as editor of *Foreign Affairs*, he returned again and again to questions of culture and cultural differences—even as his understanding of culture tended to be one of flexibility and openness to change. As for the United States, he liked the easy, open relations between people regardless of ethnicity, religion and social status. But he did not admire all that he saw:

as a total system, I find parts of it totally unacceptable: guns, drugs, violent crime, vagrancy, unbecoming behavior in public—in sum the breakdown of civil society.

Some fifteen years later, an American journalist had a two-day, book-length interview with the MM (by then in his mid-eighties). It roamed over many topics, but also over Lee's contacts with Samuel Huntington. They had met in the United States and in Singapore, and then:

> one day, he sent me a piece he was writing in the *Foreign Affairs* called the 'Clash of Civilizations'. Then I saw him and I said, look, I agree with you only where the Muslims are concerned, only there. I should have written it in a piece or in a letter to him, my thought turned out prophetic. I said, Hinduism, Chinese Confucianism, Japanese Shintoism, they are secular really. They know that to progress, you must master science and technology, and that's where they are going to compete with you in the end. But the Muslims believe that if they mastered the Quran and they are prepared to do all that Muhammad has prescribed, they will succeed. So we can expect trouble from them and so, it happened. (Plate 2010: 117–118)

One should hardly disregard here the fact that Singapore is surrounded by Muslim countries, and that Lee had had that experience of his nation-to-be being expelled from Malaysia. Yet if Islam had remained in Southeast Asia the way it had been in the past, he continued in the interview, there might not have been much of a problem. Islam had come to the region with traders and sailing ships from Yemen, merging in a milder way with what was already there of animism, Hinduism and Buddhism. The real conflict only came more lately, with the Saudi and Wahhabi influence, based on oil money, with thriving hypocrisy at home—"for weekends, they go to Dubai."

Again, Singapore has had more voices than the Minister Mentor. Another veteran, the historian Wang Gungwu (1996/97), renowned specialist on Chinese diasporas, with an academic career which had taken him from colonial Malaya (and some of his childhood under World War II Japanese occupation) through Britain, Hong Kong and Australia before settling again in Singapore, reviewed Huntington's book more gently and with some academic detachment in an American journal, *The National Interest* (at the time with Huntington, Fukuyama and Joffe on the advisory board).[33] The book and the preceding article had indeed found Asian audiences. Wang noted that in the last few years, he had made more than a dozen trips to Japan, and each time he had found Japanese intellectuals intensely interested in what Huntington's thesis meant for East Asia. Reading the book-length version a second time, he had come to think of Machiavelli:

> less powerful civilizations may be encouraged by Huntington to believe that they might become new princes, with greatly enlarged and elevated parts to play. In the end, this is what so stunning about *The Clash of Civilizations*: it is not just *about* the future, but may actually help shaping it.

And so Wang joined those seeing the possibility of a self-fulfilling prophecy.

A voice from a younger generation: by the time Simon Tay wrote *Alien Asian* (1997), in his thirties, he already had a growing public reputation. The book drew on his columns "Fax from America" (again, this was in the 1990s) published regularly in *Straits Times*, the leading Singapore newspaper, during a period when he studied for a law degree at Harvard. So like Fareed Zakaria, Benazir Bhutto, Josef Joffe and Dominique Moïsi he had had his stint at that university, but before that he had already been in a writer's program at the University of Iowa. And in a Singaporean family which was already American-oriented (and of that cosmopolitan Malay-Chinese background known as Peranakan), he had grown up under the influence of soft power.

Alien Asian indeed shows that Tay enjoyed life around Harvard Square, but he also recounts other experience and encounters in the United States. It began already on arrival at Los Angeles International Airport, as he ventured to help Mrs. Ramirez, an elderly, silver-haired Mexican woman, speaking Spanish only, through immigration control. Then it took him through a conversation with an Iowa farmer and small-town life in Vermont, and "inside the Beltway" of the national capital (finding its elite curiously encapsulated in its own way of life). At some point he found himself shopping for a handgun, for self-protection; but ending up getting a pepper spray. He followed the nationally televised road hunt for O.J. Simpson, former football star, after the bloody murder of his ex-wife, and with Singaporean friends he and his wife went shopping for groceries in Boston's Chinatown, next to the red-light district known as the Combat Zone.

Returning to Singapore, Tay could reminisce about Asian and Asian-American friends he had made in the United States. It seemed to him that although they were where they wanted to be, many of them felt that Americans were keeping a distance to them. People he met, whose notion of Asia was hazy, could not quite figure out how Tay could be a Christian, rather than a Buddhist or something. And out of that feeling of otherness came the title for his book. "Aliens" was not only the official categorization for people who are neither citizens nor permanent residents. It also suggested people who were "wholly different and perhaps dangerous." So the American mainstream had turned them into an opposite.

A bit over a decade later there was another book by Simon Tay, *Asia Alone* (2010), more directly in the global scenario genre than *Alien Asian*. His student days far behind, Tay could by now be described in the back-flap presentation as a professor of law as well as public policy, chair of a think tank, a long-time nominated member of the Singapore parliament, a speaker at the World Economic Forum, Davos, and certainly as a public intellectual. So his presentation of regional diplomacy and geopolitics becomes in part rather technocratic, even as he is also aware of how politics proceeds in a changing setting of human activities—the growing Chinese interest in soft power as demonstrated in spreading Confucius Institutes, for one example, and the new presence of Chinese tourists, for another.

Part of the story once more involves playing with maps. For Tay, Singapore, and ASEAN, the Association of Southeast Asian Nations, are at the center, but who is in and who is out in his large-scale regional scheme of things? The shadow of increasingly powerful China is surely always there—but is Japan really fully engaged? What about Australia under its variously Asia-oriented regimes? What should be done about Myanmar (aka Burma), and North Korea? To what extent does India care to look eastward? And finally, but above all, where is the United States?

It becomes clear soon enough that "Asia Alone" is not really Tay's most desirable alternative. In Chap. 4, we came across a book named *America Alone*, claiming that with Europe Eurabizing, there would indeed be only America left as a citadel of what had been the West. Very differently, Tay's *Asia Alone* is not an argument for Asian separatism, hardly material for a self-fulfilling prophecy, but rather a warning; a title suggesting a scenario intended to self-destruct. Tay wants to see the United States in close collaboration with Asia, not with part of the latter against China, but with China included. And to make his point, he plays with words as well.

He notes that when the rather new U.S. president arrived in China for his first visit, "Oba-Mao" T-shirts, with Obama's face under a Mao cap and over a Mao jacket were already popular in Beijing. He describes Singapore policy as "equi-proximate"—aiming to make Singapore a fifty-first state of USA *and* the southernmost province of China. It would be "the City of &," where "the Power of &" stands for seeking interdependence, embracing the word *and*.

One could compare Tay's point of view to Robert Kaplan's in *Asia's Cauldron* (2014)—the territory covered is more or less the same, although Kaplan's style is more reportage (and he offers one of the countless brief accounts of Lee Kuan Yew's past grip on Singapore as well). But Kaplan shows little confidence in the room for maneuver of the countries that make up ASEAN, and although he acknowledges China's internal diversity and some uncertainty about how it will conduct its external relations, the keyword for him is hardly "collaboration," but rather "containment."

For Simon Tay, again, a refashioned interdependency must to an extent entail reading globalization as "global-as-Asian," with the United States adapting to a new world situation. Things were not like what they had been in his youth, as described in his earlier book: "By the end of the Bush years, American soft power was more than soft. It had all but evaporated." (2010: 13) Here his criticisms of American life at home, and American actions abroad, resemble Lee Kuan Yew's. "Global-as-Asian" must penetrate Main Street, must reach those Americans who still do not take their shoes off when visiting an Asian home, and think sushi tastes better cooked.

Finishing *Asia Alone*, Tay looks toward a post-crisis world, after the tumultuous years of late 1990s Asian economies, and then the crisis which had more recently had its beginnings on Wall Street. He hopes for a new "post-American American leadership," and a win-win syncretism between the United States and China. Early in the book, he has a brief interview with Fareed Zakaria, whom he refers to as Mr. Post-American, and describes as "urbane, intelligent, and affable, even charming." The back cover of the book also has a blurb by Zakaria. (The two probably had no great difficulty getting together, as Tay wrote the book while spending a year as a research fellow at Asia Society, with its headquarters on Park Avenue, New York.)

Finally, the most consistently audible Singaporean voice opining on the global present and possible worlds to come is that of Kishore Mahbubani. Recently Dean of the Lee Kuan Yew School of Public Policy at the National University of Singapore, Mahbubani was in the diplomatic service for much of the time of his country's existence, including a period as its ambassador to the United Nations when Singapore had the presidency of the Security Council. He has spent time at Harvard University on a scholarly sabbatical and, to repeat, was on that *Prospect/ Foreign Policy* list, in 2005, of 100 global public intellectuals. He is a frequent Davos visitor, too, for World Economic Forum gatherings.

Which all is not a bad record for the son of poor Indian immigrants (Singapore has a sizeable South Asian population as well) who notes that he grew up in a one-bedroom house where six people lived; and that the most memorable event of progress in his childhood was at around age 10, when his home got a flush toilet. It allowed a new sense of dignity. Later came a refrigerator, and a television set. What made the stronger impression in family comedies like *I Love Lucy*, however, was hardly the plot, but the insight gained into American living standards and consumer habits. (Here is some of the early global village, in McLuhan's sense.) Finishing school at 18, young Kishore became a textile salesman, like most other youths of his background. But then he got a scholarship, and went off to the university.[34]

Mahbubani is clearly well integrated into the network of global future scenarists. In the acknowledgments for his book *Beyond the Age of Innocence* (2005), he thanks, among others, Samuel Huntington, Paul Kennedy, and Fareed Zakaria for responding "promptly and positively" to his request for blurbs. When he passes through the United States there seems to be a good chance that he will appear in Zakaria's Global Public Square TV program. Thomas Friedman (e.g. 2011a) cites him extensively too.

Before *Beyond the Age of Innocence*, however, there was *Can Asians Think?* (2002), a volume of essays, first published in Singapore, then in a slightly different version by a minor U.S. publisher. Here are a number of provocative pieces, originally intended for different audiences, some in Asia, some in the West. As for Asians—yes, certainly they can think. But coming out of Western domination, they must make a habit of thinking for themselves, making their own creative syntheses. As for Westerners, they too have sacred cows. "The freedom of the press" is one of them: sometimes the press is destructive, it can use its power irresponsibly, in following fashions it is not consistent over time, it does not respect privacy, and there is evidence that the social environment it has a part in creating is not always attractive:

I have visited the offices of four great American newspapers: the *New York Times*, the *Washington Post*, the *Los Angeles Times*, and the *Wall Street*

Journal. In any of the four offices, if you ventured out at night and strayed a few hundred yards off course, you would be putting your life in jeopardy. (2002: 74–75)

The critique of contemporary American society here is not so unlike that of both Lee Kuan Yew and Simon Tay: the social order is rather too disorderly. When Mahbubani responds to Huntington on the "clash of civilizations," it is under the rubric "The Dangers of Decadence: What the Rest can Teach the West" (2002: 92). In tone, he is reasonably friendly toward Huntington, yet he affirms that he believes not in a clash, but in a fusion of civilizations: "Western ideas and technology will over time enable other societies to accumulate enough affluence and luxury to rediscover their own cultural roots" (2002: 112). And in the twenty-first century, for the first time in centuries, there will be a "two-way street in the flow of ideas, values, and people." (2002: 111) Here, moreover, he is more favorably inclined toward the United States than toward Europe:

...the Americans are fundamentally an open and compassionate people. They carry no hubris from history, as the Europeans do. Only this can explain why the United States has been the most benevolent great power in history. (2002: 151)

Perhaps here the Mahbubani schoolboy memory lingers—a colonial subject, learning without enthusiasm to salute the British flag.

Beyond the Age of Innocence (2005) is more exclusively addressed to an American audience—beginning at a Thanksgiving dinner at the Mahbubani apartment in New York, with his Irish-American wife and her family (for the sixth year in a row). It is in the period, we may again remember, when Europeans are from Venus and Americans from Mars, but in the rest of the world there are more people who also find Americans difficult to understand—or if they understand them, are not too pleased. So the subtitle of the book is "Rebuilding Trust Between America and the World."

The United States was a more reliable partner, and world power, in Mahbubani's view, during the Cold War than after. Since then it has become more like a "normal country"—inconsistent, inward-turning, often unaware of the consequences of its actions (here is the innocence) for others in the world. But these others are still sharing global space with this elephant. In the late 1990s, when international speculation against local currencies caused an economic crisis in Southeast Asia, the United

States offered bad advice and little support. When cotton growing in the American South is heavily subsidized, as a matter of local pork barrel politics, it contributes to the poverty of cotton growers in the Global South, such as in Burkina Faso or Mali. Washington fails to appreciate that the meritocracy of Beijing can also be a way of running a very large country (and does not recognize that Deng Xiaoping had to do what he did in Tiananmen Square, to avoid, as Mahbubani sees it, a collapse of order). When there is little international support for Islamic moderates in Pakistan or elsewhere in their attempts to improve schools, they can only offer weak competition for the *madrasas* churning out prospective jihadists by the thousands. It is true that opening up America's own first-class universities to the best and brightest young people from elsewhere in the world is a major contribution to global development—but then soft power must not be undermined in the exercise of other sorts of power.

Returning momentarily to the map-making endeavors of Chap. 3, we may realize that the period and the regions Mahbubani refers to here are more or less the same as Robert Cooper referred to as "premodern," and Thomas Barnett as "the Gap." So he seems to suggest that the elephant had a part in their making. Even so, more and more people in the world, Mahbubani concludes, want a way of life in line with enduring American values. One of them is a sense of human equality. After many years in Manhattan, he appreciates the way the doormen of its buildings look him straight in the eye, ready to exchange stories or opinions. But these people out there in the world are capable of discerning when the United States does not act in ways meeting their interests, or even in line with its own professed values. What is needed to rebuild trust is not a new Empire, for which the American heritage is not suited anyway. It is a return to, and a renewal of, those institutions of global multilateralism, not least the United Nations, which it had once done so much to build. Here, certainly, is the voice of both the Singapore diplomat and the New Yorker.

By the time of Mahbubani's next book, *The New Asian Hemisphere* (2008), there seems to be less of the New Yorker. In the acknowledgments he notes that it might have been "an act of sheer folly" to take on a book project while trying to build a new school of public policy (the one in Singapore, named after Lee Kuan Yew). This time, however, he has the help of a whole team of research assistants. It is not that between books Mahbubani has changed views dramatically. Being back in the middle of developing Asia, however, he seems to have less faith in innocence, with its own capacity of generating problems. The new, harsher keywords in characterizing the West are rather "arrogance" and "incompetence." In the intervening years, the United States and its main allies may have continued to provoke mistrust and dislike, but it is also that China, India and a number of other Asian countries have continued to tell their success stories.

For the veteran diplomat, one example of the Western disregard for meritocratic ideals is the American habit of reserving top ambassadorships as rewards for domestic political services, including cash contributions to campaigns—a habit dispiriting for young professionals in the foreign service. Failures, however, occur at the very top as well—invading Iraq in 2003, "neither Bush nor Blair had malevolent intentions, yet their mental approach was trapped in a limited cultural context: the Western mindset." (2008: 4) And Mahbubani points to the early gentleness of the Japanese occupation of Singapore in 1942, when even the British curator of the famous Botanic Gardens was asked to stay on and continue his work—contrasting this with the wholesale dismantling of existing Iraqi structures, which allowed looting of antiquities in the Baghdad Museum. "Stuff happens," Secretary of Defense Donald Rumsfeld had noted laconically in another of his memorable comments.

Now Kishore Mahbubani sees three possible scenarios for the twenty-first century world. One, that which he favors, is The March to Modernity. It is in line with his previous books: in large part it originated in the West, in its philosophy, science and technology. The good news is that it is spreading to China, India and elsewhere, and the bad news is that the West is reluctant to accept the implications of this fact. The second scenario is The Retreat into Fortresses. Mahbubani draws attention to Western economic protectionism, while one may feel for example that "clash of civilizations" thinking and Eurabia visions likewise belong here. And then the third scenario is The Triumph of the West—very popular in that West after the end of the Cold War, and exemplified not least in simplistic understandings of Fukuyama's "end of history" thesis (even as we have seen, again, that more carefully read, Fukuyama himself was not altogether enthusiastic).

We can discern that The March of Modernity scenario is possibly somewhat utopian, although on its way to becoming a reality. The other two, from Mahbubani's point of view, are dystopic. Yet we can also see that the three do not actually appear well marked off from each other, but mix and mingle in the world.

Accelerating the March of Modernity, he sees a number of issues to be dealt with. Overall, there is a need for more global governance.

Institutions should be reformed—to begin with, his old home, the United Nations: why should both Great Britain and France have permanent seats on the Security Council, and not Japan, India, Brazil, or for that matter Germany? The World Bank and the International Monetary Fund also need to be de-Occidentalized. There are ways of dealing with matters like nuclear non-proliferation and global warming. The Western dominance in upscale international media of news and opinion—the *New York Times*, *The Economist*, CNN, BBC—is problematic. As Mahbubani notes the already decades-long adversary relationship, or non-relationship, between the United States and Iran, he advises that the American leadership should follow the example set by President Nixon with his Beijing trip to visit the erstwhile arch-enemy Mao. Most originally perhaps, he recalls the scholarly glory of Damascus and Baghdad under medieval caliphates, and proposes that to improve its relationship to the Arab world, Europe could make a major effort to help revive these centers of learning.

A conspicuous aspect of *The New Asian Hemisphere* is the favorable view of China's emergent place in the world. Mahbubani treads rather lightly around China's internal weaknesses, and points for one thing to its heritage of cosmopolitanism from the Tang Dynasty, a millennium or so earlier. (A striking instance, one might reflect, of resort to a Braudelian *longue durée* history.) With a Westward bow of recognition, he regrets that his own early academic education dwelt mostly on British and Continental philosophy, and took so little notice of that most useful tradition of American Pragmatism. And then he concludes the book by citing the man whom he regards as the greatest of twentieth century pragmatists, Deng Xiaoping: "It does not matter whether a cat is black or white; if it catches mice, it is a good cat."[35]

Some years later, a kinder, gentler Mahbubani is back, as he sees things going his way. As the title of his new book has it, there is now *The Great Convergence* (2013). Fareed Zakaria's endorsement on the back cover says that "Kishore Mahbubani has done it again…Rudyard Kipling said, 'East is East and West is West and never the twain shall meet.' But they do in this book."

Still the situation is complicated, with a number of global contradictions. The world has to move toward an emphasis on global interests, away from the habitual, divisive preoccupation with national interests. There are still the tensions between Islam and the West. Mahbubani does find a "strong hint" of a real clash of civilizations here, while he considers Samuel Huntington to have been entirely wrong in seeing a clash of this nature between the West and China. And he wonders how the United States will take becoming Number Two, in economic terms. Will it be a crisis? The overall prognosis, however, is "Up!," for the world. The very broad base of the great convergence consists of people around the world arriving at a level of some material security and comfort, who want more of this. At the top, there are the best and the brightest young people from everywhere making it to the best U.S. universities, and then coming back home to take charge.

So the great convergence is more or less another term for the March of Modernity. That base of people seeking more of an improved material life may remind us of Mahbubani's own childhood experience—and then, at the vanguard top, we learn of his pride when two of his children were admitted to Yale University (where – who knows?—they may find Amy Chua among their teachers). It appears that Kishore Mahbubani is turning his life's experience into his global scenario.

The "global village" also becomes a key term in *The Great Convergence*. Indeed, with Mahbubani's early viewing of *I Love Lucy*, the original, television-emphasizing McLuhan sense of the term may come to mind, but for his own purposes the old diplomat draws it instead from Kofi Annan, the former Secretary-General of the United Nations. This global village needs village councils, of various kinds. While like many other observers he recognizes that the political landscape now includes a variety of kinds of actors (such as NGOs), not just states, he sees the continued convergence in large part in a global governance through negotiation, negotiation, and more negotiation, and reformed institutions. This time Europe (something like Robert Cooper's postmodern Europe, as encountered in Chap. 3), a continent ready to negotiate just about everything, stands out as a model; together with Southeast Asia, once more Balkanized than Balkan itself, now through ASEAN eliminating all traces of bamboo curtains.

The reform of global institutions must involve removing all the hidden injuries of Empire. Mahbubani points to the evolution of the International Cricket Council as an illuminating case. Originally it was the Imperial Cricket Conference, run by the white Anglosphere. As especially India has turned cricket into a mass spectator sport, the power balance in the organization has shifted. Now, in world organization generally, the West has to give up its presumptions of standing as the morally superior civilization. He notes how foreign aid has often benefited the donors rather more than the supposed beneficiaries. Getting to some concrete proposals, Mahbubani the United Nations veteran argues that the great powers, especially the five permanent members of the Security Council, have made the offices and branches of the organization into something less than a meritocracy. To serve the great convergence well, it must be updated to reflect the world as it is, rather than as it was at the end of World War II. Yet one cannot deny that there are great powers, and it is a good thing if there is some arena where they habitually get together to sort some things out. Mahbubani's solution of some changes of membership at the top, and a more multi-tiered global village council, still blends in a measure of *Realpolitik*.

The great convergence involves the people of the world "moving toward creating a set of common values." Yet:

> This does not mean that humanity will become homogeneous. We will continue to worship different gods, enjoy different cultures, eat different foods, marry in different ways, and so on. Global diversity will not disappear. Indeed, with the resurgence of long-dormant cultures and societies, especially in Asia, cultural diversity will grow. (Mahbubani 2013: 83–84)

Tourism, too, plays some part in Mahbubani's vision of the opening of minds (and it is no longer a case of long-distance travel only by Europeans and Americans). Here, it seems, worried-face cosmopolitanism is also beginning to smile.

So *The Great Convergence* is basically an optimistic endeavor, by an activist. One cannot get everything in between the covers of one book, and that is true here as well. It dwells on relationships between Asia and the West, and between China and India, but Russia hardly shows up. There is not much mention of those noticeable people in early twenty-first century politics who are not great convergers, but more like the people Francis Fukuyama referred to in his first "end of history" essay as "crackpot messiahs." Nor do we really see the people somehow making their way over the USA-Mexico border, nor the Africans, and refugees from elsewhere, trying to get across the Mediterranean. Then, however, these may also be people trying to join the great convergence, even if they are still further away from it. Yet in the reception of the boat people, and in some other ways, that ever-negotiating Europe has turned out not to be so successful. And then, too, at the top, if as Mahbubani points out, people from everywhere try to get into American universities, one might take note of the voices warning that these (probably Harvard, Yale and a few others excluded) are not what they used to be.

With his several books, then, Kishore Mahbubani clearly takes his place among the leading, most original and eloquent contributors to the global scenario genre. But he is not heard from only by way of his books. He frequently writes articles and op-ed pieces, in the *New York Times* and elsewhere. In a brief, not so kind and gentle, contribution to the *Harvard International Review* in 2010, "Beyond the Universal: The Cultural Myopia of US Social Science," he addresses academic issues in a way relating to those raised toward the end of Chap. 5. The fundamental mistake of American economics, political science, sociology and psychology, he proposes, has been to extrapolate natural science thinking and methodology to their own fields:

> Quantification, abstraction, and emphasis on model-building and replicability led to a fundamental failure to understand the differences in human societies. The destruction of "area studies" made things worse... a new approach of humility and willingness to absorb new perspectives will be needed to repair the enormous damage that US social science has done to US relations with the world.

CONCLUSION: DEBATING GLOBAL FUTURES

Between the halfies of the United States and the voices of that Southeast Asian "red dot," there are many opinions on the shared world future. One conclusion, drawing at least on those summarized here, is that an anxious American question, occasionally heard in the early twenty-first century, may be in large part misplaced: "Why do they hate us?" Mostly there seems to be little direct anti-Americanism, with the possible exception of one commentator in Paris, and at least by implication some in Moscow. It is hardly that one wants the United States to go away, but rather that one wants it to adjust the way it plays its part.

For one thing, it should remember that Americans are only five percent of the world population. But in considerable part, it is a matter of knowledge, or ignorance. Kishore Mahbubani the academic has his tough view of American scholarship. Mahbubani the diplomat shows up in a quote from Fareed Zakaria (2008: 226):

> To foreigners, American officials seem clueless about the world they are supposed to be running. "There are two sets of conversations, one with the

Americans in the room and one without," says Kishore Mahbubani, who was formerly Singapore's foreign secretary and ambassador to the United Nations. Because Americans live in a "cocoon," they don't see the "sea change in attitudes towards America throughout the world."

Just before that, in the *Post-American World* (2008: 225), Zakaria himself has made an observation on high-level international exchange:

President Bush's foreign trips seem designed to require as little contact as possible with the countries he visits. He is usually accompanied by two thousand or so Americans, as well as several airplanes, helicopters, and cars. He sees little except palaces and conference rooms. His trips involve almost no effort to demonstrate respect and appreciation for the country and culture he is visiting. They also rarely involve any meetings with people outside the government—businessmen, civil society leaders, activists.

Turning more Americans into informed citizens of the world thus seems to be a priority on the agenda of many commentators. Dominic Moïsi's optimistic scenario of Americans' new curiosity about other languages and cultures, and their rush to get passports for foreign travel, points in the same direction. So, in more general terms, does Benazir Bhutto's plea, referred to in Chap. 4, for a "dialogue between civilizations."

How much of a global dialogue do we hear, then? What do the future scenarios and the responses to them, the topic of this book, contribute to it? It seems there is room for improvement. The dialogue need not take the form of an in-your-face brawl like that between Niall Ferguson and Pankaj Mishra. There could be some heated but indeed civil debate, and there might at least sometimes be a tone of relaxed conversation.

Clifford Geertz, the anthropologist on that original *Prospect/Foreign Policy* list of global public intellectuals, also became increasingly preoccupied with this question. In his last book, as he portrayed the world at the end of the twentieth century, he noted that "a much more pluralistic pattern of relationships among the world's peoples seems to be emerging," but that "its form remains vague and irregular, scrappy, ominously indeterminate"; there was a need for "a practical politics of cultural conciliation" (Geertz 2000: 256). And in another book before that, he had argued that "the next necessary thing," was

to enlarge the possibility of intelligible discourse between people quite different from one another in interest, outlook, wealth, and power, and yet contained in a world where, tumbled as they are into endless connection, it is increasingly difficult to get out of each other's way.

A global public sphere, then—so how do we get there? We may first identify one practical, but central, challenge: language diversity. As Benjamin Barber puts it in *Jihad vs. McWorld* (1995: 84), "American English has become the world's primary transnational language in culture and the arts as well as in science, technology, commerce, transportation, and banking." The language of George Orwell's *1984* Oceania, plus much of what was once the British Empire, has a position of its own. As for other languages, they mostly offer construction materials for the Tower of Babel. We come across the question of language with the scenarists encountered in this chapter as well. Amin Maalouf, no doubt with the situation of French in mind, offers an argument for multilingualism which may appear admirable but unrealistic. Kishore Mahbubani, providing materials for his Retreat into Fortresses scenario, notes unenthusiastically that the administrative machine of the European Union, generous toward the national languages of member states, employs more than 3,400 interpreters and translators, whose services cost the Union over US $ 1,400 million per year. Perhaps this could be better spent.

So Mahbubani says that among his diplomat colleagues, there may be two sets of conversations—"one with the Americans in the room and one without." But with the Americans out of the room, those who remain will probably continue to speak English. That is the way the global language system works.[36] To put it differently, English is the only "hyperlanguage." If it is not your first language, but you also know a second language, this is likely to be it. The editors who had compiled that first *Prospect/Foreign Policy* list of top "global public intellectuals" admitted that to get on it, it helped if you were active in the Anglophone West.

If those of us who are not first-language Anglophones want to keep something secret from those who are (and mostly also from one another), we will be fairly safe if we write it in our own other languages. If, on the other hand, we want to talk back, engage in a transnational dialogue, as things stand now, we had better also do it in English. (Back in the seventeenth century, Olof Rudbeck the Elder's *Atlantica* had editions in his native language and in Latin, the nearest thing to a hyperlanguage in its time.)

This takes us to the question of translations. Just about all the texts dealt with in this chapter are available in English, whether in the original or in translation; the main exception would be those by Russians, such as

Gumilev. We have noted (in Chap. 2) that many of the major scenario texts have also been translated from English into other languages: *Das Ende der Geschichte*, *La terre est plate*, *Il paradosso del potere Americano*. In the later paperback edition of *The New Asian Hemisphere*, Kishore Mahbubani notes that the original had had an unfavorable Anglo-American reception, but was well received in Asia, and in continental Europe where there had been French, German and Dutch translations.

But the direction of these translations may seem a bit puzzling. In the global world of publishing, there are many more translations *from* English into other languages than vice versa.[37] Given the status of English as *the* hyperlanguage, a fair proportion of the people reading those translations of the scenario texts could conceivably also have read them in the original. To make more of the writing of the world available, not only to Anglophones but to humanity generally, there should really be more translations *into* English.

In that way there could be less of the West talking to the Rest (even if, given the multitude of European languages, there might also be a greater diversity in Western talk), more of a real global debate over shared and interlinked futures. Yet beyond the translations in themselves, to be fully effective, their messages might also need to make their ways recirculated into public consciousness—whether through oneliners, soundbites or in other slightly more complex forms—as the early global scenarios did. Here may be a greater challenge of cultural translation.

The language issue apart, however, the wider question is which voices are or are not in the conversations over global scenarios. Even with a rather wide range of visitors, the Global Public Square sometimes seems to turn into Harvard Square. In *Free World* (2004: 73), Timothy Garton Ash finds Europeans arguing about Francis Fukuyama, Samuel Huntington and Robert Kagan, and asks: "Couldn't Europeans have a big idea of their own for a change? Or did intellectual hegemony inevitably go with political hegemony?" Yet *Free World* is in large part for the British to read. (Although Ash might lately have found himself in agreement on many things with Mahbubani.) A number of commentators in Hamburg, Paris, Moscow and Singapore respond to the main American scenarists, such as that original "One Big Thing" quintet. American participants in the scenario genre seldom, and very selectively, refer to contemporaries elsewhere.

It is true, too, that Kishore Mahbubani places himself in conversations and debates with Francis Fukuyama, Samuel Huntington and Thomas Friedman. There is no sign here of Amin Maalouf, and certainly not of

Lev Gumilev. Exchanges are still with the scenarists in North America, not laterally among those elsewhere.

That "possibility of intelligible discourse" which Clifford Geertz argued for is not confined, of course, to scenario exchanges: it could be sought in many forms. Here and there, again, one could imagine a more symmetrical exchange of views. Thomas Friedman and Fareed Zakaria can have direct access to the American president, and can show their extended video interviews with him on the screens of their media outlets; moreover, they may have face-to-face encounters with many other heads of state or government as well. So why not let, say, Amin Maalouf or Simon Tay into the White House for comparable visits? Perhaps for the interviewee there could be some domestic political risk, but audiences elsewhere would probably appreciate it.

Kishore Mahbubani may still be generally right about Western news-media dominance: CNN, BBC, and so forth. But now more or less global television also includes Al Jazeera English, a Qatar enterprise. Toward the end of *Monsoon*, Robert Kaplan (2010: 322) notes that from its home base in Doha, this channel can "focus equally on the four corners of the Earth rather than on just the flash points of any imperial or post-imperial interest." However, it is not easily available for most American viewers.[38]

As far as reading and responding is concerned, new cosmopolitan habits may at this point be more noticeable in fiction—acknowledged fiction—than in scenario debates. Remember Joseph Nye's suggestion to students, referred to in Chap. 6, that they should take in novels and films to supplement their academic readings? There is now a twentieth/twenty-first century "world literature" of African, Asian, Latin American and Caribbean writers to portray the everyday life, not least what I have referred to as the consociality, of the present in many places, and it seems to find readers everywhere. Again, many of these writers are in the sort of in-between positions that Amin Maalouf refers to. Among recent African writers, on the move between Africa, Europe and North America, there is an emerging set described as "Afropolitans."

With regard to the scenario writers, again, it does seem desirable to search for them in many sites—and at the same time, we should perhaps be wary of assuming that they are always representatives, "spokesmen," for everybody in their home regions. Two Singaporeans, Kishore Mahbubani and Lee Kuan Yew, dwell on the infrastructure of a good life—a flush toilet for one, air-conditioning for the other. Such amenities can bring dignity and comfort, and the latter in its turn allows efficiency, getting things done. With the television screen, and American sitcoms, notes Mahbubani, may come the imagination of other domestic technology. But he also dwells on the empowerment which goes with cellphones. The Square People we met in Chap. 7 would agree. Yet their pioneers, with only fax technology, were in Tiananmen Square, and they might not agree with him on the dangers of a free press—a stance for which he certainly found immediate critics in the West. Indeed it may be that many people in regions now on The March of Modernity, joining the Great Convergence, value order and comfort more than the full range of civil and political liberties, but for many, the time comes when they want those, too. China, or India, or Russia, have their internal debates as well, with more voices to listen to.[39]

And then one final point relating to mutual understandings across the West/Rest divide: Ethan Casey, American journalist, we may remember, suggested that it could have been a good thing if Pankaj Mishra had been to South Dakota. Again, for all the soft power of the United States, many visitors to, and commentators on, the country are not acquainted with very much of it. Bernard-Henri Lévy and Simon Tay are among those who have moved around in it, but there seem to be many non-Americans who take for granted that they know more about it than they actually do. Very few foreign correspondents reporting from the United States for news media elsewhere in the world are based anywhere else than in Washington or New York, and many of them travel little elsewhere in the country (except perhaps in election campaign contexts). At times, "inside-the-Beltway" expertise may appear somewhat comparable to old-style Kremlinology. More knowledge of Joel Garreau's Nine Nations—on and off campus, along Wall Street but also on Main Street, and in the MexAmerican borderlands—could be desirable. For one thing, it might sometimes explain those modes of American conduct toward the outside world which commentators from elsewhere find mysterious and objectionable—occasionally even ridiculous. Here are yet more voices, speaking with or without accents, contributing to the diversity of the global ecumene.

Notes

1. The year before, Mishra (2010) had also reviewed a book by Ferguson's wife Ayaan Hirsi Ali (with "A Personal Journey Through the Clash of Civilizations" for a subtitle), for the *New Yorker*. That review was likewise critical.
2. Arnold Toynbee, world-historian-to-be, was also at the conference as a member of the British delegation.

3. Pankaj Mishra (2014) for his part took on another reporting journey, with a book on China and its East and Southeast Asian neighbors.
4. In a note, Abu-Lughod acknowledges that she got the term in a personal communication from Kirin Narayan, another member of the category.
5. Among the critical reviews of *How to Run the World* are those by Ikenberry (2011) and Wieseltier (2011).
6. In book acknowledgments, Zakaria expresses his debt to his parents Rafiq and Fatma. Look for Rafiq Zakaria in the Wikipedia, and you learn that he was an Islamic scholar, with a doctorate from the School of Oriental and African Studies, University of London (with a thesis on the turn-of-the-century politics of Islam in India), and a prominent member of the Indian National Congress (politically active primarily in his home state of Maharashtra). He was called to the bar in London, practiced law in Bombay, and wrote some fifteen books. Fatma Zakaria, for her part, was for some time an editor of the *Sunday Times of India.*
7. Concluding *The Post-American World* (2008: 259) Zakaria remembers, a little nostalgically, his arrival, at age eighteen: "It was a feeling that I had never had before, a country wide open to the world, to the future, and to anyone who loved it." Some years later, after more experience of economic difficulties and political deadlock, he has a more somber view of the future of the United States and of Western democracies: "Muddling through the crisis will mean that these countries stay rich but slowly and steadily drift to the margins of the world. Quarrels over how to divide a smaller pie may spark some political conflict and turmoil but will produce mostly resignation to a less energetic, interesting, and productive future." (Zakaria 2013c: 33)
   More recently, in a short book in defense of a liberal arts education increasingly under attack in the United States as the country focuses more narrowly on business and technology, Zakaria (2015) has taken his own story as a point of departure for arguing that the broad educational experience offers knowledge, and skills in thinking critically and creatively, writing, speaking, conversing as a way of learning... He approaches the topic with a comparative perspective, and offers food for thought also about what changes open online courses will bring to global higher education. The book has a back cover blurb by Malcolm Gladwell—"Zakaria's book couldn't have come at a more valuable moment"—and climbed quickly on the *New York Times* bestseller list. It is relevant to Kishore Mahbubani's emphasis on the global role of American universities (see below in the text) as well.
8. While of a Muslim family background, Zakaria recognizes the problematic internal conflicts within contemporary Islam, yet finds contemporary Western views of the religion sometimes bizarre. One marginal Republican presidential aspirant, he points out, had suggested that the U.S. military

should threaten to "take out" Mecca. Closer to his own intellectual milieu, noting that Bernard Lewis had claimed that the Iranian president Ahmadinejad planned to celebrate an auspicious date in the Islamic calendar by ending the world, Zakaria (2008: 15) added, for emphasis, that "yes, he actually wrote that." Obviously he was less impressed with the elderly Orientalist's expertise than Samuel Huntington had been—and one might reflect that back in the 1990s, Huntington would have been better off taking in more of his young Harvard student's sense of what Islamic civilization was about.

9. See for example Zakaria (2013a, b).
10. That was in 1984, not a good period in his old country. For one thing, Indira Gandhi was assassinated that year, an event preceded as well as followed by violent conflicts between Hindus and Sikhs.
11. Joffe is also associated with Fukuyama's journal *The American Interest*.
12. One could note that with a total of six mentions, Africa gets little attention in *Überpower*—a tendency in much of the scenario literature, with the exception of the dark imagery exemplified by Kaplan's "coming anarchy."
13. Huntington (1988) in his turn takes his point of departure in Paul Kennedy's *The Rise and Fall of the Great Powers*.
14. The Frankfurt School, starting out between the world wars as the Institut für Sozialforschung, was in large part in exile during the Nazi years, after which some members returned to Germany; Theodor Adorno, Walter Benjamin and Herbert Marcuse were among its early members, Jürgen Habermas among the later (after its post-war revival).
15. The historian Christopher Lasch, probably best remembered for his rather declinist *The Culture of Narcissism* (1978), is understood to have advised President Carter, to confront, in a speech, the "national malaise." This was evidently not a good idea.
16. The aim here is certainly not to review that tradition, or recent global scenario efforts, comprehensively. For one thing I leave out Jacques Attali's *A Brief History of the Future* (2009), which is wide-ranging, entertaining and well worth reading (and has a blurb by Henry Kissinger), but is somewhat unfocused and stands rather apart from those writings which have been more central here.
17. Todd's demographic specialization is exemplified, for one thing, in his later co-authored book *A Convergence of Civilizations* (Courbage and Todd 2011), referred to in Chap. 5, note 11.
18. Josef Joffe (2006: 92), on the other hand, comments on *After the Empire* that "Todd ruthlessly selects facts to predict that the United States will do itself in."
19. For a wide-ranging perspective toward ambivalence, see the sociologist Neil Smelser (1998).

20. One could note that Fouad Ajami, the Middle East specialist who advised the U.S. State Department on the 2003 Iraqi invasion (see note 20, Chap. 5), was also born in Lebanon, and spent parts of his childhood and youth in Beirut at much the same time as Maalouf was there; then as migrants their lives certainly took different directions.

21. The historian Natalie Zemon Davis has also devoted a book to Leo Africanus, under the title *Trickster Travels* (2006), including some comment on Maalouf and his book.

22. Batu Ferringhi, "Foreigner's Rock," I discovered on a recent visit to Penang, Malaysia, is a suburban beach area in large part given up to tourists and expatriates. A colleague with Penang roots considers it likely that ferringhi is a term of Arabic origins.

23. For a well-rounded and entertaining view of *la mission civilisatrice*, by an American foreign correspondent long in France, see Rosenblum (1988).

24. See on this Kingston-Mann (1999: 76–81).

25. Encounters with members of the perestroika/post-Soviet intelligentsia offer a range of personal views of the period—see for example Elfimov (2000), Grant (1993), Wolfe (1997). With regard to contacts with colleagues abroad, however, one of Elfimov's (2000: 249) interlocutors concludes that there is also some recurrent disappointment: "the West by and large maintains the image of a Russian scholar as some sort of ethnographic curiosity, an ethnographic informant of a kind who sits there in Russia and studies nothing but their native customs."

26. I base my understanding of Gumilev on Shnirelman and Panarin (2001) and other less accessible writings by Shnirelman, as well as on Goudakov (2006) and Oushakine (2009: 86–95).

27. In mainstream Soviet academic ethnography that view still seems to have been regnant, with theoretical elaborations and conceptual discussions, into the 1980s, to judge from an overview by a dominant scholar-politician (Bromley 1984).

28. Among these anthropologists of the perestroika years were Grant (1995), Ries (1997), Pesmen (2000), and Yurchak (2006).

29. Oushakine's study is interestingly complementary here to the documentary reporting by the Belarus writer Svetlana Alexievich (Nobel Prize winner in literature in 2015) on the experience of Soviet soldiers in *Zinky Boys* (1992)—so referred to as the bodies of many of them returned home from Afghanistan in zinc coffins. This reporting on lives in uniform, one could note, is very different from that of Robert Kaplan on American "imperial grunts;" moreover, one might guess that the quick appearance of Alexievich's book in English-language translation was an indication of the wider interest in the fall of the Soviet Union.

A breezy reportage by Peter Pomerantsev, *Nothing is True and Everything is Possible* (2015), offers closeups of another Russia: Janus-faced kleptocrats and their consorts, perhaps putting on a patriotic mien at home, while appearing as happy-face or straight-face (but hardly somber-face) cosmopolitans in their new habitats abroad, in "Moscow-on-Thames" and elsewhere. Pomerantsev, English-born son of Soviet-era exiles, is another instance of the kind of in-between people to whom Maalouf draws our attention; although his variant of mediation really amounts to whistleblowing.

30. My thanks to Goh Beng-lan for drawing my attention to the Singaporean use of the "red dot on the map," responding originally to a depreciatory comment by a former Indonesian president.

31. Cherian George (2000: 14), Singaporean political commentator, draws on this in subtitling his collection of essays "The Air-Conditioned Nation."

32. For a series on ideas consigned to "the dustbin of history," Zakaria (2002: 38) commented retrospectively on Asian Values that "It's not Confucius but Lee Kuan Yew that explains Singapore's success." In her book *Flexible Citizenship*, the anthropologist Aihwa Ong (1999: 73–77)—Malaysian-American and thus another halfie—offers her critique of Asian Values as an alibi for government regulation of newly affluent, possibly more individualistically free-thinking populations, and also has some comments on writings by Kishore Mahbubani. That book, and her later *Neoliberalism as Exception* (2006), offer closeup views of contemporary Southeast and East Asia which are usefully complementary to writings by Mahbubani and others.

33. This was in the same issue with Pierre Hassner's review of the book, referred to (with Huntington's reaction) in Chap. 2. A book of interviews with Wang Gungwu (2010), a kind of Festschrift at his eightieth birthday, offers a view of his scholarly career as well as of East and Southeast Asian academic and public life during a large part of the twentieth century.

34. The parents left Sindh, the South Asian region, at the time of the partition between India and Pakistan, when Hindus like them more or less had to choose between escaping and being killed by members of the Muslim majority. As a great many fled, to different parts of the world, Mahbubani notes that he now has first cousins in most parts of the world. The information about Mahbubani's background, childhood and youth is from Mahbubani (2005: 5, 65–67) and (2008: 14–16).

35. The most-cited variant of Deng's utterance seems to have the colors wrong: he actually talked about white and yellow cats (Leijonhufvud 2014: 438). But then the color of the cat does not matter—it is a good cat as long as it catches the imagination.

36. De Swaan (2001) provides an overview of the global sociology of languages.

37. A central article on the global sociology of translation by Johan Heilbron (1999) may by now be somewhat dated, but gives a clear view of the overall situation; the dominance of translations from English into other languages may even have grown since then.

38. Alexa Robertson (2015) has made a comparative study of four major television news channels, Al Jazeera English, BBC World, CNN International and Russia Today, finding rather like Kaplan that the first of these is the least affected by national or commercial biases; she finds the style of Russia Today reminiscent of Fox News.

39. Mark Leonard, British think tank denizen, offers some of this in *What Does China Think?* (2008). With this and his previous book, *Why Europe Will Run the 21ˢᵗ Century* (2005), a brief volume reminiscent of Robert Cooper's understanding of European postmodernism, Leonard is another writer active at the margins of the global future scenario genre.

REFERENCES

Abu-Lughod, Lila. 1991. Writing Against Culture. In *Recapturing Anthropology*, ed. Richard G. Fox. Santa Fe, NM: School of American Research Press.
———. 2013. *Do Muslim Women Need Saving?* Cambridge, MA: Harvard University Press.
Acemoglu, Daron, and James A. Robinson. 2012. *Why Nations Fail.* New York: Random House.
Adorno, Theodor W. 1991. In *The Culture Industry*, ed. J.M. Bernstein. London: Routledge.
Ajami, Fouad. 2008. Samuel Huntington's Warning. *Wall Street Journal*, December 30.
Alexievich, Svetlana. 1992. *Zinky Boys.* New York: Norton.
al-Saleh, Asaad, ed. 2015. *Voices of the Arab Spring.* New York: Columbia University Press.
Alvarez, Robert R. Jr. 1995. The Mexican-US Border: The Making of an Anthropology of Borderlands. *Annual Review of Anthropology* 24: 447–470 . Palo Alto, CA: Annual Reviews
Amselle, Jean-Loup. 2003. *Affirmative Exclusion.* Ithaca, NY: Cornell University Press.
Anderson, Elijah. 2011. *The Cosmopolitan Canopy.* New York: Norton.
Andersson, Ruben. 2014. *Illegality, Inc.* Berkeley, CA: University of California Press.
Ang, Ien. 1985. *Watching Dallas.* London: Methuen.
Appadurai, Arjun. 1996. *Modernity at Large.* Minneapolis, MN: University of Minnesota Press.
Appiah, Kwame Anthony. 1992. *In My Father's House.* New York: Oxford University Press.

————. 1996. Cosmopolitan Patriots. In *For Love of Country*, ed. Joshua Cohen. Boston: Beacon Press.

Aronczyk, Melissa. 2013. *Branding the Nation*. New York: Oxford University Press.

Ash, Timothy Garton. 1989. *The Uses of Adversity*. New York: Random House.

————. 1990. *We The People*. London: Granta.

————. 1997. *The File*. London: Harper Collins.

————. 2004. *Free World*. New York: Random House.

————. 2009. *Facts Are Subversive*. London: Atlantic Books.

Atran, Scott. 2010. *Talking to the Enemy*. London: Allen Lane.

Attali, Jacques. 2009. *A Brief History of the Future*. New York: Arcade.

Avey, Paul C., and Michael C. Desch. 2014. What Washington Wants. *Foreign Policy*, March/April, pp. 63–64.

Azaryahu, Maoz. 2000. McIsrael? On the "Americanization of Israel". *Israel Studies* 5(1): 41–64.

Bangstad, Sindre. 2014. *Anders Breivik and the Rise of Islamophobia*. London: Zed.

Barber, Benjamin R. 1981. *Marriage Voices*. New York: Summit Books.

———— 1992. Jihad vs. McWorld. *Atlantic Monthly*, March, pp. 53–65.

———— 1995. *Jihad vs. McWorld*. New York: Ballantine.

———— 1996. Constitutional Faith. In *For Love of Country*, ed. Joshua Cohen. Boston: Beacon Press.

———— 2001. *The Truth of Power*. New York: Columbia University Press.

———— 2003. *Fear's Empire*. New York: Norton.

———— 2007. *Consumed*. New York: Norton.

———— 2011. Benjamin Barber Responds. *The Nation*, March 6.

———— 2013. *If Mayors Ruled the World*. New Haven, CN: Yale University Press.

Barma, Naazneen, Ely Ratner, and Steven Weber. 2007. A World Without the West. *The National Interest* 90: 23–30.

Barnett, Thomas P.M. 2004. *The Pentagon's New Map*. New York: Berkley.

———— 2005. *Blueprint for Action*. New York: Putnam.

———— 2009. *Great Powers*. New York: Putnam.

Barth, Fredrik, ed. 1969. *Ethnic Groups and Boundaries*. Oslo: Universitetsforlaget.

Bastide, Roger. 1971. *African Civilisations in the New World*. London: Hurst.

Bawer, Bruce. 2006. *While Europe Slept*. New York: Doubleday.

Bayoumi, Moustafa. 2015. *This Muslim American Life*. New York: New York University Press.

Beattie, Alan. 2011. New World Disorder. *Financial Times*, February 26/27, section 2, p 13.

Beck, Ulrich. 1999. *World Risk Society*. Cambridge: Polity.

————. 2005. *Power in the Global Age*. Cambridge: Polity.

————. 2006. *Cosmopolitan Vision*. Cambridge: Polity.

Beeman, William O. 2005. *The "Great Satan" vs. the "Mad Mullahs."*. Chicago: University of Chicago Press.

Bell, Martin. 1996. *In Harm's Way*. London: Penguin.

Benedict, Ruth. 1946. *The Chrysanthemum and the Sword*. Boston: Houghton Mifflin.

Besteman, Catherine, and Hugh Gusterson, eds. 2005. *Why America's Top Pundits are Wrong*. Berkeley: University of California Press.

Bhutto, Benazir. 2008. *Reconciliation*. New York: Harper Collins.

Biehl, Joao, Byron Good, and Arthur Kleinman, eds. 2007. *Subjectivities*. Berkeley: University of California Press.

Bildt, Carl. 2006. An Expanding Union: Open Wide Europe's Doors. *International Herald Tribune*, November 8.

Bilici, Mucahit. 2012. *Finding Mecca in America*. Chicago: University of Chicago Press.

Booth, Michael. 2015. *The Almost Nearly Perfect People*. London: Vintage.

Borneman, John, and Abdellah Hammoudi. 2009. *Being There*. Berkeley, CA: University of California Press.

Bottici, Chiara, and Benoît Challand. 2006. Rethinking Political Myth: The Clash of Civilizations as a Self-Fulfilling Prophecy. *European Journal of Social Theory* 9(3): 315–336.

Bourdieu, Pierre. 1977. *Outline of a Theory of Practice*. Cambridge: Cambridge University Press.

Bowen, John R. 2007. *Why the French Don't Like Headscarves*. Princeton, NJ: Princeton University Press.

———— 2010. *Can Islam Be French?* Princeton, NJ: Princeton University Press.

Boyer, Dominic. 2013. *The Life Informatic*. Ithaca, NY: Cornell University Press.

Boynton, Robert S. 1999. Thinking the Unthinkable. *New Yorker*, April 12: 43-50.

Bradburd, Daniel. 1998. *Being There*. Washington, DC: Smithsonian Institution Press.

Braudel, Fernand. 1980. *On History*. Chicago: University of Chicago Press.

Brenneis, Don. 2009. Anthropology in and of the Academy: Globalization, Assessment and Our Field's Future. *Social Anthropology* 17: 261–275.

Brettell, Caroline B. 2015. *Anthropological Conversations*. Lanham, MD: Rowman & Littlefield.

Bromley, Yu.V. 1984. *Theoretical Ethnography*. Moscow: General Editorial Board for Foreign Publications, "Nauka" Publishers.

Brooks, David. 2004. The Americano Dream. *New York Times*, February 24.

————. 2011. Huntington's Clash Revisited. *New York Times*, March 3.

Brumann, Christoph. 1999. Writing for Culture: Why a Successful Concept Should not be Discarded. *Current Anthropology* 40: S1–S27.

Buchanan, Patrick J. 2006. *State of Emergency*. New York: St. Martin's Press.

Caldwell, Christopher. 2009. *Reflections on the Revolution in Europe*. London: Penguin.

Casey, Ethan. 2011. Has Pankaj Mishra Ever Been to South Dakota? *Open*, December 10.

Chase, Robert, Emily Hill, and Paul Kennedy, eds. 1999. *The Pivotal States*. New York: Norton.

Calhoun, Craig. 1994. *Neither Gods nor Emperors*. Berkeley: University of California Press.

———. 2012. Libyan Money, Academic Missions, and Public Social Science. *Public Culture* 24: 9–45.

Chafetz, Zev. 2007. The Huckabee Factor. *New York Times*, December 12.

Chua, Amy. 2003. *World On Fire*. New York: Doubleday.

———. 2007. *Day of Empire*. New York: Doubleday.

———. 2011. *Battle Hymn of the Tiger Mother*. New York: Bloomsbury.

Chua, Amy, and Jed Rubenfeld. 2014. *The Triple Package*. New York: Penguin.

Cohen, Eliot. 2001. World War IV: Let's Call This Conflict What It Is. *Wall Street Journal*, November 20.

Comaroff, John L., and Jean Comaroff. 2009. *Ethnicity, Inc.* Chicago: University of Chicago Press.

Confino, Alan. 2014. *A World Without Jews*. New Haven, CT: Yale University Press.

Conover, Ted. 1987. *Coyotes*. New York: Random House.

Cooper, Robert. 2002. The Post-modern State. *The Observer*, April 7.

———. 2003. *The Breaking of Nations*. London: Atlantic Books.

Coupland, Douglas. 2010. *Marshall McLuhan: You Know Nothing of My Work!* New York: Atlas & Co.

Courbage, Youssef, and Emmanuel Todd. 2011. *A Convergence of Civilizations*. New York: Columbia University Press.

Cowell, Alan. 2006. A Russian Outpost With More Freedom: Londongrad. *New York Times*, December 17.

Davis, Natalie Zemon. 2006. *Trickster Travels*. New York: Hill and Wang.

De Swaan, Abram. 2001. *Words of the World*. Cambridge: Polity.

Dirlik, Arif, ed. 1998. *What Is in a Rim?* Lanham, MD: Rowman & Littlefield.

Dowd, Maureen. 2006. Velvet Elvis Diplomacy. *New York Times*, July 1.

Dressler, William W. 2015. "Culture"…Again. *Anthropology News* 56(5-6): 20.

DuBois, W.E.B. 1903. *The Souls of Black Folk*. Chicago: A.C. McClurg & Co.

Eisenstadt, S.N. 2000. Multiple Modernities. *Daedalus* 129(1): 1–29.

Elfimov, Alexei. 2000. Academics and the Production of an Intellectual Discourse of Modernity in Russia. In *Para-Sites*, ed. George E. Marcus. Chicago: University of Chicago Press.

Epstein, Helen. 2014. Ebola in Liberia: An Epidemic of Rumors. *New York Review of Books, December* 18: 91–95.

Eriksen, Thomas Hylland. 2006. *Engaging Anthropology*. Oxford: Berg.

Evans-Pritchard, E.E. 1940. *The Nuer*. Oxford: Oxford University Press.

Fabian, Johannes. 1983. *Time and the Other*. New York: Columbia University Press.

Fallaci, Oriana. 2006. *The Force of Reason*. New York: Rizzoli.

Fassin, Didier. 2013. *Enforcing Order*. Cambridge: Polity.

———. 2015. In the Name of the Republic: Untimely Meditations on the Aftermath of the *Charlie Hebdo* attack. *Anthropology Today* 31(2): 3–7.

Ferguson, James. 1999. *Expectations of Modernity*. Berkeley: University of California Press.

Ferguson, Niall, ed. 1997. *Virtual History*. London: Picador.

———. 1998. *The Pity of War*. London: Allen Lane.

———. 2003. *Empire*. New York: Basic Books.

———. 2004a. *Colossus*. New York: Penguin.

———. 2004b. Eurabia? *New York Times*, April 4.

———. 2008. Is This the End of Banks? *Vanity Fair*, December.

———. 2011. *Civilisation*. London: Allen Lane.

———. 2012. *The Great Degeneration*. New York: Penguin.

Ferguson, Niall, and Moritz Schularick. 2009. The Great Wallop. *New York Times*. November 16

Fernández, Bélen. 2011. *Imperial Messenger*. London: Verso.

Finnström, Sverker. 2008. *Living with Bad Surroundings*. Durham, NC: Duke University Press.

Frank, Thomas. 2004. *What's the Matter With Kansas?* New York: Henry Holt.

Fraser, Nancy. 2007. Transnationalizing the Public Sphere: On the Legitimacy and Efficacy of Public Opinion in a Post-Westphalian World. *Theory, Culture and Society* 24(4): 7–30.

Freeland, Chrystia. 2012. *Plutocrats*. New York: Penguin.

French, Howard W. 2014. *China's Second Continent*. New York: Knopf.

Freyre, Gilberto. 1956. *The Masters and the Slaves*, 2 edn. New York: Knopf.

Friedman, George. 2009. *The Next 100 Years*. New York: Doubleday.

———. 2011. *The Next Decade*. New York: Random House.

Friedman, Thomas L. 1989. *From Beirut to Jerusalem*. New York: Farrar Straus & Giroux.

——— 1998. The Mouse That Roars: A Global Tale. *New York Times*, July 18.

——— 1999. *The Lexus and the Olive Tree*. New York: Farrar, Straus & Giroux.

——— 2005. *The World is Flat*. New York: Farrar, Straus & Giroux.

——— 2008. *Hot, Flat, and Crowded*. New York: Farrar, Straus & Giroux.

——— 2011. The Whole Truth and Nothing But. *New York Times*, September 6.

——— 2014a. Obama on the World: President Obama Talks to Thomas L. Friedman About Iraq, Putin and Israel. *New York Times*, August 8.

——— 2014b. Stampeding Black Elephants. *New York Times*, November 22.

——— 2014c. What is News? *New York Times*, July 26.

————— 2014d. Order vs. Disorder, Part 4. *New York Times*, September 30. (ch5)

————— 2014e. The Square People, Part 1. *New York Times*, May 13.

————— 2014f. The Square People, Part 2. *New York Times*, May 17.

Friedman, Thomas L., and Robert D. Kaplan. 2002. States of Discord. *Foreign Policy*.March–April, 64–70

Friedman, Thomas L., and Michael Mandelbaum. 2011. *That Used To Be Us*. New York: Farrar, Straus & Giroux.

Fukuyama, Francis. 1989. The End of History? *The National Interest* 16: 3–18.

—————. 1992. *The End of History and the Last Man*. New York: Free Press.

—————. 1995a. *Trust*. New York: Free Press.

—————. 1995b. Reflections on The End of History, Five Years Later. *History and Theory* 34(2): 27–43.

—————. 1999. *The Great Disruption*. New York: Simon & Schuster.

—————. 2004. Identity Crisis: Why We Shouldn't Worry About Mexican Immigration. *Slate* .June 4

—————. 2006. *America at the Crossroads*. New Haven, CT: Yale University Press.

—————, ed. 2007. *Blindside*. Washington, DC: Brookings Institution Press.

—————. 2011. *The Origins of Political Order*. New York: Farrar, Straus and Giroux.

—————. 2014. *Political Order and Political Decay*. New York: Farrar, Straus and Giroux.

Fuller, Graham E. 2010. *A World Without Islam*. New York: Little, Brown.

Funt, Danny. 2015. Bill Keller's Crusade: The Marshall Project Stakes Out High Ground on Journalism's Slippery Slope. *Columbia Journalism Review* 54(3): 16–19.

Gammeltoft-Hansen, Thomas, and Ninna Nyberg Sörensen, eds. 2013. *The Migration Industry and the Commercialization of International Migration*. London: Routledge.

Gaonkar, Dilip, ed. 2001. *Alternative Modernities*. Durham, NC: Duke University Press.

Garfinkle, Adam. 2000. The Sky is Always Falling: Internationally, Robert Kaplan says, nothing is very likely to go right. *New York Times Book Review*, March 19, p. 27.

Garreau, Joel. 1981. *The Nine Nations of North America*. Boston, MA: Houghton Mifflin.

—————. 2014. U.S., Mexico and Canada: Nine Nations. *New York Times*, July 3.

Geertz, Clifford. 1973. *The Interpretation of Cultures*. New York: Basic Books.

—————. 1988. *Works and Lives*. Stanford, CA: Stanford University Press.

—————. 2000. *Available Light*. Princeton, NJ: Princeton University Press.

George, Cherian. 2000. *Singapore: The Airconditioned Nation*. Singapore: Landmark.

Gilroy, Paul. 2005. *Postcolonial Melancholia*. New York: Columbia University Press.

Gingrich, Andre, and Marcus Banks, eds. 2006. *Neo-nationalism in Europe and Beyond*. Oxford: Berghahn.

Gladwell, Malcolm. 2000. *The Tipping Point*. New York: Little, Brown.

Glick Schiller, Nina, and Andrew Irving. 2015. *Whose Cosmopolitanism?* Oxford: Berghahn.

Goodenough, Ward H. 1971. *Culture, Language, and Society*. Reading, MA: Addison-Wesley.

Goody, Jack. 2006. *The Theft of History*. Cambridge: Cambridge University Press.

———. 2010. *The Eurasian Miracle*. Cambridge: Polity.

Gordon, David F., and Howard Wolpe. 1998. The Other Africa: An End to Afro-Pessimism. *World Policy Journal* 15(1): 49–59.

Goudakov, Vladimir. 2006. Gumilev and Huntington: Approaches and Terminologies. *Diogenes* 210: 82–90.

Gourevitch, Philip. 1996. Misfortune Tellers. *New Yorker*, April 8, pp. 96–100.

Gramsci, Antonio. 1971. *Selections from the Prison Notebooks*. London: Lawrence and Wishart.

Grant, Bruce. 1993. Dirges for Soviets Passed. In *Perilous States*, ed. George E. Marcus. Chicago: University of Chicago Press.

———. 1995. *In the Soviet House of Culture*. Princeton, NJ: Princeton University Press.

Gray, John. 1992. *Men Are from Mars, Women Are from Venus*. New York: Harper Collins.

Gray, John. 1998a. *False Dawn*. London: Granta.

———. 1998b. Global Utopias and Clashing Civilizations: Misunderstanding the Present. *International Affairs* 74(1): 149–164.

Guardiola-Rivera, Oscar. 2010. *What if Latin America Ruled the World?* New York: Bloomsbury.

Guiso, Luigi, Paola Sapienza, and Luigi Zingales. 2006. Does Culture Affect Economic Outcomes? *Journal of Economic Perspectives* 20(2): 23–48.

Guldi, Jo, and David Armitage. 2014. *The History Manifesto*. Cambridge: Cambridge University Press.

Gupta, Akhil. 2012. *Red Tape*. Durham, NC: Duke University Press.

Hacker, Andrew. 2004. Patriot Games. *New York Review of Books*. June 24

Hall, John A., and Charles Lindholm. 1999. *Is America Breaking Apart?* Princeton, NJ: Princeton University Press.

Hannerz, Ulf. [1969] 2004. *Soulside*. Chicago: University of Chicago Press.

———. 1989. Notes on the Global Ecumene. *Public Culture* 1(2): 66–75.

———. 1990. Cosmopolitans and Locals in World Culture. In *Global Culture*, ed. Mike Featherstone. London: Sage.

———. 1992a. *Cultural Complexity*. New York: Columbia University Press.

———. 1992b. The Global Ecumene as a Network of Networks. In. Adam Kuper (ed.), *Conceptualizing Society*. London: Routledge.

————. 1996. *Transnational Connections.* London: Routledge.

————. 1997. Borders. *International Social Science Journal* 154: 537–548.

————. 1998. Other Transnationals: Perspectives Gained from Studying Sideways. *Paideuma* 44: 109–123.

————. 1999. Reflections on Varieties of Culturespeak. *European Journal of Cultural Studies* 2: 393–407.

————. 2003. Macro-scenarios: Anthropology and the Debate over Contemporary and Future Worlds. *Social Anthropology* 11(169–187): 2003.

————. 2004a. *Foreign News.* Chicago: University of Chicago Press.

————. 2004b. Cosmopolitanism. In *Companion to the Anthropology of Politics*, eds. David Nugent, and Joan Vincent. Oxford: Blackwell.

————. 2007. Geokulturella scenarier. In *Kulturstudier i Sverige*, eds. Bodil Axelsson, and Johan Fornäs. Studentlitteratur: Lund.

————. 2008. Scenarios for the Twenty-first Century World. *Asian Anthropology (Hong Kong)* 7: 1–23.

————. 2009. Geocultural Scenarios. In *Frontiers of Sociology*, eds. Peter Hedström, and Björn Wittrock. Brill: Leiden.

————. 2010a. "The First Draft of History": Notes on Events and Cultural Turbulence. In *The Benefit Of Broad Horizons*, eds. Hans Joas, and Barbro Klein. Brill: Leiden.

————. 2010b. *Anthropology's World.* London: Pluto.

————. 2015a. Die Rhetorik der Kultur in globalen Zukunftsszenarien. In Ingo Schneider und Martin Sexl (eds.), *Das Unbehagen an der Kultur.* Hamburg: Argument.

————. 2015b. Writing Futures: An Anthropologist's View of Global Scenarios. *Current Anthropology* 56(6): 797–818.

Harden, Nathan. 2013. The End of the University as We Know It. *The American Interest* 8(3): 55–62.

Hardt, Michael, and Antonio Negri. 2000. *Empire.* Cambridge, MA: Harvard University Press.

————. 2004. *Multitude.* New York: Penguin.

Harrison, Lawrence E. 2006. *The Central Liberal Truth.* New York: Oxford University Press.

Harrison, Lawrence E., and Samuel P. Huntington, eds. 2000. *Culture Matters.* New York: Basic Books.

Hartmann, Heinz. 1995. Clash of Cultures, When and Where? Critical Comments on a New Theory of Conflict—and Its Translation into German. *International Sociology* 10: 115–125.

Hassner, Pierre. 1996/97. Morally Objectionable, Politically Dangerous. *The National Interest* 46: 63–69.

Haugerud, Angelique. 2005. Globalization and Thomas Friedman. In *Why America's Top Pundits Are Wrong*, eds. Catherine Besteman, and Hugh Gusterson. Berkeley: University of California Press.

Heilbron, Johan. 1999. Toward a Sociology of Translation: Book Translations as a Cultural World-System. *European Journal of Social Theory* 2(4): 429–444.

Hersh, Seymour M. 2004. The Gray Zone: How a Secret Pentagon Program Came to Abu Ghraib. *New Yorker*, May 24.

Hertsgaard, Mark. 2002. *The Eagle's Shadow*. London: Bloomsbury.

Hertz, Ellen, and Laura Nader. 2005. On *The Lexus and the Olive Tree*, by Thomas L. Friedman. In *Why America's Top Pundits Are Wrong*, eds. Catherine Besteman, and Hugh Gusterson. Berkeley: University of California Press.

Herzfeld, Michael. 1997a. Anthropology and the Politics of Significance. *Social Analysis* 41: 107–138.

———. 1997b. *Cultural Intimacy*. London: Routledge.

Heyman, Josiah McC., and Howard Campbell. 2009. The Anthropology of Global Flows: A Critical reading of Appadurai's 'Disjuncture and Difference in the Global Cultural Economy.' *Anthropological Theory*, 9: 131–148.

Hiro, Dilip. 2010. *After Empire*. New York: Nation Books.

Hodgson, Marshall G.S. 1993. *Rethinking World History*. Cambridge: Cambridge University Press.

Hoffman, Danny. 2011. *The War Machines*. Durham, NC: Duke University Press.

Holdar, Sven. 1992. The Ideal State and the Power of Geography: The Life-work of Rudolf Kjellén. *Political Geography* 11: 307–323.

Horowitz, Jason. 2014. Historian's Critique of Obama Foreign Policy Is Brought Alive by Events in Iraq. *New York Times*, June 15.

Houellebecq, Michel. 2015. *Submission*. New York: Farrar, Straus and Giroux.

Hughes, Everett C. 1961. *Students' Culture and Perspectives*. Lawrence: University of Kansas School of Law.

Huntington, Samuel P. 1988. The U.S.—Decline or Renewal? *Foreign Affairs*. 67: 76–96.

——— 1993. The Clash of Civilizations? *Foreign Affairs* 72(3): 22–49.

——— 1996. *The Clash of Civilizations and the Remaking of World Order*. New York: Simon & Schuster.

——— 1997. Hassner's Bad Bad Review. *The National Interest* 47: 97–102.

——— 2004. *Who Are We?* New York: Simon & Schuster.

Hutchinson, Sharon E., and Naomi R. Pendle. 2015. Violence, Legitimacy, and Prophecy: Nuer Struggles with Uncertainty in South Sudan. *American Ethnologist* 42: 415–430.

Ibrahimovic, Zlatan. 2013. *I am Zlatan Ibrahimovic*. London: Penguin.

Ignatieff, Michael. 1993. *Blood and Belonging*. London: Chatto & Windus.

———. 1997. *The Warrior's Honor*. New York: Henry Holt.

———. 2003. *Empire Lite*. London: Vintage.

———. 2007. Getting Iraq Wrong. *New York Times Magazine*, August 5.

Ikenberry, G. John. 1997. Just Like the Rest. *Foreign Affairs* 76(2): 162–163.

———. 2011. Review of Parag Khanna, How to Run the World. *Foreign Affairs* 90(2): 170.

Illich, Ivan. 1973. *Tools for Conviviality*. New York: Harper & Row.

Inoguchi, Takashi. 1999. Peering into the Future by Looking Back: The Westphalian, Philadelphian, and Anti-Utopian Paradigms. *International Studies Review* 1(2): 173–191.

Iwabuchi, Koichi. 2002. *Recentering Globalization*. Durham, NC: Duke University Press.

Jacques, Martin. 2009. *When China Rules the World*. London: Allen Lane.

Joffe, Josef. 2006. *Überpower*. New York: Norton.

———. 2014. *The Myth of America's Decline*. New York: Liveright.

Kagan, Robert. 2000. The Return of Cheap Pessimism: Inside the Limo. *New Republic*, April 10.

———. 2003. *Paradise and Power*. New York: Knopf.

———. 2006. *Dangerous Nation*. New York: Alfred Knopf.

Kaldor, Mary. 1999. *New and Old Wars*. Cambridge: Polity.

———. 2003. *Global Civil Society*. Cambridge: Polity.

Kaplan, Robert D. 1993a. *Balkan Ghosts*. New York: St. Martin's Press.

——— 1993b. *The Arabists*. New York: Free Press.

——— 1994. The Coming Anarchy. *Atlantic Monthly*, February, pp. 44–76.

——— 1996. *The Ends of the Earth*. New York: Random House.

——— 1998. *An Empire Wilderness*. New York: Random House.

——— 2000. *The Coming Anarchy*. New York: Random House.

——— 2001a. *Warrior Politics*. New York: Random House.

——— 2001b. *Looking the World in the Eye*, 68–82. December: *Atlantic Monthly*.

——— 2004. *Mediterranean Winter*. New York: Random House.

——— 2005. *Imperial Grunts*. New York: Random House.

——— 2007. *Hog Pilots, Blue Water Grunts*. New York: Random House.

——— 2010. *Monsoon*. New York: Random House.

——— 2012. *The Revenge of Geography*. New York: Random House.

——— 2014. *Asia's Cauldron*. New York: Random House.

Kearney, Michael. 1991. Borders and Boundaries of State and Self at the End of Empire. *Journal of Historical Sociology* 4: 52–74.

Kearns, Gerry. 2009. *Geopolitics and Empire*. Oxford: Oxford University Press.

Kennedy, Paul. 1987. *The Rise and Fall of the Great Powers*. New York: Random House.

———. 1988. Pointers from the Past. *Foreign Affairs* 66(5): 1108–1113.

———. 1993. *Preparing for the Twenty-first Century*. New York: Random House.

———. 2006a. *The Parliament of Man*. New York: Random House.

———. 2006b. The Worst of Times? *New York Review of Books*, November 2.

Khanna, Parag. 2008. *The Second World*. New York: Random House.

———. 2011. *How to Run the World*. New York: Random House.

King, Charles. 2015. The Decline of International Studies: Why Flying Blind Is Dangerous. *Foreign Affairs* 94(4): 88–98.

King, David. 2005. *Finding Atlantis*. New York: Crown.

Kingston-Mann, Esther. 1999. *In Search of the True West*. Princeton, NJ: Princeton University Press.

Klausen, Jytte. 2005. *The Islamic Challenge*. Oxford: Oxford University Press.

Kluckhohn, Clyde, and H.A. Murray, eds. 1948. *Personality in Nature, Society, and Culture*. New York: Knopf.

Knörr, Jacqueline, and Wilson Trajano Filho, eds. 2010. *The Powerful Presence of the Past*. Leiden: Brill.

Krastev, Ivan, and Alan McPherson, eds. 2007. *The Anti-American Century*. Budapest: Central European University Press.

Kristof, Nicholas D. 2009. The Daily Me. *New York Times*, March 19, 2009.

———— 2014. Professors, We Need You! *New York Times*, February 15.

Kristof, Nicholas D., and Sheryl WuDunn. 2009. *Half the Sky*. New York: Knopf.

————. 2014. *A Path Appears*. New York: Knopf.

Kroeber, Alfred L. 1939. *Cultural and Natural Areas of Native North America*. Berkeley, CA: University of California Press.

———— 1945. The ancient *Oikoumené* as an historic culture aggregate. *Journal of the Royal Anthropological Institute* 75: 9–20.

———— 1952. *The Nature of Culture*. Chicago: University of Chicago Press.

———— 1962. *A Roster of Civilizations and Culture*. Chicago: Aldine.

———— 1963. *An Anthropologist Looks at History*. Berkeley: University of California Press.

Kroeber, Alfred L. and Clyde Kluckhohn. [1952]1963. *Culture: A Critical Review of Concepts and Definitions*. New York: Random House/Vintage.

Kroeber, Karl, and Clifton Kroeber, eds. 2003. *Ishi in Three Centuries*. Lincoln: University of Nebraska Press.

Kroeber, Theodora. 1961. *Ishi in Two Worlds*. Berkeley: University of California Press.

————. 1970. *Alfred Kroeber*. Berkeley: University of California Press.

Kuper, Adam. 1999. *Culture*. Cambridge, MA: Harvard University Press.

Kuper, Simon. 2011. The End of Eurabia. *Financial Times*, September 10–11.

————. 2013. How Books about Sport Got Serious. *Financial Times*, November 22.

Kurlantzick, Joshua. 2007. *Charm Offensive*. New Haven, CT: Yale University Press.

Kurtz, Howard. 2001. Thomas Friedman Comes Out Swinging in His Columns on the Middle East. *Washington Post*, December 6.

Kwarteng, Kwasi. 2011. *Ghosts of Empire*. London: Bloomsbury.

Lapham, Lewis. 1998. *The Agony of Mammon*. London: Verso.

Lasch, Christopher. 1978. *The Culture of Narcissism*. New York: Norton.

Lash, Scott, and Celia Lury. 2007. *Global Culture Industry*. Cambridge: Polity.

Lash, Scott, and John Urry. 1994. *Economies of Signs and Space*. London: Sage.

Lave, Jean. 2011. *Apprenticeship in Critical Ethnographic Practice*. Chicago: University of Chicago Press.

Lave, Jean, and Etienne Wenger. 1991. *Situated Learning.* Cambridge: Cambridge University Press.

Leibovich, Mark. 2013. *This Town.* New York: Blue Rider Press.

Leijonhufvud, Göran. 2014. *Pionjär och veteran.* Stockholm: Bonniers.

Leonard, Mark. 2005. *Why Europe Will Run the 21ˢᵗ Century.* London: Fourth Estate.

———. 2008. *What Does China Think?* London: Fourth Estate.

LeVine, Donald. 1965. *Wax and Gold.* Chicago: University of Chicago Press.

LeVine, Mark. 2005. *Why They Don't Hate Us.* Oxford: Oneworld.

———. 2008. *Heavy Metal Islam.* New York: Three Rivers Press.

Lévy, Bernard-Henri. 2006. *American Vertigo.* New York: Random House.

Lewis, Bernard. 1990. *The Roots of Muslim Rage*, 47–60. September: *The Atlantic.*

Liebes, Tamar, and Elihu Katz. 1993. *The Export of Meaning.* Cambridge: Polity.

Lilla, Mark. 2015. Slouching Toward Mecca. *New York Review of Books*, April 2, 41–43.

Linton, Adeline, and Charles Wagley, eds. 1971. *Ralph Linton.* New York: Columbia University Press.

Linton, Ralph. 1936. *The Study of Man.* New York: Appleton-Century-Crofts.

Lomnitz, Claudio. 2005. American Soup: Are We All Anglo-Protestants? *Boston Review*, February/March.

Long, Nicholas J., and Henrietta L. Moore, eds. 2013. *Sociality: New Directions.* Oxford: Berghahn.

Lozada, Carlos. 2009. A How-to Guide for Putting Your Big-Think on the Map. *Foreign Policy*, December, pp. 58–61.

Lucht, Hans. 2011. *Darkness before Daybreak.* Berkeley, CA: University of California Press.

Lutz, Catherine, ed. 2009. *The Bases of Empire.* New York: New York University Press.

Maalouf, Amin. 1984. *The Crusades through Arab Eyes.* London: Saqi.

———. 1988. *Leo Africanus.* New York: Norton.

———. 1995. *The Rock of Tanios.* London: Abacus.

———. 2001. *In the Name of Identity.* New York: Arcade.

———. 2011. *Disordered World.* London: Bloomsbury.

Mahbubani, Kishore. 2002. *Can Asians Think?* South Royalton, VT: Steerforth Press.

———. 2005. *Beyond the Age of Innocence.* New York: Public Affairs.

———. 2008. *The New Asian Hemisphere.* New York: Public Affairs.

———. 2010. Beyond the Universal: The Cultural Myopia of US Social Science. *Harvard International Review* 31(4): 72.

———. 2013. *The Great Convergence.* New York: Public Affairs.

Malkki, Liisa. 1992. National Geographic: The Rooting of Peoples and the Territorialization of National Identity Among Scholars and Refugees. *Cultural Anthropology* 7: 24–44.

Mamdani, Mahmood. 2005. Whither Political Islam? Understanding the Modern Jihad. *Foreign Affairs* 84(1): 148–155.

Marks, Robert. 2000. The Clash of Civilizations and the Remaking of World Order (review). *Journal of World History* 11(1): 101–104.

Martin, Douglas. 2014. Fouad Ajami is Dead at 68; Expert in Arab History. *New York Times*, June 22.

Mathews, Jessica. 1997. Power Shift. *Foreign Affairs* 76(1): 50–66.

Matory, J. Lorand. 2005. *Black Atlantic Religion*. Princeton, NJ: Princeton University Press.

Mbembe, Achille. 2001. *On the Postcolony*. Berkeley, CA: University of California Press.

McConnell, Scott. 2009. Not so Huddled Masses: Multiculturalism and Foreign Policy. *World Affairs* 171(4): 39–50.

McGeary, Johanna, and Marguerite Michaels. 1998. Africa Rising. *Time*, March 30.

McGovern, Mike. 2011. *Making War in Côte d'Ivoire*. London: Hurst.

McLuhan, Marshall. 1962. *The Gutenberg Galaxy*. Toronto: University of Toronto Press.

———. 1964. *Understanding Media*. New York: McGraw-Hill.

McNeill, William H. [1963]1991. *The Rise of the West*. Chicago: University of Chicago Press.

McNeill, William H. 1995. The Changing Shape of World History. *History and Theory* 34(2): 8–26.

——— 1997. Decline of the West? *New York Review of Books*, January 9, pp. 18–22.

——— 2000. A Short History of Humanity. *New York Review of Books*, June 29, pp. 9–11.

McNeill, J.R., and William H. McNeill. 2003. *The Human Web*. New York: Norton.

Mead, Walter Russell. 2004. America's Sticky Power. *Foreign Policy*, March/April, 46–53.

Melko, Matthew, and Leighton R. Scott, eds. 1987. *The Boundaries of Civilizations in Space and Time*. Lanham, MD: University Press of America.

Menand, Louis. 2010. *The Marketplace of Ideas*. New York: Norton.

Meyer, John W. 1999. The Changing Cultural Content of the Nation-State: A World-Society Perspective. In *State/Culture*, ed. George Steinmetz. Ithaca, NY: Cornell University Press.

Meyer, John W., John Boli, George M. Thomas, and Francisco O. Ramirez. 1997. World Society and the Nation-State. *American Journal of Sociology* 103: 144–181.

Mishra, Pankaj. 2006. *Temptations of the West*. New York: Farrar, Straus and Giroux.

———. 2010. Islamismism. *New Yorker*, June 7, pp. 68–73.

———. 2011. Watch This Man. *London Review of Books*, November 3.pp. 10–12.

————. 2012. *From the Ruins of Empire*. London: Allen Lane.

————. 2014. *A Great Clamour*. Gurgaon: Penguin Books India.

Mitchell, Joshua. 2013. *Tocqueville in Arabia*. Chicago: University of Chicago Press.

Mitchell, Timothy. 2002. McJihad: Islam in the U.S. Global Order. *Social Text* 20(4): 1–18.

Moeller, Susan D. 1999. *Compassion Fatigue*. New York: Routledge.

Moïsi, Dominique. 2009. *The Geopolitics of Emotion*. New York: Doubleday.

Morgan, Marcyliena, and Dionne Bennett. 2011. Hip-Hop & the Global Imprint of a Black Cultural Form. *Daedalus* 140(2): 176–196.

Nader, Laura. 1972. Up the Anthropologist—Perspectives Gained from Studying Up. In *Reinventing Anthropology*, ed. Dell Hymes. New York: Pantheon.

Naisbitt, John. 1984. *Megatrends*. New York: Warner Books.

Napoleoni, Loretta. 2014. *The Islamist Phoenix*. New York: Seven Stories Press.

Nash, Kate, ed. 2014. *Transnationalizing the Public Sphere*. Cambridge: Polity.

Newcomer, Peter J. 1972. The Nuer are Dinka: An Essay on Origins and Environmental Determinism. *Man* 7: 5–11.

Nordstrom, Carolyn. 1997. *A Different Kind of War Story*. Philadelphia: University of Pennsylvania Press.

————. 2004. *Shadows of War*. Berkeley: University of California Press.

Nussbaum, Bruce. 1997. Capital, Not Culture. *Foreign Affairs* 76(2): 165.

Nussbaum, Martha C. 1996. Patriotism and Cosmopolitanism. In *For Love of Country*, ed. Joshua Cohen. Boston: Beacon Press.

Nye, Joseph S. Jr. 1990. *Bound to Lead*. New York: Basic Books.

————. 2002. *The Paradox of American Power*. New York: Oxford University Press.

————. 2003. The Velvet Hegemon: How Soft Power Can Help Defeat Terrorism. *Foreign Policy* 136: 74–75.

————. 2004a. *Soft Power*. New York: Public Affairs.

————. 2004b. The Decline of America's Soft Power. *Foreign Affairs* 83(3): 16–20.

————. 2005. Meanwhile: Searching for Truth. *I Turn to Fiction. New York Times* .March 11

————. 2006. *The Power Game*. New York: Public Affairs.

————. 2008. *The Powers to Lead*. New York: Oxford University Press.

————. 2011a. Joseph Nye Responds to Criticism of His TNR Article on Qaddafi. *The New Republic* .March 10

————. 2011b. *The Future of Power*. New York: Public Affairs.

————. 2011c. The War on Soft Power. *Foreign Policy* .April 2011

————. 2015. *Is the American Century Over?* Cambridge: Polity.

Ong, Aihwa. 1999. *Flexible Citizenship*. Durham, NC: Duke University Press.

————. 2006. *Neoliberalism as Exception*. Durham, NC: Duke University Press.

Ortner, Sherry B. 1973. On Key Symbols. *American Anthropologist* 75: 1338–1346.
——— 2010. Access: Reflections on Studying Up in Hollywood. *Ethnography* 11: 211–233.
Orwell, George. 1949. *Nineteen eighty-four.* London: Secker and Warburg.
Oushakine, Serguei Alex. 2009. *The Patriotism of Despair.* Ithaca, NY: Cornell University Press.
Parker, Ian. 2008. The Bright Side: The Relentless Optimism of Thomas Friedman. *New Yorker*, November 10, pp. 52–63.
Parkin, David. 1978. *The Cultural Definition of Political Response.* London: Academic Press.
Pautz, Hartwig. 2005. The Politics of Identity in Germany: the Leitkultur Debate. *Race and Class* 46(4): 38–52.
Pesmen, Dale. 2000. *Russia and Soul.* Ithaca, NY: Cornell University Press.
Pfaff, William. 1997. The Reality of Human Affairs. *World Policy Journal* 14(2): 89–96.
Phillips, Melanie. 2006. *Londonistan.* London: Gibson Square.
Plate, Tom. 2010. *Conversations with Lee Kuan Yew.* Singapore: Marshall Cavendish.
Podhoretz, Norman. 2007. *World War IV.* New York: Vintage Books.
Pomerantsev, Peter. 2015. *Nothing is True and Everything is Possible.* London: Faber and Faber.
Ramo, Joshua Cooper. 2009. *The Age of the Unthinkable.* New York: Little, Brown.
Rao, Ursula. 2006. News from the Field: the Experience of Transgression and the Transformation of Knowledge during Research in an Expert-site. In *Celebrating Transgression*, eds. Ursula Rao, and John Hutnyk. Oxford: Berghahn.
Revel, Jean-Francois. 1971. *Without Marx or Jesus.* Garden City, NY: Doubleday.
Ribeiro, Darcy. 1971. *The Americas and Civilization.* New York: Dutton.
Richards, Paul. 1996. *Fighting for the Rain Forest.* Oxford: James Currey.
———. 1999. Out of the Wilderness? Escaping Robert Kaplan's Dystopia. *Anthropology Today* 15(6): 16–18.
———, ed. 2005. *No Peace, No War.* Athens, OH: Ohio University Press.
Rieff, David. 1998. In Defense of Afro-Pessimism. *World Policy Journal* 15(4): 10–22.
Ries, Nancy. 1997. *Russian Talk.* Ithaca, NY: Cornell University Press.
Ritzer, George. 1993. *The McDonaldization of Society.* Thousand Oaks, CA: Pine Forge Press.
———. 1998. *The McDonaldization Thesis.* London: Sage.
Robertson, Alexa. 2015. *Global News.* New York: Peter Lang.
Robertson, Roland. 1992. *Globalization.* London: Sage.
Rockefeller, Stuart Alexander. 2011. Flow. *Current Anthropology* 52: 557–578.

Roitman, Janet. 2005. *Fiscal Disobedience.* Princeton, NJ: Princeton University Press.

Rosaldo, Renato. 1988. Ideology, Place, and People without Culture. *Cultural Anthropology* 3: 77–87.

Rosenblum, Mort. 1988. *Mission to Civilize.* New York: Doubleday.

Ross, Andrew, and Kristin Ross, eds. 2004. *Anti-Americanism.* New York: New York University Press.

Rothkopf, David. 2008. *Superclass.* New York: Farrar, Straus and Giroux.

Sahlins, Marshall. 2014. *Confucius Institutes: Academic Malware.* Chicago: Prickly Paradigm.

Said, Edward W. 1978. *Orientalism.* New York: Pantheon.

——— 1994. *Representations of the Intellectual.* New York: Pantheon.

——— 2000. *The End of the Peace Process.* New York: Pantheon.

Sanderson, Stephen K., ed. 1995. *Civilizations and World Systems.* Walnut Creek, CA: AltaMira Press.

Sanjek, Roger. 1998. *The Future of Us All.* Ithaca, NY: Cornell University Press.

Sardar, Ziauddin, and Merryl Wyn Davies. 2002. *Why Do People Hate America?* Cambridge: Icon.

Schlesinger, Arthur M. Jr. 1992. *The Disuniting of America.* New York: Norton.

Schudson, Michael. 1984. *Advertising, The Uneasy Persuasion.* New York: Basic Books.

———. 1987. Deadlines, Datelines, and History. In *Reading the News,* eds. Robert Karl Manoff, and Michael Schudson. New York: Pantheon.

Schutz, Alfred. 1967. *Collected Papers, I: The Problem of Social Reality.* The Hague: Martinus Nijhoff.

Schwartz, Theodore. 1978. Where is the Culture? Personality and the Distributive Locus of Culture. In *The Making of Psychological Anthropology,* ed. George D. Spindler. Berkeley, CA: University of California Press.

Scott, James C. 2009. *The Art of Not Being Governed.* New Haven, CT: Yale University Press.

Seierstad, Åsne. 2015. *One of Us.* New York: Farrar, Straus and Giroux.

Sen, Amartya. 2006. *Identity and Violence.* New York: Norton.

Senghaas, Dieter. 1998. *The Clash Within Civilizations.* London: Routledge.

Servan-Schreiber, Jean Jacques. 1969. *The American Challenge.* New York: Penguin.

Shambaugh, David. 2015. China's Soft-Power Push. *Foreign Affairs* 94(4): 99–107.

Shils, Edward A., and Morris Janowitz. 1948. Cohesion and Disintegration in the Wehrmacht in World War II. *Public Opinion Quarterly* 12: 280–315.

Shnirelman, Victor, and Sergei Panarin. 2001. Lev Gumilev: His Pretensions as Founder of Ethnology and his Eurasian Theories. *Inner Asia* 3: 1–18.

Shore, Cris. 2000. *Building Europe.* London: Routledge.

Silver, Nate. 2012. *The Signal and the Noise.* New York: Penguin.

Skidelsky, William. 2011. Niall Ferguson: 'Westerners don't understand how vulnerable freedom is.' *The Observer*, February 20.

Small, Helen, ed. 2002. *The Public Intellectual*. Oxford: Blackwell.

Smelser, Neil J. 1998. The Rational and the Ambivalent in the Social Sciences. *American Sociological Review* 63: 1–16.

Smith, Tony. 1997. Dangerous Conjecture. *Foreign Affairs* 76(2): 163–164.

Smith, Woodruff D. 1991. *Politics and the Sciences of Culture in Germany, 1840–1920*. New York: Oxford University Press.

Solomon, Erika. 2014. Consumers of the Caliphate Retain Taste for Gadgets from the West. *Financial Times*, November 29/30.

Sontag, Susan. 1966. *Against Interpretation*. New York: Farrar, Straus & Giroux.

Stade, Ronald. 2010. Emergent Concept Chains and Scenarios of Depoliticization: The Case of Global Governance as a Future Past. In Thomas Hylland Eriksen, Christina Garsten and Shalini Randeria (eds.), *Anthropology Now and Next*. Oxford: Berghahn.

Starn, Orin. 2004. *Ishi's Brain*. New York: Norton.

Steyn, Mark. 2006. *America Alone*. Washington, DC: Regnery.

Stolcke, Verena. 1995. Talking Culture: New Boundaries, New Rhetorics of Exclusion in Europe. *Current Anthropology* 36: 1–13.

Strathern, Marilyn, ed. 2000. *Audit Culture*. London: Routledge.

Talbot, Margaret. 2006. The Agitator: Oriana Fallaci Directs Her Fury toward Islam. *New Yorker*, June 5, pp. 58–67.

Taleb, Nassim Nicholas. 2007. *The Black Swan*. New York: Random House.

Tay, Simon. 1997. *Alien Asian*. Singapore: Landmark.

———. 2010. *Asia Alone*. Singapore: Wiley.

Tenold, Vegas. 2014. Detroit Love, Swedish Style. *New York Times*, August 1.

Tharoor, Shashi. 2003. The New Global Mantra. *The Hindu*, September 28.

———. 2007. *The Elephant, the Tiger and the Cellphone*. London: Penguin.

Tiryakian, Edward A. 1997. Review of The Clash of Civilizations and the Remaking of World Order by Samuel P. Huntington. *American Journal of Sociology* 103: 475–477.

Tobar, Héctor. 2005. *Translation Nation*. New York: Berkley.

Todd, Emmanuel. 2003. *After the Empire*. New York: Columbia University Press.

Toffler, Alvin. 1970. *Future Shock*. New York: Random House.

Toynbee, Arnold J. 1947. *A Study of History*. New York: Oxford University Press.

Trefon, Theodore, ed. 2004. *Reinventing Order in the Congo*. London: Zed.

Tsygankov, Andrei P. 2003. The Irony of Western Ideas in a Multicultural World: Russians' Intellectual Engagement with the "End of History" and "Clash of Civilizations.". *International Studies Review* 5: 53–76.

Tunander, Ola. 2001. Swedish-German Geopolitics for a New Century: Rudolf Kjellén's 'The State as a Living Organism. *Review of International Studies* 27: 451–463.

Turner, Frederick Jackson.[1893] 1961. The Significance of the Frontier in American History. In *Frontier and Section*. Ray A. Billington, ed. Englewood Cliffs, NJ: Prentice-Hall.

Turner, Victor. 1977. Process, System, and Symbol: A New Anthropological Synthesis. *Daedalus* 106(3): 61–80.

Underhill, William. 2009. Why Fears of a Muslim Takeover Are All Wrong. *Newsweek*, July 20.

Vaïsse, Justin. 2010. Eurabian Follies: the shoddy and just plain wrong genre that refuses to die. *Foreign Policy*, January/February, pp. 86–88.

Van der Veer, Peter. 2014. *The Modern Spirit of Asia*. Princeton, NJ: Princeton University Press.

Vertovec, Steven, and Robin Cohen, eds. 2002. *Conceiving Cosmopolitanism*. Oxford: Oxford University Press.

Vertovec, Steven, and Susanne Wessendorf, eds. 2009. *The Multiculturalism Backlash*. London: Routledge.

Vulliamy, Ed. 2010. *Amexica*. London: Bodley Head.

Wallace, Anthony F.C. 1961. *Culture and Personality*. New York: Random House.

Wallerstein, Immanuel. 1991. *Geopolitics and Geoculture*. Cambridge: Cambridge University Press.

Wang Gungwu. 1996/97. A Machiavelli for Our Times. *The National Interest* 46: 69–73.

Wang, Gungwu. 2010. *Junzi: Scholar-Gentleman*. Singapore: Institute of Southeast Asian Studies.

Wasserstrom, Jeffrey. 2014. China & Globalization. *Daedalus* 143(2): 157–169.

Watson, C.W. 1999. *Being There*. London: Pluto.

Watson, James L., ed. 1997. *Golden Arches East*. Stanford, CA: Stanford University Press.

Wedeen, Lisa. 2003. Beyond the Crusades: Why Huntington, and Bin Ladin, are Wrong. *Middle East Policy* 10(2): 54–61.

Wedel, Janine R. 2014. *Unaccountable*. New York: Pegasus.

Weisman, Alan. 2007. *The World Without Us*. London: Virgin Books.

Werbner, Pnina. 1999. Global Pathways: Working Class Cosmopolitans and the Creation of Transnational Ethnic Worlds. *Social Anthropology* 7: 17–35.

———, ed. 2008. *Anthropology and the New Cosmopolitanism*. Oxford: Berg.

Wieseltier, Leon. 2011. The New Thinking. *New Republic*, January 27.

Wikan, Unni. 2002. *Generous Betrayal*. Chicago: University of Chicago Press.

———. 2008. *In Honor of Fadime*. Chicago: University of Chicago Press.

Wildavsky, Ben. 2010. *The Great Brain Race*. Princeton, NJ: Princeton University Press.

Wimmer, Andreas, and Nina Glick Schiller. 2002. Methodological Nationalism and Beyond: Nation-state Building, Migration and the Social Sciences. *Global Networks* 2: 301–334.

Wodak, Ruth, Majid KhosraviNik, and Brigitte Mral, eds. 2013. *Right-Wing Populism in Europe*. London: Bloomsbury.

Wolf, Eric R. 1981. Alfred L. Kroeber. In *Totems and Teachers*, ed. Sydel Silverman. New York: Columbia University Press.

——— 1982. *Europe and the People without History*. Berkeley: University of California Press.

——— 2001. *Pathways of Power*. Berkeley: University of California Press.

Wolfe, Alan. 2004. Native Son: Samuel Huntington Defends the Homeland. *Foreign Affairs* 83(3): 120–125.

Wolfe, Thomas C. 1997. The Most Invisible Hand: Russian Journalism and Media-Context. In *Cultural Producers in Perilous States*, ed. George E. Marcus. Chicago: University of Chicago Press.

Wulff, Helena. 1992. Young Swedes in New York: Workplace and Playground. In *Networks of Americanization*, eds. Rolf Lundén, and Erik Åsard. Uppsala: Department of English, Uppsala University.

Yates, Joshua J. 2009. Mapping the Good World: The New Cosmopolitans and Our Changing World Picture. *The Hedgehog Review* 11(3): 7–27.

Ye'or, Bat. 2001. *Islam and Dhimmitude*. Madison, NJ: Fairleigh Dickinson University Press.

———. 2005. *Eurabia*. Madison, NJ: Fairleigh Dickinson University Press.

Yoshimi, Shunya. 2003. 'America' as Desire and Violence: Americanization in Postwar Japan and Asia during the Cold War. *Inter-Asia Cultural Studies* 4: 433–450.

Yurchak, Alexei. 2006. *Everything Was Forever, Until it Was No More*. Princeton, NJ: Princeton University Press.

Zakaria, Fareed. 1994. Culture is Destiny: A Conversation with Lee Kuan Yew. *Foreign Affairs* 73(2): 109–126.

———. 1998. *From Wealth to Power*. Princeton, NJ: Princeton University Press.

———. 2002. *Asian Values*, 38–39. November-December: *Foreign Policy*.

———. 2004. *The Future of Freedom*. New York: Norton.

———. 2008. *The Post-American World*. New York: Norton.

———. 2013a. Statecraft and Stagecraft. *Time*, October 14.

———. 2013b. The Saudis Are Upset? Tough! *Time*, November 11.

———. 2013c. Can America Be Fixed? The New Crisis of Democracy. *Foreign Affairs* 92(1): 22–33.

———. 2014. Natural Americans: The United States Should Not Turn its Back on Immigrants who Broke the Rules. *Washington Post*, November 28.

———. 2015. *In Defense of a Liberal Education*. New York: Norton.

Index

A

Abu-Lughod, Lila, 109n7, 214, 258n4
Acemoglu, Daron, 136, 137, 157n1
Afghanistan, 13, 68, 70, 86, 101, 216, 239
Africa, 12, 13, 17, 20–2, 41, 43, 51, 55, 57, 58, 62, 64, 65, 68, 71, 74, 77n12, 78n22, 78n26, 132n14, 146, 152, 180, 200, 202, 209, 214, 216, 217, 226–8, 229, 256, 259n12
Afro-pessimism, 64, 68, 69, 78n22, 187
Afropolitans, 256
Ajami, Fouad, 127, 129, 133n20, 168, 260n20
Åkesson, Jimmie, 110n14
Al-Afghani, Jamal al-Din, 210
Alexievich, Svetlana, 260n29
Algeria, 17, 77n18, 230
Al Jazeera, 182

Amsterdam, 55, 84
anarchy, 12, 20–2, 35, 53, 55, 62, 78n24, 78n26, 107, 113, 117, 124, 127, 143, 146, 154, 166, 178, 259n12
Anderson, Elijah, 176
Anglo-Protestants, 105, 106, 179
Annan, Kofi, 250
Anthropocene, 113
anthropology, anthropologists, 50, 53, 54, 68, 74, 75n3, 77n15, 79n32, 111n20, 127, 132n17, 149, 157n3, 158n14, 160n21, 162, 165, 170, 179, 188n2, 189n7, 190n16
anti-Americanism, 87, 108n2, 181, 193, 223, 252
Anti-Semitism, 92, 238
Appadurai, Arjun, 158n15
Appiah, Kwame Anthony, 77n12, 173
Arabs, 51, 82, 89, 93, 97, 138, 165, 227, 229

Note: Page numbers followed by "n" refer to notes.

U

Ukraine, 59, 71, 80n36, 114, 131n8, 216, 228

United Nations, 18, 61, 66, 79n33, 142, 146, 164, 228, 245, 247, 249, 250, 253

United States, 12, 13, 15, 24, 25, 27, 28, 29n8, 33, 36, 43, 48n20, 49, 53, 61, 62, 64, 66, 68, 70, 71, 73–5, 76n9, 78n26, 81, 88, 91, 92, 95, 103, 104, 106, 107, 106n1, 114, 118, 130, 130n5, 133n41, 140, 158n14, 159n17, 163, 179, 181, 188n2, 189n6, 191n20, 191n24, 193, 195, 202–5, 209, 212–16, 218–27, 235, 240–9, 252, 253, 257, 258n7

Uppsala, University of, 53, 76n6, 77n10, 142

V

Van der Veer, Peter, 47n14

Venus, 26, 39, 52, 69–73, 81, 82, 123, 139, 140, 225, 246

Vietnam, 22, 68, 80n37, 139

W

Wahhabism, 88

Waldseemüller, Martin, 51

Wallace, Anthony, 157n7

Wallerstein, Immanuel, 45n1

Wall Street, 24, 42, 47n12, 63, 66, 87, 127, 177, 178, 203, 210, 240, 244, 245, 257

Wang Gungwu, 241, 261n33

Washington, D.C., 109n10, 189n9

Watson, James, 132n11

Wedel, Janine, 48n20

Weisman, Alan, 117

Westphalian Peace, 73, 131n5, 146

Wiesel, Elie, 169

Wikan, Unni, 109n7

Wikileaks, 44, 48n20

Wilders, Geert, 99

Wilson, Woodrow, 146

Wolfe, Alan, 105, 260n25

Wolf, Eric, 75n2, 157n8, 166, 188n2

world citizens, 172

World Economic Forum, 41, 57, 168, 169, 185, 190n9, 215, 243, 245

world music, 152

World Social Forum, 169, 174

World Trade Center, 63, 186

World War II, 14, 50, 51, 55, 66, 82, 86, 87, 104, 139, 163, 173, 181, 194, 198, 199, 206n1, 211, 224, 237, 241, 251

World War IV, 87–9

Wulff, Helena, 204

Y

Yale University, 17, 214, 250

Yemen, 241

Ye'or, Bat, 27, 52, 81–5, 87, 89, 92, 95, 101, 103, 105, 120, 233

Yoruba, 77n10

Yoshimi, Shunya, 207n6

Z

Zakaria, Fareed, 27, 32, 44, 218–22, 223, 226, 234, 240, 242, 244, 245, 249, 252, 256

Zomia, 79n28

THE AUTHOR

Ulf Hannerz is Professor Emeritus of Social Anthropology, Stockholm University, Sweden, and has taught at and held research appointments at several American, European, Asian, and Australian universities. He is a member of the Royal Swedish Academy of Sciences, the Austrian Academy of Sciences, and the American Academy of Arts and Sciences, and is a former Chair of the European Association of Social Anthropologists. His research has been especially in urban anthropology, media anthropology, and transnational cultural processes, with field studies in West Africa, the Caribbean, and the United States. He has also conducted a multi-sited study of the work of news media foreign correspondents.

Among his books are *Soulside*, *Exploring the City*, *Cultural Complexity*, *Transnational Connections*, *Foreign News*, and *Anthropology's World*. In 2005 he was awarded an honorary doctorate at the University of Oslo.

The manufacturer's authorised representative in the EU is Springer
Nature Customer Service Centre GmbH, Europaplatz 3, 69115 Heidelberg,
Germany. If you have any concerns regarding our products, please
contact ProductSafety@springernature.com

Printed and bound by CPI Group (UK) Ltd, Croydon, CR0 4YY
27/04/2026
02097625-0002